Conrad Shawcross

The Steady States

The New Art Gallery Walsall

Walker Art Gallery, National Museums Liverpool

Foreword

Conrad Shawcross is a relatively young artist, yet he has already attracted significant critical attention for his work which has been shown nationally and internationally. He has become renowned, above all, for his large-scale kinetic sculptures that combine interests in art, science and philosophy. These often complex works incorporate mechanised systems that appear functional yet have no useful application in the real world. They remain intriguing and compelling to the viewer, demonstrating intellectual rigour, technical dexterity and an intense sense of drama.

This collaborative project has presented an opportunity for Conrad to develop a whole new body of sculptural work which continues to draw upon his interest in science, philosophy and art. This particular group of sculptures is intended to be a cohesive body of work that combines elements of quantum mechanics and musical theory, in particular, string theory and harmonics.

Importantly, the project also marks the first major collaboration between The New Art Gallery Walsall and the Walker Art Gallery. The support of living artists and the engagement of ever broader audiences with contemporary art of the highest quality have been clear priorities for The New Art Gallery in its five-year history. The Walker Art Gallery presents a diverse programme of exhibitions of art, design and applied art and is committed to showing contemporary art and developing audiences for it. We hope that this project marks the start of a rewarding partnership that will continue to benefit both contemporary artists and our audiences locally and further afield.

We are grateful to Jenny Uglow and Andrea Bellini for their insightful and informative yet extremely diverse contributions to this publication. Also, Fraser Muggeridge has developed a consistently imaginative response to the initial design brief. All three have generously engaged in dialogue with the curators and the artist and have been sensitive and responsive throughout.

Conrad Shawcross is represented by Victoria Miro Gallery, London and staff at the gallery have been extremely helpful and supportive, particularly Victoria Miro, Andrew Silewicz, Kathy Stephenson and Erin Manns. Early discussions around the project were facilitated by Monica Chung, formerly of Entwistle, and we are grateful to her for her initial contributions to the project.

We are also indebted to the hard work of many members of staff at both The New Art Gallery Walsall and the Walker Art Gallery, National Museums Liverpool, especially Myra Brown, Rachel Dagnall and Emily Marsden.

The project would not have been possible without funding support from The Arts Council's National Touring Fund and The Henry Moore Foundation, our core funders, Walsall Council, National Museums Liverpool and Arts Council England.

Finally, thank you to Conrad Shawcross from committing wholeheartedly and passionately to an ambitious and challenging project and for producing a body of visually exciting and intellectually stimulating sculpture. He has been generous in his support and contribution to the development of the publication, interpretation and education programmes, demonstrating his recognition of the audience as a vital component in the realisation and validation of his work.

Stephen Snoddy
Director, The New Art Gallery Walsall

Deborah Robinson
Senior Exhibitions Curator, The New Art Gallery Walsall

Julian Treuherz
Keeper of Art Galleries, National Museums Liverpool

Ann Bukantas
Curator of Fine Art, National Museums Liverpool

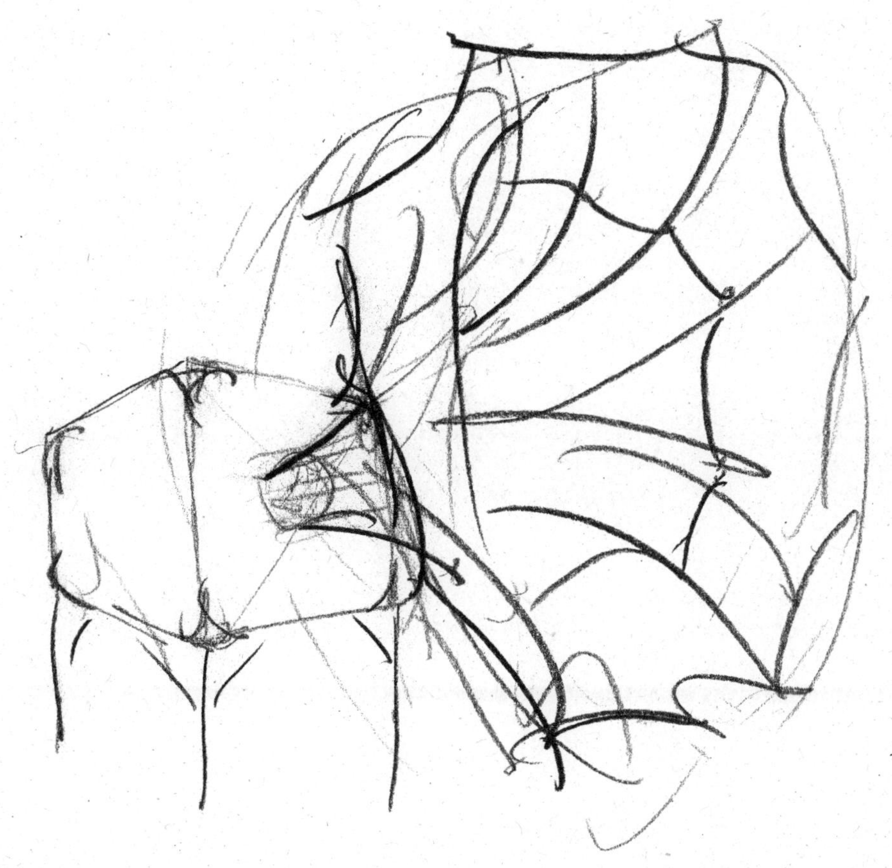

Models of harmony

by Jenny Uglow

Ring out ye Crystall sphears,
Once bless our human ears,
(If ye have power to touch our senses so)
And let your silver chime
Move in melodious time:
And let the base of Heaven's deep organ blow,
And with your ninefold harmony
Make up full consort to th'Angelicke symphony

Milton's 'Hymn', one of his earliest poems, makes one think of infinity and time, of our smallness in the cosmos and the greatness of our ambition. It leads us to puzzle over our desire to order and model, as if we are always searching for a lost pattern, a key to proportion and harmony at one with the great rhythms that surround us like the ocean tides.

In *The Tempest*, as soon as Ferdinand is cast ashore from the chaos of the sea, he notices the ubiquity of sound. But he is bewildered by the source of Ariel's song:

Where should this music be? I'the air, or the earth?
It sounds no more: – and sure it waits upon
Some god of the island. Sitting on a bank,
Weeping again the king my father's wrack
This music crept by me upon the waters
Allaying both their fury and their passion,
With its sweet air: thence have I follow'd it,
Or it hath drawn me rather: –

From the myths of Orpheus onwards music has seduced us with its promise, its offer of a charm to soothe the wild beast and the savage heart, to calm the stormy waters and appease – but not quite – the horrors of hell. We distinguish between harmony, Ariel's 'sweet air', and unwanted noise. And the search for pattern in sound is as ancient as Western culture. At the centre of the Greek scientific revolution of the 6th century BC was the idea that the world is regulated by a hidden order that can be perceived by human reason if only we try hard enough: indeed the word *Kosmos* itself means a kind of supreme rational order and beauty.

Building on earlier teachings from Egypt, Pythagoras and his followers, the *mathematikoi*, sought this answer in numbers. They were especially intrigued by the numbers that seemed to govern music: the different tones Pythagoras distinguished – according to an ancient story – when he heard a blacksmith striking the anvil with blows of different weight. When a string of a certain length was plucked, and then one of half that length, the difference was an octave. Every time a string was halved it produced a new dominant note: a harmonic series. And if the string was divided by 2/3 you could create an unending, spiralling cycle of harmonious notes. The most pleasing sounds came, the Pythagoreans thought, from the simplest ratios 2:1, 3:2, 4:3 – intervals which were named the diapason (octave), the diapente (fifth), the diatesseron (fourth).

This was the first known translation of an experienced quality – sound – into quantity. In Aristotle's words, once the Pythagoreans saw that the ratios of musical scales could be expressed in numbers, then 'all things seemed to be modelled on numbers… they supposed the elements of numbers to be the elements of all things, and the whole heaven to be a musical scale and a number.'[1] The world was composed of invisible particles of matter, each with its resonance, sounding at a level inaudible to the human ear. The only person who could hear this universal music was Pythagoras himself, a demi-god, an Apollonian being.

Numbers as 'elements of all things' flowed into the personal and social spheres: even numbers were masculine, odd ones feminine and their relationships infused all human institutions whether it be marriage, or justice, or medicine. Numbers are the wires that hold the material and spiritual world together, fighting the destroying desert of infinity.[2] Inherent in matter they merge into solid mathematics, geometric beauty – and we recognise today that life is indeed inscribed in geometry, from the spirals of DNA to the wondrously varied angles of atoms within molecules, or the growing, starry lattice of crystals. And in geometry the Pythagoreans also discovered that there were five 'regular solids' – and only five: the tetrahedron (4), cube (6), octahedron (8), dodecahedron (12) and icosahedron (20). Now comes the magic: if you fit any regular solid just inside a sphere all of its points will touch the inside of the sphere: if you fit a sphere inside a solid, it will touch all the faces. These shapes were counterparts to the four elements Earth, Water, Air and Fire, and to the summation, Quintessence.

The Pythagorean universe was thus modelled on the harmonious relationships of sounds and geometrical forms. At its heart was the unmoving earth, a still sphere, surrounded by one of the regular solids, in turn enclosed in a crystalline sphere bounded by another solid, and so on. Attached to these concentric spheres were the moon, sun and planets, creating exquisite sounds as they spun and whooshed through the air, as if whirled on a string varying in length with its distance from earth.

The closer spheres hummed lower tones while those further away, whirling faster, were sweeter and higher pitched. The correspondences were not fixed, but fluid and harmonious, governing the seasons, the tides and all the rhythms of earthly life.

The five known planets of the ancient world, plus the sun and moon, balanced the seven notes of the ancient scale, and philosophers from Plato to Ptolemy brooded on their relationship. In the first century AD Pliny the Elder defined the 'scale' of the solar system in relation to the strings of the lyre, with the shortest distance – from Earth to Moon – representing the shortest string. In the 1601 translation of his *Historia Naturalis*, this appears as follows. Pythagoras, writes Pliny, 'calleth the space between the earth and the Moone a Tonus (tone), saying that from here to *Mercurius* is halfe a tone (semi-tone), and from him to *Venus* in manner the same space. But from her to the Sunne as much and halfe againe' (a minor third).[3] And so it flows on: Sun to Mars, a tone; Mars to Jupiter, semi tone; Jupiter to Saturn, semi-tone; Saturn to the fixed stars – the Signifier Sphaere or Zodiake, a minor third. 'Thus are composed seven tunes, which harmonie they call Diapason, that is to say the Generalitie or whole state of concent and accord, which is perfect musicke'.

To some people a mathematical equation is a form so rich that you can return to it time and time again and find something new. 'Much like a work of art, writes Graham Farmelo, a beautiful equation, 'has among its attributes much more than attractiveness – it will have universality, simplicity, inevitability and an elemental power'.[4] Physicists and mathematicians see elegance as an indicator. Graham de Sautoy, who works on 'group theory and symmetry' finds mathematical patterns in palindromes. He is, he says, searching for 'some deep and subtle structure at the heart of my subject which I don't yet understand.' If he can understand the internal symmetry of a zeta function, he writes, ' I am convinced it will go hand in hand with revealing a huge vista of structure that we are currently too blind to see'.[5] But for those like me, who find abstract thought difficult, the real excitement comes when these equations and patterns are conveyed in other ways. I understand a palindrome, but not the maths. I can 'see' the crystalline spheres and solids, but cannot do the calculations.

Sometimes, too, complex theories suddenly make sense in relation to poetic metre, or musical notation. To the medieval mind there was a strange, mystical power in musical modes, where some dominant notes exert a 'pull' on the others, like planets in orbit. But there was no clearly visible musical hierarchy, no map of sound that explained this pull until Guido of Arezzo invented his system of written notation at the start of the eleventh century, with his red and yellow lines foreshadowing the modern clef. This was supplemented by his technique of hand signals and his enduring 'sol-fa' mnemonic, its indicators (with the 'ut' later replaced by 'sol') aptly taken from the first syllables of the hymn to John the Baptist:

Ut queant laxis
Resonare fibris
Mira gestorum
Famuli thorum
Solve polluti
Labii reatum, Sancte Johannes
(That your servants may with relaxed throats sing the wonder of your deeds; take away sin from their unclean lips, O Saint John).[6]

We feel similar leaps and links in architecture. The great Gothic cathedrals were designed in relation to musical and geometrical proportions, and in High Renaissance Italy, Alberti and Palladio both applied Pythagorean mathematics to building, hunting for the secrets of proportion, harmonies of space.' I conclude that the same numbers, by means of which the Agreement of Sound affects our ears with delight', wrote Alberti, 'are the very same which please our eyes and mind. We shall therefore borrow all our Rules for the Finishing our Proportions, from the Musicians, who are the greatest Masters of this Sort of Numbers, and from those Things wherein Nature shows herself most excellent and compleat'.[7] At the same time, Alberti longed to make an engine, beautifully geared, 'some unheard of machine to move and carry weights, making it possible to create great and wonderful things', levering his dreams into three dimensions.[8]

In the next generation Copernicus dismantled the Aristotelian universe. Instead of revolving around the earth, the kingly sun governed his family of wheeling stars.[9] But Copernicus still believed that this 'government' could be understood in harmonious, transcendent mathematical terms and when Johannes Kepler discovered that the planets orbited in ellipses rather than circles, he still placed them in a musical progression, related to the dimensions of the regular solids. Each orbital plane, he declared in his *Harmonia Mundi*, created the great harmonic chords: 'Henceforth it is no longer a harmony made for the benefit of our planet, but the song which the cosmos sings to its Lord and centre, the Solar Logos'.[10]

Kepler designed a model, a scooped sphere whose clumsiness belies the fluid beauty of his thinking. This was the dawn of a great age of model-making in Europe, as instrument makers and clock makers reached new levels of precision. Charting space, the flurry of exploration led to finer astrolabes, quadrants and compasses. Measuring time, Galileo suggested using a pendulum, and in 1656 Christian Huygens built the first clock with a freely suspended pendulum, transmitting its regular movement to the mechanism. Huygens – a devout Copernican – also built a planetarium, driven by clockwork: the six planets were moved simultaneously by a central slanting axle, and the orbiting times (determined by the new mathematics of continued fractions) were governed by pairs of cog-wheels.

After the publication of Newton's *In Principia* the new cosmic mechanics seemed to impose a different order, a modality of gravity and weight. But to many these new laws still seemed to compose a social as well as a universal melody, as J T Desagulier's verse proclaims:

What made the planets in such Order move
He said, was harmony and mutual Love
The Music of his Spheres did represent
The ancient Harmony of Government.

Travelling lecturers were soon displaying the wonders of electricity, magnetism and astronomy to an enthralled public, while aristocratic patrons requested orreries or armillary spheres, beautiful objects in brass and silver, models of the solar system in which the planets rotated round the sun within a ring engraved with signs of the zodiac.

But was the world really so orderly? In the 1760s Joseph Wright painted a famous pair of pictures, displaying instruments that could clarify the workings of the universe to old and young, men and women. But they also showed two sides to forces and rhythms of nature. In the first painting, of 1766, *A Philosopher giving that Lecture on the Orrery, in which a lamp is put in place of the sun*, the lecturer uses the lamp to explain an eclipse: events that were once thought frightening, mysterious, supernatural, are now explained. The orrery presents a system that is rational, harmonious, serene. Yet in the companion picture the mood is different. *An Experiment on a Bird in an Air pump*, 1768, is shocking, violent, uncertain: as the experimenter sucks the air, creating a vacuum, so the bird flutters near to death – instead of experiencing delight, the children now recoil in terror. The music of the spheres has been replaced by a rasp, a rattle of breath. The pale moon still floats on high, glimpsed through the window. But Wright seems to say that art must recognise tumult and chaos as well as the mathematical proportion of natural forces.

In Wright's day science and technology had not yet become divorced from the arts. Galileo worked on sound and vibrating strings; Huygens experimented with the layout of the keyboard; Benjamin Franklin invented a 'glassychord', a mechanised version of musical glasses. On his arrival in

England in 1757 Franklin apparently heard an Irishman playing Gluck's *Concerto upon Twenty-six Drinking-Glasses'*: fascinated, he redesigned the instrument by attaching the glasses to an horizontal spindle in a trough of water in which the glasses were half-submerged. When the spindle was turned (by a pedal or treddle) their wet edges would come up and the player would draw sounds from them by the friction of his fingers on the wet rims, the note varying with the size of the glass. Franklin's scribbled directions to the glassmaker are minutely precise. And his invention worked – allegedly the young Mozart wanted one, but his father couldn't afford it.[11]

At the same time, James Watt, the improver of the steam engine, was working as an instrument maker in Glasgow, and although he was tone deaf he proudly built a perfect organ for a local Masonic Lodge simply through brilliant calculations. 'Though we all knew he could not tell one note from another', remembered his friend John Robison, he went ahead, 'noting a thousand things no Organ builder would have dreamt of', delving into books on harmony, following the new science of Equal Temperament, worked out by Bach in his *Well-Tempered Clavier* of 1722. [12]

It may seem, literally, a plunge from the sublime to the ridiculous to move from the music of the spheres to a home-made organ in Glasgow. But the harmony of numbers knows no bounds. Indeed a good mathematician and engineer – or sculptor – can create music without sound. I felt this when I first saw Charles Babbage's Difference Engine in the Science Museum in London. Babbage had become obsessed with building a machine to assist in the complex compiling of tables, based on the principle of finite differences. Invented in the 1830s and 40s, his machine was not finally built until the 1990s: on one side are the stacks of intricate, balanced gear wheels and cogs, of bronze, steel and cast iron. But on the other, as the cogs move and lock according to the numbers entered, the 'fairground whirl' of levers makes the keys spiral up steel poles, a sculptural ballet of numbers.[13]

It is tempting, but fanciful, to think that Babbage was engineering an harmonic series all his own. The translation of numerical proportion creates a ripple of excitement – a wave. In the 1880s the poet Gerald Manley Hopkins responded with intense interest to the work of Hermann von Helmholtz on vision and acoustics, and the way the human eye and ear grasp order intuitively. Hopkins wrote vigorous letters to *Nature*, and planned works of his own on the science of music and metre and light. He was fascinated by the tension between stability and flux and in reconciling scientific insights with his passionate religious faith. His own metrical experiments with 'sprung rhythm', 'inscape' and 'instress' reflect a belief that identity can be conveyed in sound as well as image:

As kingfishers catch fire, dragonflies draw flame
As tumbled over rim in roundy wells
Stones ring; like each tucked string tells, each hung bell's
Bow swung finds tongue to fling out broad its name;
Each mortal thing does one thing and the same;
Deals out that being indoors each one dwells.[14]

It is not surprising that as well as the clattering stone and plucked string, Hopkins chooses the bell's great note, the sound where we most clearly hear a dominant note amid an aura of others: every note contains a spectrum of sounds, just as there is a range of colour within light, and indeed sounds share the properties of light waves shimmering outwards from a star. We can tell if sound waves are moving towards us if there seems to be an increase in frequency and a decrease in wavelengths, as the Austrian physicist Christian Doppler demonstrated in the early 1800s with an orchestra on a moving railroad car, the music changing pitch as it whizzed past its audience. Within a decade physicists proved that the principle also applied to light waves. Now astronomers measure 'red shift' to see if stars and galaxies are moving away from us, as the lengthening of the wavelengths causes the light to move toward the red end of the spectrum.

Contemporary science still finds the links made in the past between music and the cosmos, notably in String Theory, which also ties into the notion of Quintessence, since it treats the essence of matter as a loop of energy/(light) rather than the original 'atomistic' particle. And in its balance of number and resonance, this provides a Theory of Everything, a single explanatory model for forces and matter, standing as a modern, and equally poetic version of the Pythagorean quest for a universal harmony.

String theorists argue that the fundamental particles – electrons, neutrinos, quarks, and so on – are not point-like but infinitely small, one-dimensional *loops*, each containing a single 'vibrating, oscillating, dancing filament'. As explained by the mathematician and physicist Brian Greene:

> *Just as the strings on a violin or on a piano have resonant frequencies at which they prefer to vibrate – patterns that our ears sense as various musical notes and their higher harmonics – the same holds true for the loops of string theory. But rather than producing musical notes, each of the preferred mass and force charges are determined by the string's oscillatory pattern. The electron is a string vibrating one way, the up-quark is a string vibrating another way, and so on... hence everything, all matter and all forces, is unified under the same rubric of microscopic string oscillations – the 'notes' that strings can play.*[15]

If electrons vibrate on this almost unimaginably infinitesimal plane, radio signals can reach seventy light years beyond the solar system. Through them we can hear the stars. The sun gives off waves of radiation in a flaring range of frequencies: 'chords' with different resonance depict the leaping and flying of sunspots and storms. Pulsars spin with such regular pulses of radiation that a radio telescope can detect a synchronized rhythm as planets orbit them. To return to *The Tempest*, in Caliban's words 'the isle is full of noises/ Sounds and sweet airs', a thousand instruments humming around our ears. Sounds in every wavelength ripple out from the heart of the cosmos, scribbling their tracks into infinity. We need ears to hear them, and pulses to feel their time-bound, timeless rhythm – and art to show their ravelled mystery.

1. Aristotle, *Metaphysics*, trs. W.D.Ross (1924), I, Part 5
2. John D. Barrow, *The Infinite Book* (2005)
3. Plinius Secundus, *The Historie of Nature*, trs. Philemon Holland (1601), II, xii
4. Graham Farmelo, *It Must be Beautiful: An Anthology of the Great Equations of Modern Science*
5. Quoted in Sian Ede, *Art and Science* (2005), 14
6. Howard Goodall, *Big Bangs* (2000), 24
7. Leon Battista Alberti (1407–1472)
8. Ross King, Brunelleschi's Dome (2000)
9. Nicholas Copernicus, *De Revolutionibus*, trs C.G. Wallis, 1939
10. Joscelyn Godwin, *Harmonies of Heaven and Earth* (1997) 130
11. Soho Archive, Birmingham Central Library MS 3782/12/108/9, with thanks to Shena Mason
12. 'Robison's Narrative' in Eric Robinson and A.E.Musson (eds), *James Watt and the Steam Revolution: a Documentory History* (1969)
13. See Doron Swade, *Charles Babbage and his Calculating Engines* (1991)
14. Hopkins, *Poetical Works*, (1990), 141. See Gillian Beer, *Open Fields: Science in Cultural Encounter (1996) and David Cahan, ed, Hermann con Helmholtz and the Foundations of Nineteenth-century Science* (1993)
15. Brian Greene, *The Elegant Universe: Superstrings, Hidden Dimensions, and the Quest for the Ultimate Theory* (1999): see his article under NOVA, *The Elegant Universe* homepage on www.pbs.org

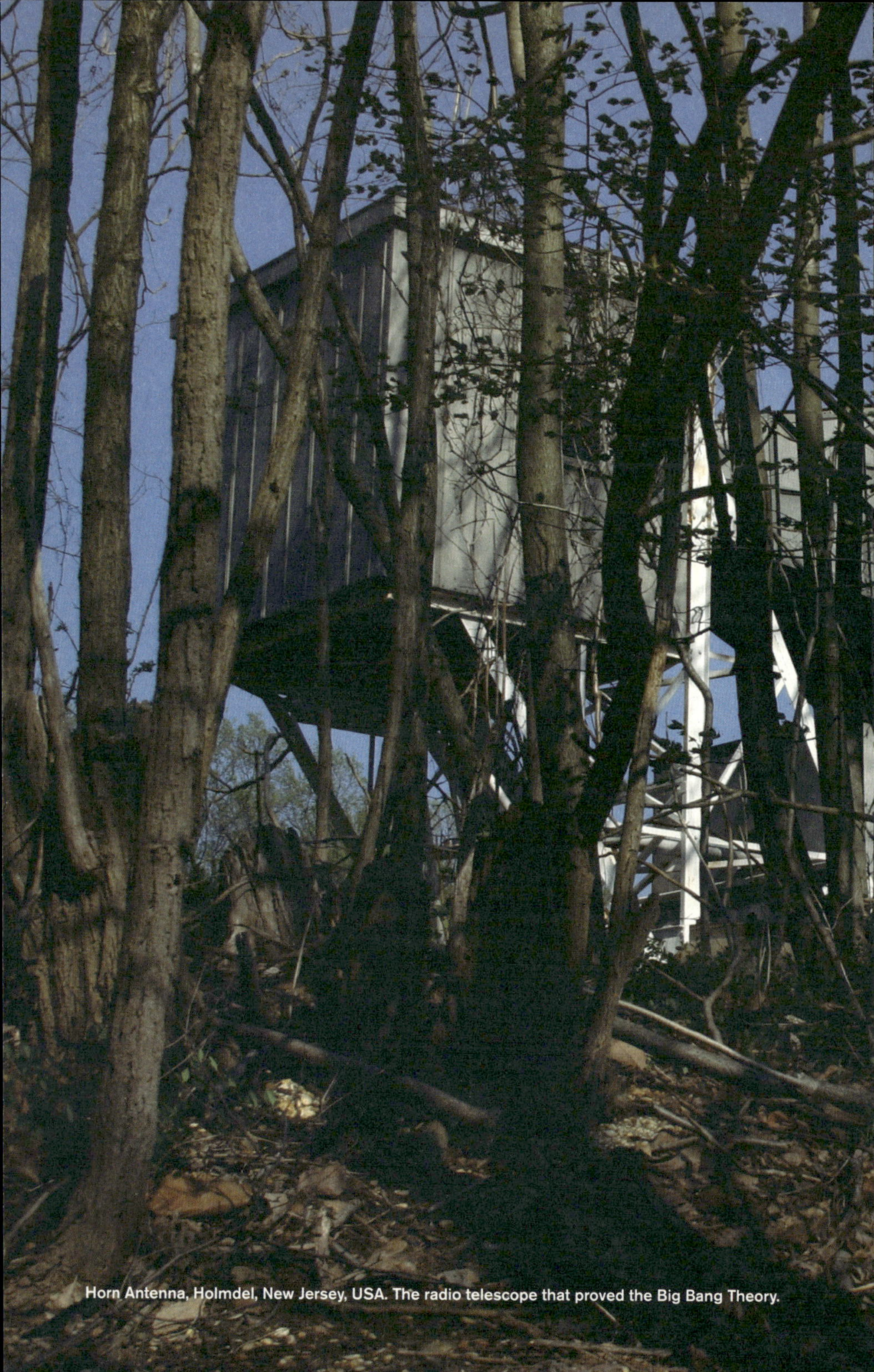

Horn Antenna, Holmdel, New Jersey, USA. The radio telescope that proved the Big Bang Theory.

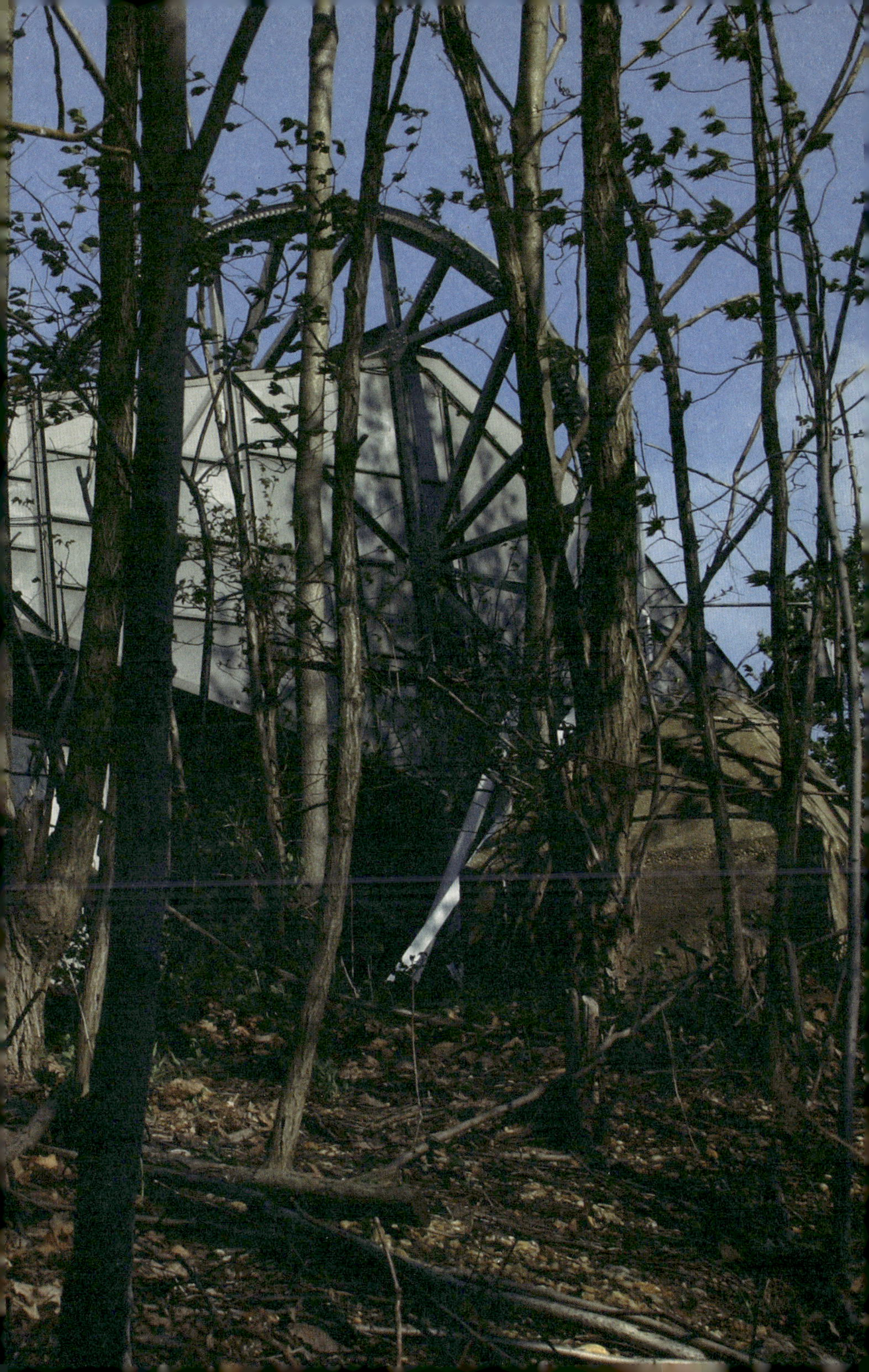

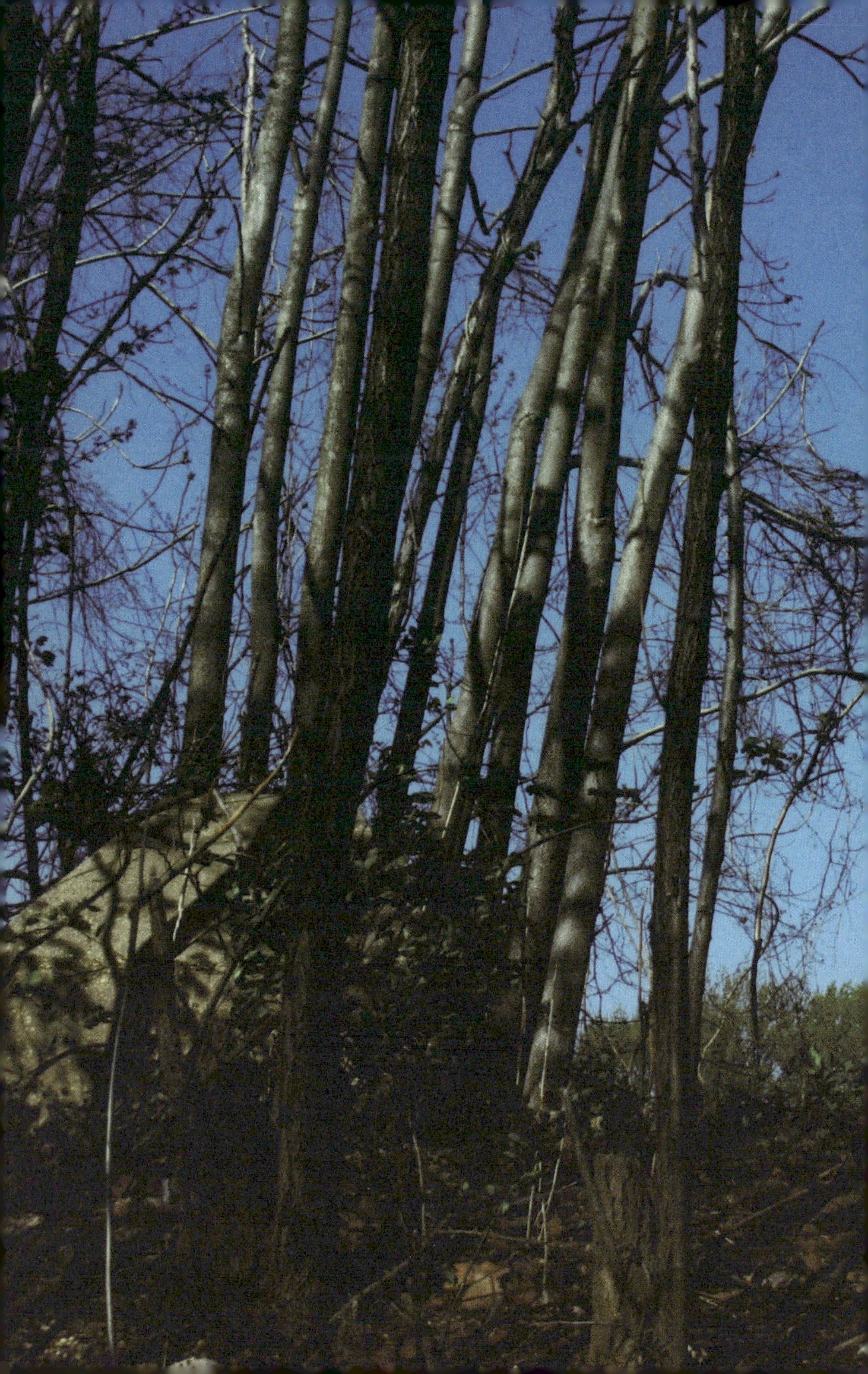

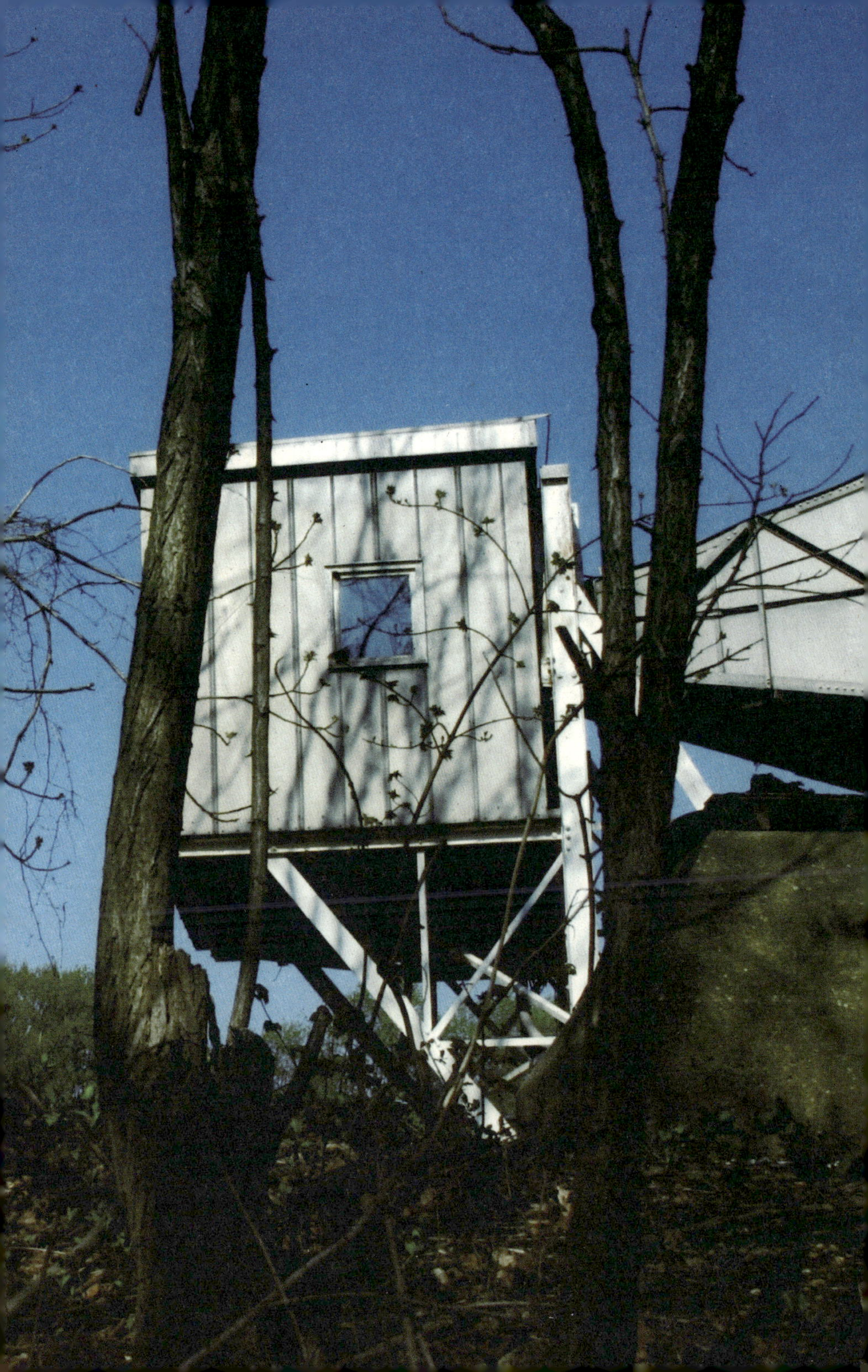

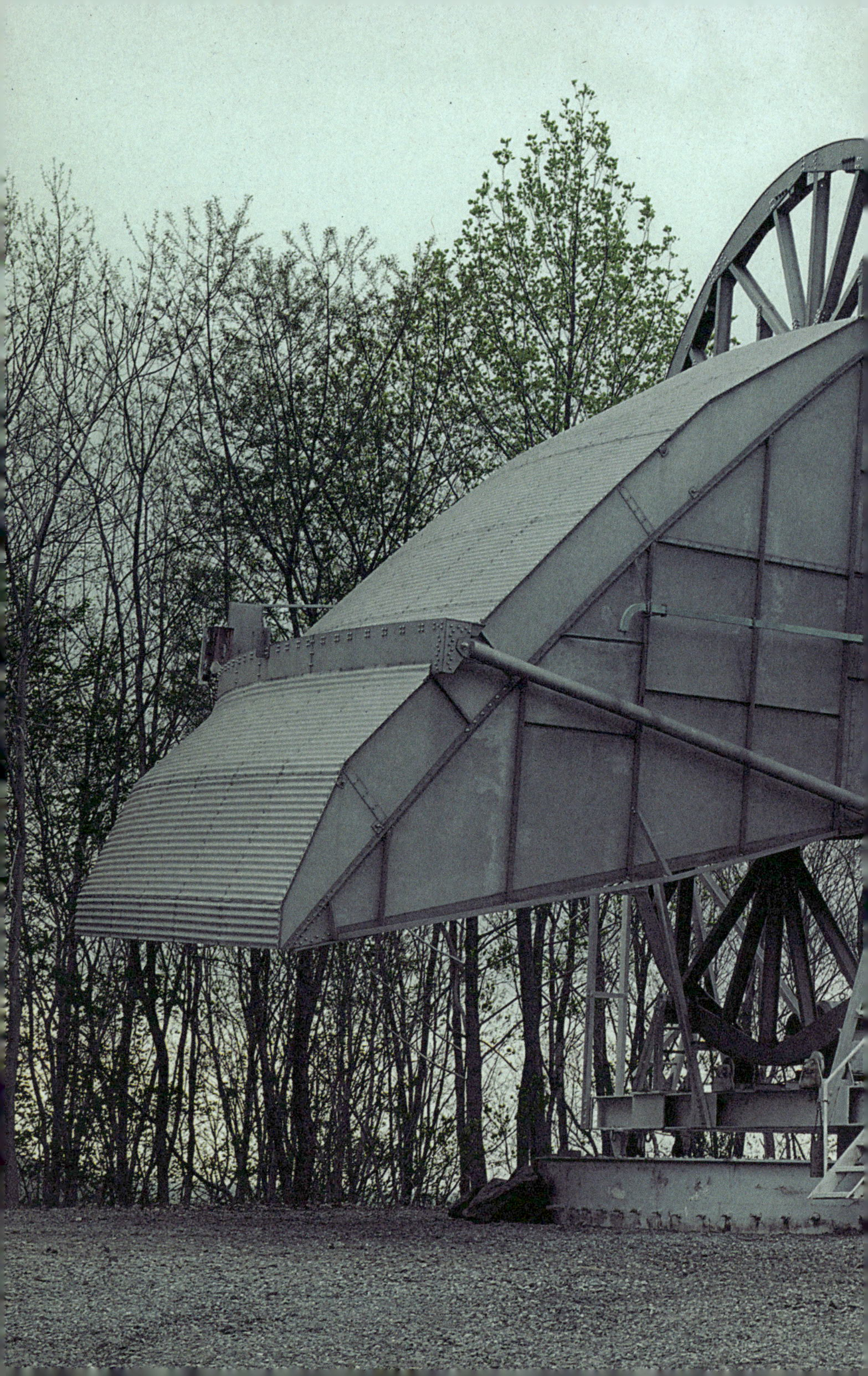

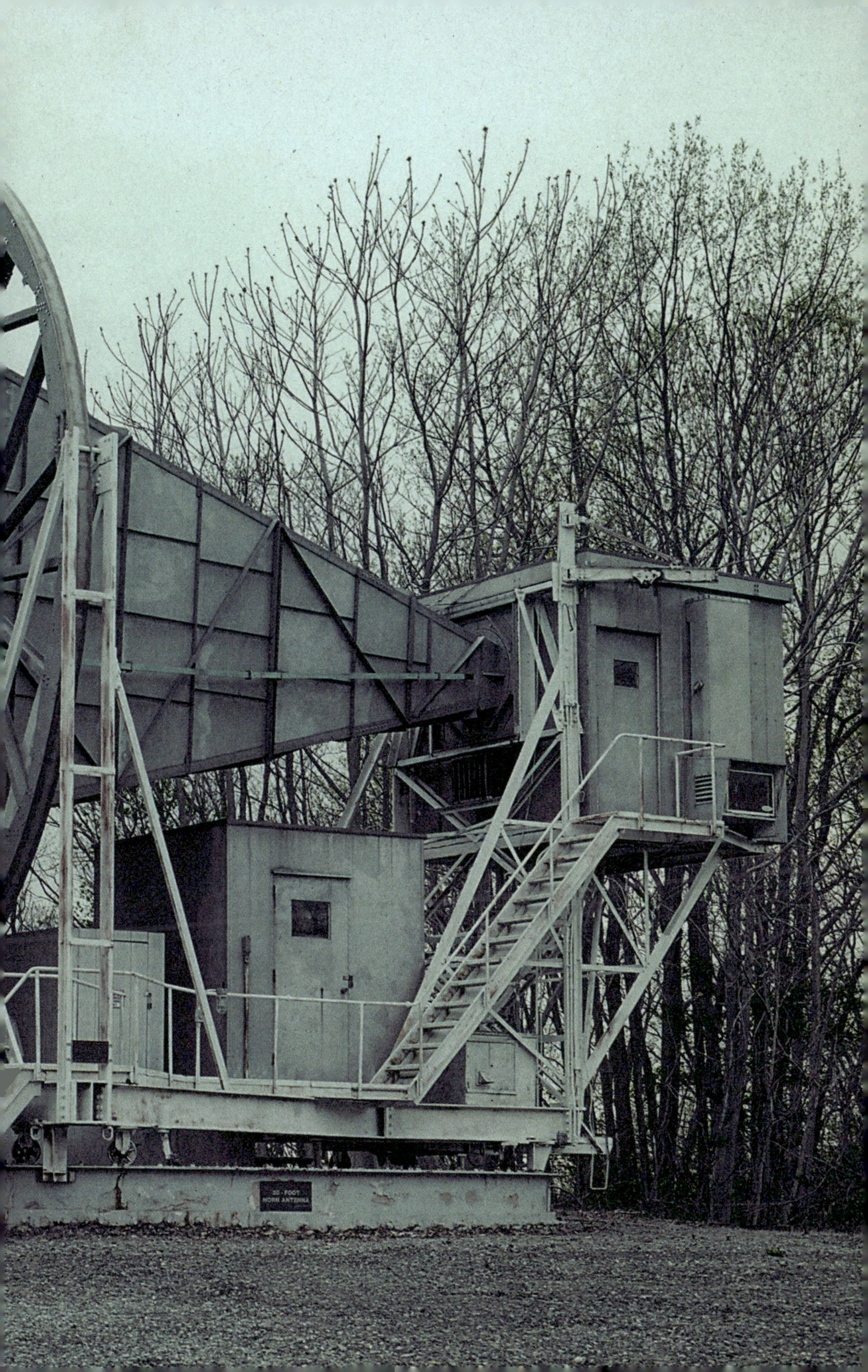
HORN ANTENNA

Conrad Shawcross's Studiolo in London

By Andrea Bellini

Autonomy. One of the most evident and also intriguing aspects of Conrad Shawcross's work is the degree of autonomy and originality that distinguishes him in the context of contemporary British sculpture. This autonomy becomes evident by comparing his work with those of a recent, interesting generation of artists gathered together three years ago at the exhibition *Early One Morning* at the Whitechapel Gallery in London. For the occasion, Iwona Blazwick and Andrea Tarsia presented sculptural installations by Shahin Afrassiabi, Claire Barclay, Jim Lambie, Eva Rothschild and Gary Webb: five diverse artists that had been grouped together under a series of common characteristics, although perhaps lacking a true poetic denominator. In the exhibition catalogue, the curators speak of non-figuration, assemblages, installations, synthetic materials, of a relationship with painting and of the visual impact of the works. To juxtapose Shawcross's work with these artists is to highlight a radical departure from a decisive neo-Pop influence. The ultimate significance of his work must be found in the young British artist's ability to achieve a heroic dimension of art – a cognitive explorative dimension – without abandoning himself to the self-reassuring game of yet another manipulation of the object. This characteristic places Shawcross's art in an international context more than a national one.

The Studiolo. To satisfy our desire to simplify things, we could draw a continuous line from Shawcross's work to the Kinetic Art movement, pinpointing the mechanical and surrealistic sculptures of Jean Tinguely. But the need for differentiation immediately presents itself. Shawcross distinguishes himself from Tinguely and other representatives of Kinetic Art by his lack of interest in movement for the sake of movement. Movement is not a key element in his work. While many of his works incorporate movement using complex motorized mechanisms, others are static and aspire to the emblematic exactness of pure form. In his case, movement is functional with a precise goal in view: the construction of metaphors, the representation of a process that reflects the 'becoming' of things. Perhaps he can be likened to a new Leonardo Da Vinci, who imagined human flight using complex and fascinating wooden structures; Shawcross, with his kinetic sculptures, first imagines and then attempts to visually assess, the functionality of the universe, the nature of time and the eternal essence of things. The leap of faith, the enthusiasm and nature of Conrad Shawcross's imagination make him look like a young scientist-artist of the Renaissance, hard at work in his 'studiolo' to interpret the nature of matter, to decipher the sense of life and the mysterious origin of the universe. And just like a scientist-artist from the

1500s, Shawcross prefers not to delegate construction to specialists and relies on his own hands as instruments of his fantastic imagination, philosophy and pseudo-science. In his hands, wood – that antique and noble material – becomes a malleable material, re-imagined and reconfigured into complex mechanisms destined to provoke stupor and wonder, which speak to us of the cosmos and its admirable laws.

A soul catcher. His nature as a visionary post-modern bard is clearly seen in his first work: a black Ford Capri Soul Catcher. It consists of an apparatus resembling the chairs that fishermen attach to the back of boats, mounted on the top of a Ford Capri. This apparatus, thanks to kites, roads, lines and hooks, is meant to catch souls and then reel them in. The imaginary story behind the work is a beautiful tale. After World War II, the British government set up an organization to locate the human soul as part of the welfare state. *The Investigative Bureau into the Location of the Soul (IBLS),* after an optimistic start, enjoyed only minor success. In 1984, a young technician called Bruce Springshaw had the intuition that souls were not to be found in the human body but outside it, most likely in the sky. To this end, twelve Ford Capris called Soul Catchers were created and twelve bold IBLS employees set off to the four corners of the earth. According to Shawcross, they all disappeared without a trace and the IBLS was closed down and forgotten. The artist claimed to have spent two years combing Europe for

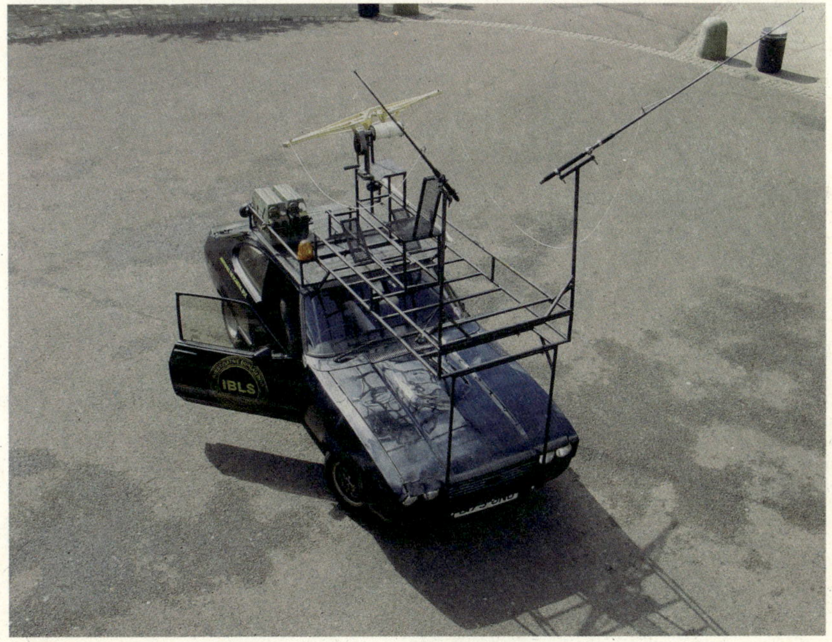

Bruce Springshaw's IBLS Soul Catcher, 1984

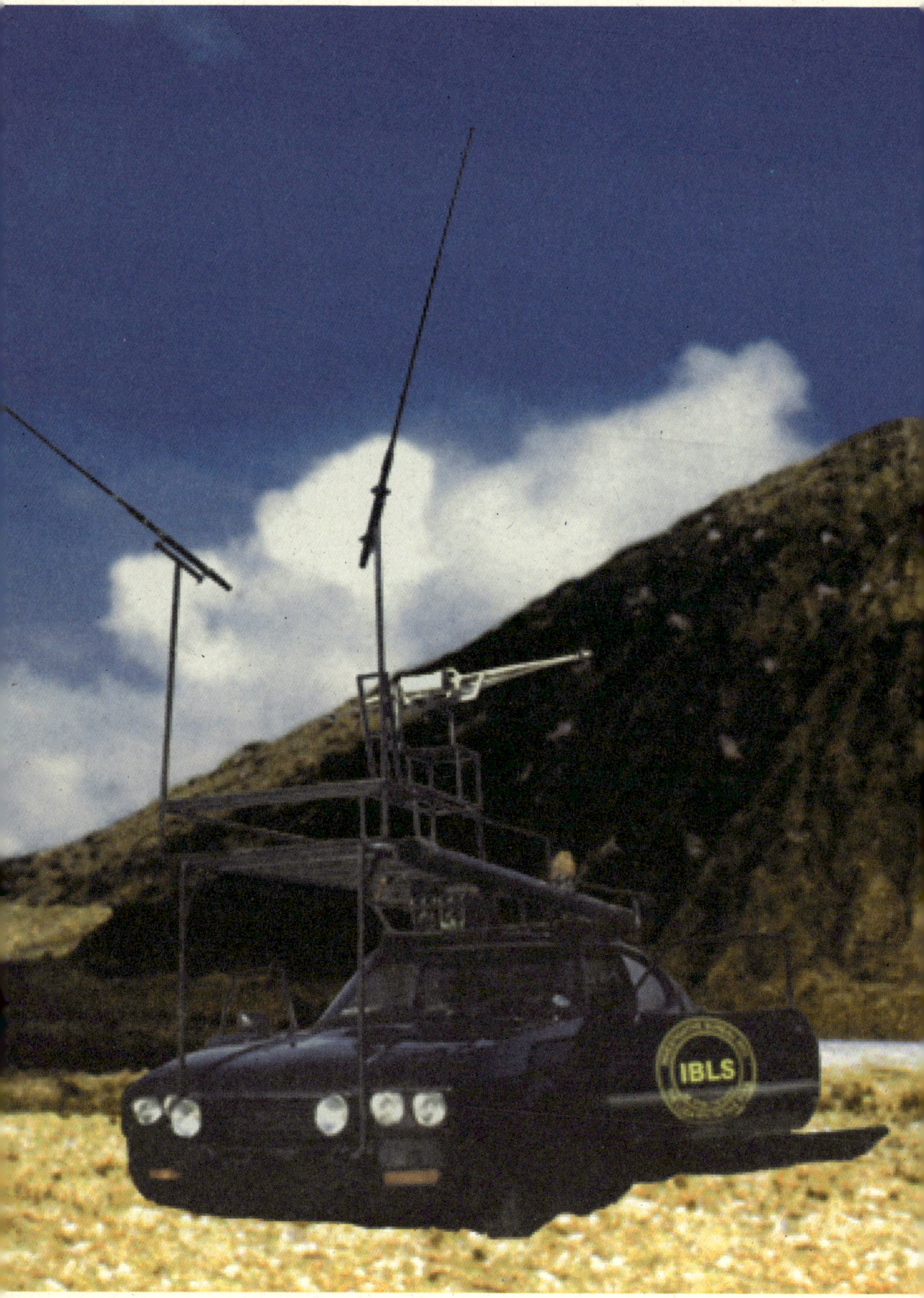
IBLS

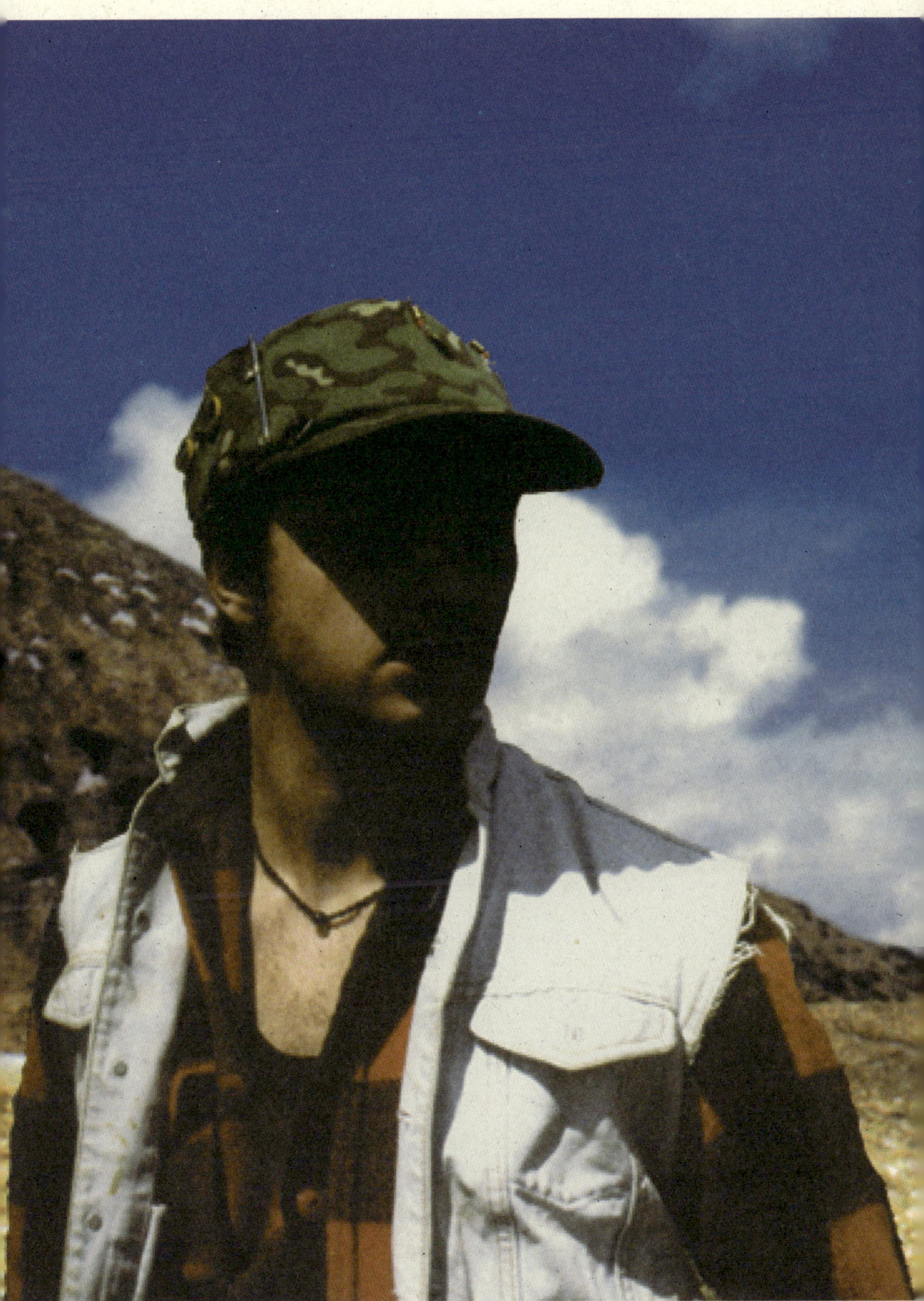

The last photo of Bruce Springshaw, 1984

IBLS-related objects until he discovered Bruce Springshaw's own Capri Soulcatcher in a Russian field. With this first work, the young British artist had already identified himself as a singular creator of those myths and legends on which the human spirit depends.

Metaphors. Every metaphor retains its enigmatic nature and all-powerful metaphors – as we know – stimulate the intellect. I mention metaphors because Conrad Shawcross's sculptures reveal themselves as traces of an archaic level of theoretical curiosity and experience. Shawcross does not create a theoretical or scientific structure to represent the world or universal laws. Science and abstract thought refer to the norms of a language which tends

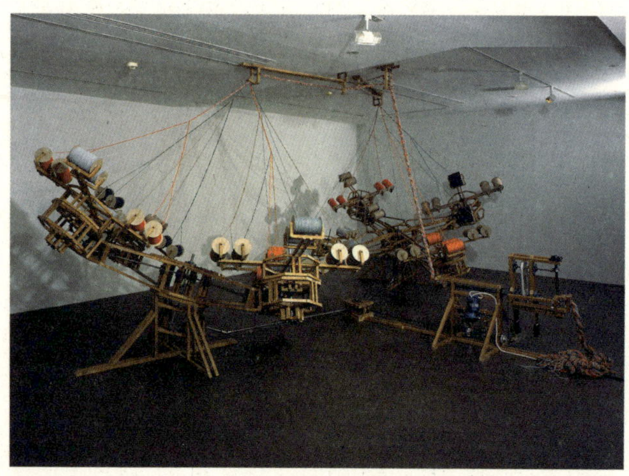

The Nervous Systems, 2003

towards objective unambiguity, towards that which can be verified, while Shawcross works in the indefinite zone of art, of a fantastic and poetic imaginary that does not want to be and cannot be dissolved into communication. His works maintain an incommunicable nucleus that breeds infinite interpretations. *The Nervous Systems* (2003), for example, a monumental spinning machine, recalls a model of the planets used by early astronomers, with its complex system of movements and orbits. This machine endlessly weaves a length of coloured rope into the form of a double helix, the shape of human DNA, evoking an idea of evolutionary process. It combines two classical theories about time: that of time as a circle, prevalent in the ancient world, and that of time as a line, typical of modern, and particularly western society. But it also recalls something organic, the two hemispheres of the brain from which the entire human nervous system originates.

Time and Space. Shawcross really loves to elaborate on these themes in his '*Studiolo*'. Let us consider, for example, *Inversal* (loop system) (2003) and *Continuum* (2004). These sculptures, different in size but alike in concept,

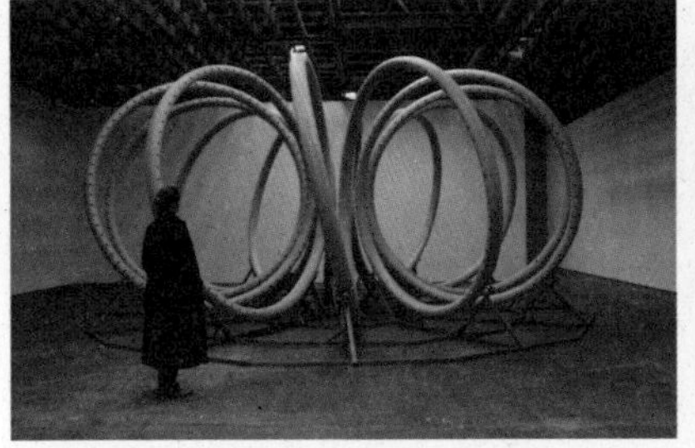
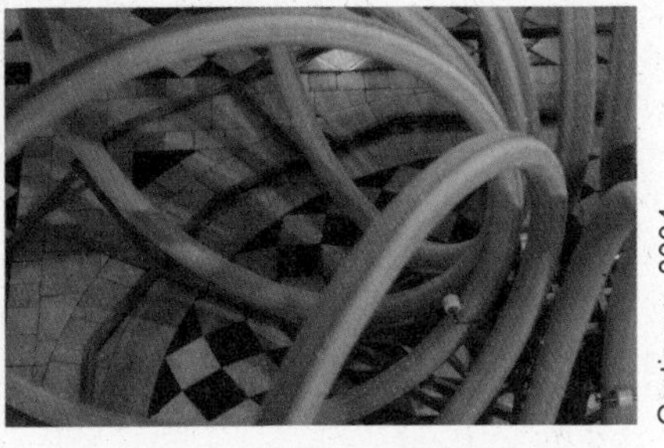

Continuum, 2004

are two continuous wooden spirals that revolve slowly, propelled by small motorized wheels. The movement of these works evokes the infinite process of death and rebirth, and the idea of time as a dramatic succession. Plywood is an organic material and thus suffers the passage of time more than iron or steel. Wood revolving around its central axis groans and shudders, alive and fragile. *Inversal* and *Continuum* seem to represent not only the destiny of matter through time, but also the idea of time as something uncatchable. The present itself is something that eludes both grasp and observation in the exact moment in which it happens. In 1905, Einstein theorized the impossibility of the simultaneous perception of events. In the morning, the sun rises above the horizon about eight minutes before we can first see it, a result of the finiteness of the speed of light. Thus, the idea of an objective point of view that is exact and global, comes from classic physics and the dimension of human desires rather than reality. The *Pre-retroscope* (2002) addresses this

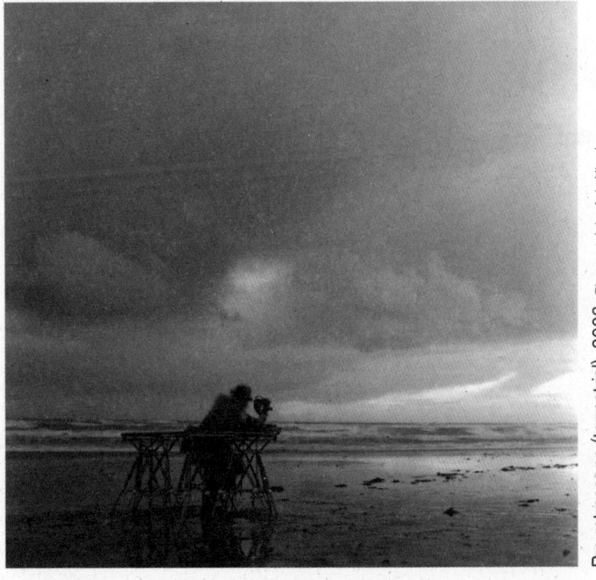

Pre-retroscope (terrestrial), 2002 Photograph by Anja Niemi

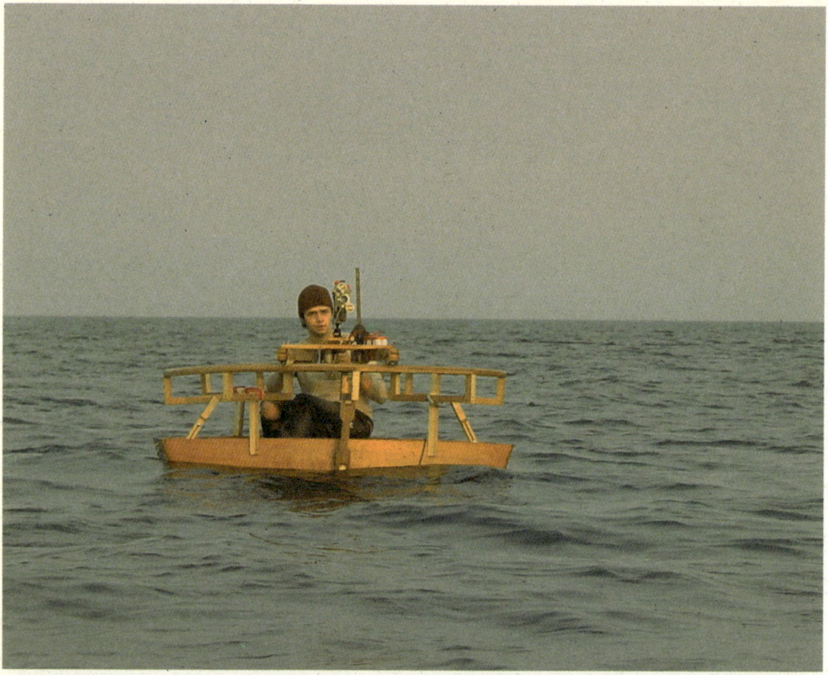

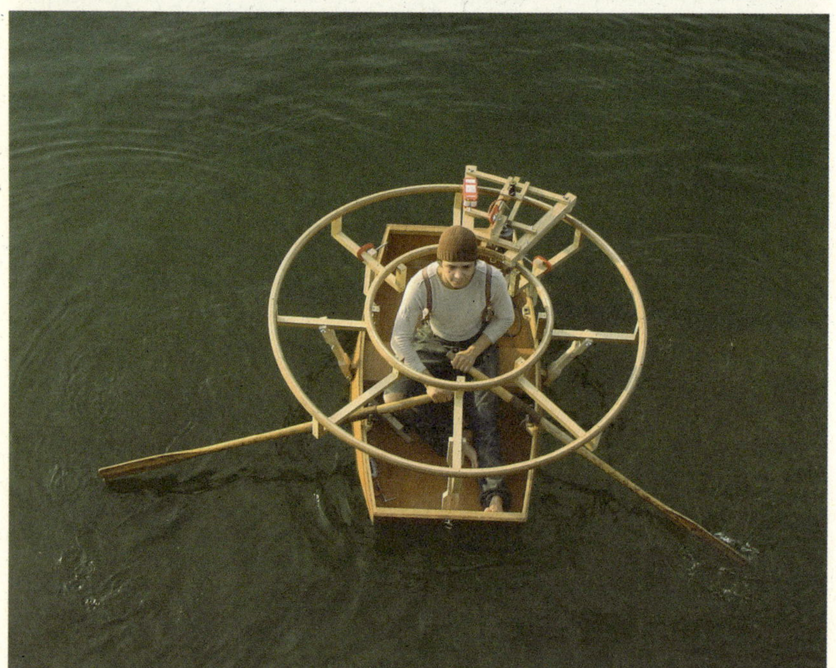

Pre-retroscope (marine), 2002

desire for and the impossibility of simultaneous perception. It is built in two versions: terrestrial and marine. These machines attempt to capture continual 360° panoramas of their surroundings. The *Pre-retroscope (terrestrial)* is composed of eight wooden tripods supporting a circular guide rail, which in turn supports a rotating motorized arm with a 16mm camera. The *Pre-retroscope (marine)* operates on the same principle but the horizontal wooden runner is mounted on a one-seater rowing boat. In the gallery, when the *Pre-retroscope* is not recording, the arm holds a video projector casting an image onto a flat screen at its end. The arm with the screen spins at the same speed as the camera's original movement. For the viewer, it is quite impossible to watch the continual image as one is forced to pursue the screen around the sculpture, losing sight of where one is going.

Magister lignaminis. If the reader is familiar with Tuscany, as many British people are, they will perhaps know the beautiful convent of Monte Oliveto Maggiore, just outside Siena. I studied art in that city and during my time at university, I often found myself at Monte Oliveto admiring the frescos by Sodoma and Signorelli preserved in the famous cloisters. Besides the frescos, the convent holds extraordinary choir-stalls (1503–1505), the work of 'magister lignaminis' Fra Giovanni da Verona. He decorated the stalls with an unforgettable succession of musical instruments and abstract objects in bold compositions and daring angles, showing not only an unequalled craftsmanship but also the scientific culture of his time, steeped in the new theories of perspective and geometry. The *tarsia lignea* of the choir-stalls and the Italian *studioli* reflect the very brief period of 'archimedean' culture in which science, technology and art came together to elaborate forms. This was a time when the specific intellectual experience of perspective and of mathematics informed both mechanics and the arts, adding a feverish dimension to the quest for knowledge. Therefore, if it does not seem too bold a comparison, I would like to suggest a connection between certain sculptures by Shawcross and various elements of Fra Giovanni's choir-stalls and other humanistic *studioli:* their enigmatic isolation, their ability to represent the very paradigm of the desire for knowledge and a propensity towards the future.

Let's take as an example *The Winnowing Oar* (2003), a fascinating and apparently incomprehensible oak object that combines a traditional paddle with that of a winnowing fan. This strange object is reminiscent of a curious and, in the end, useless precision instrument – almost the result of an impossible riddle of mathematical perspective – in the style of Fra Giovanni. Shawcross's oar is in fact useless but represents an interesting poetic metaphor, a metaphor of physical travel in space and of immaterial travel into the world of knowledge. The artist is inspired by a passage in Homer's

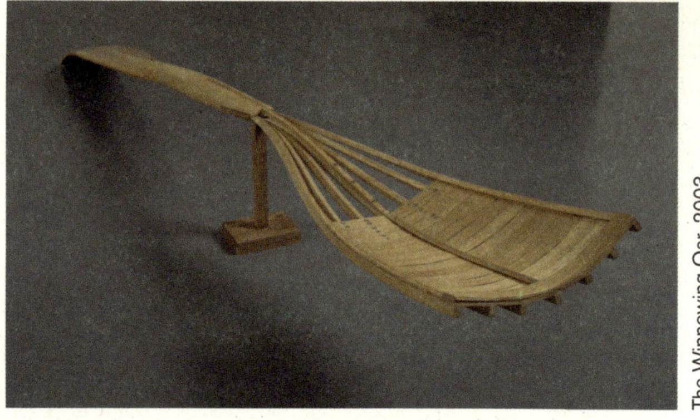
The Winnowing Oar, 2003

Odyssey where it is prophesied that before his death, Odysseus will travel until he reaches a land where people have never heard of the sea. There, a man will mistake the oar Odysseus carries for a winnowing fan. Only then can his journey end. But in reality the journey will never end because such a place does not exist. Shawcross's *Winnowing Oar* represents the emblem of infinite search: Ulysses's nostalgia for his homeland, but also a nostalgia for the unexplored, for the unknown, to measure the world with perspective and mathematics and then to measure time and the universe. Shawcross is attracted to this hypothesis and to the ontological, metaphysical and mystic dimensions that it opens up. Another sculpture that is perfect for a Renaissance *studiolo* is *Measurement and Control for the Infinite* (2002). It consists of a group of seven portable 'instruments' that the artist exhibits sometimes together, sometimes separately, that are vaguely reminiscent of navigation tools. Once opened, these instruments reveal a miniature maze of mirrors inside. A portable instrument that can measure the infinite brings

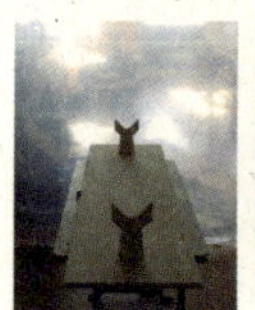
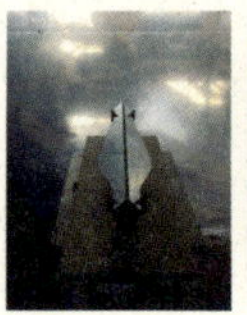
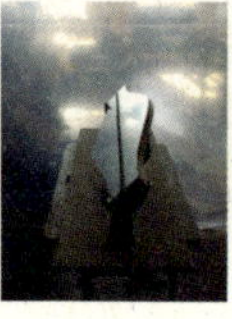
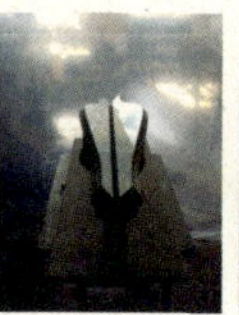
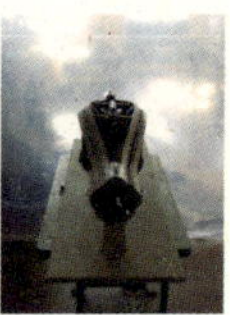

us back to ideas of travel and human adventure, back to a dream of a small and heroic explorer thrown towards the discovery of the mystery of the cosmos and life.

Beauty. Shawcross's works possess their own specific, fascinating beauty. In his hands, wood sheds both its antiquity and familiarity and is transformed with artisan knowledge into something completely new, into an equation of intelligence, a virtuosity of the imagination. The tight, pure form and almost metaphysical beauty that characterizes *The Winnowing Oar* and

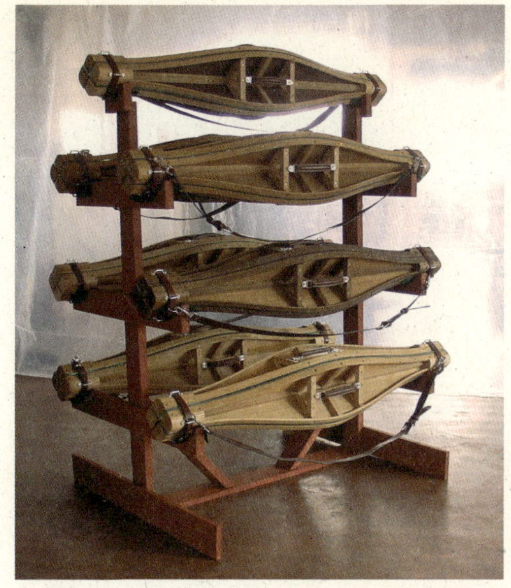

Measurement and Control for the Infinite, 2002

Measurement and Control for the Infinite leaves room in other, kinetic works for more spectacular mechanical complexity and a greater degree of showiness. In one series of works, for example in *Skelter* (2003) and *Light Perpetual* (2004), the artist uses sources of light, attaching a bulb to the extremity of a wooden arm that rotated around itself. The speed of movement and the intensity of the light ensure that the sculpture produces a luminous design in the space. In each of the works, this design assumes a particular significance according to the type of movement of the arm. The ethereal light shape of *Skelter*, for example, is an updated version of the rounded patterns drawn by the Harmonograph – a kind of Victorian spirograph – but can also be read as the circle of energy related to string theory. *Light Perpetual* also refers to string theory, which unites two sectors of modern physics: Einstein's theory of general relativity and Quantum mechanics, which postulates the existence

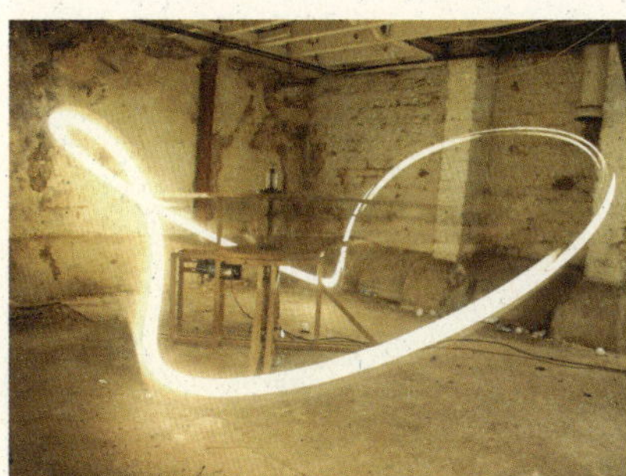

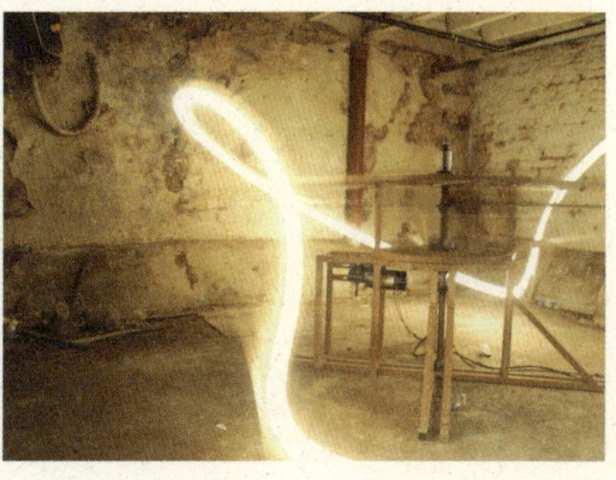

Skelter, 2003

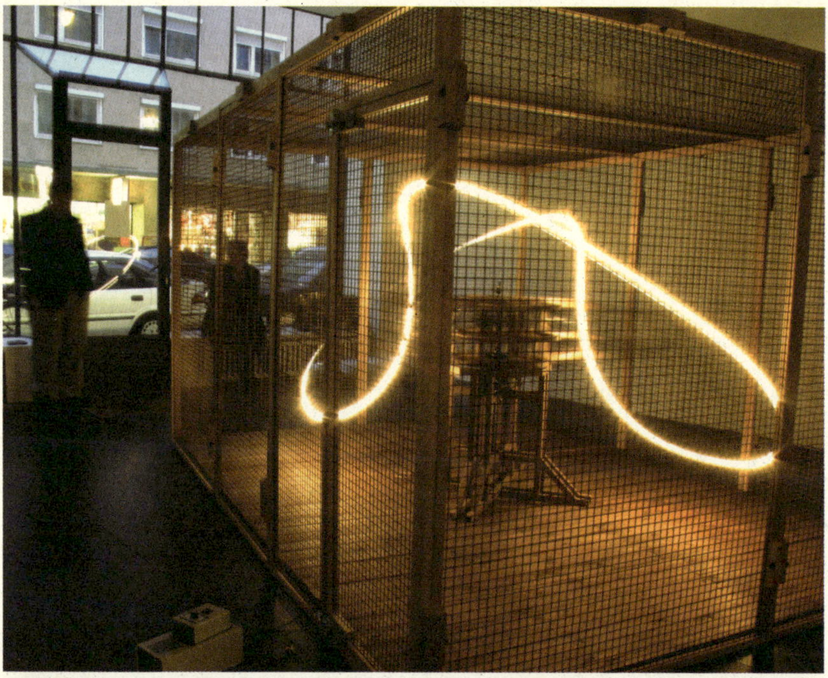

Light Perpetual, 2004

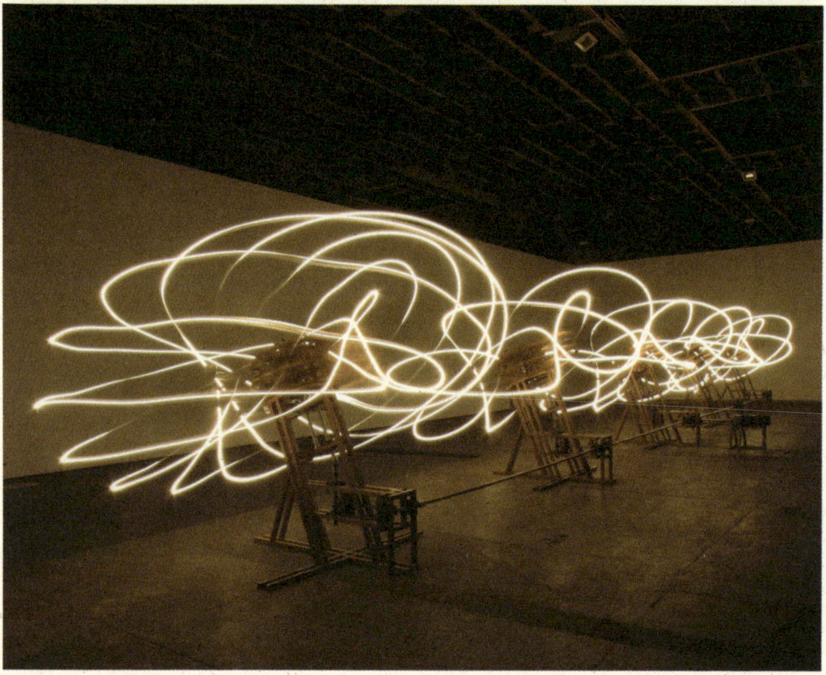

Loop System Quintet, 2005

of a multidimensional universe. From this work, the artist has developed *Loop System Quintet*, a series of five similar machines shown in the present exhibition at The New Art Gallery Walsall and the Walker Art Gallery, Liverpool. These machines are driven by a single drive-shaft leading to a motor and are visual transcriptions of harmonic chords, each tying – as the artist says – a different 'knot in space'.

Sound is a new frontier of Shawcross's work. *Harmonic Tower*, also included in the exhibition, is a tall construction equipped with two huge

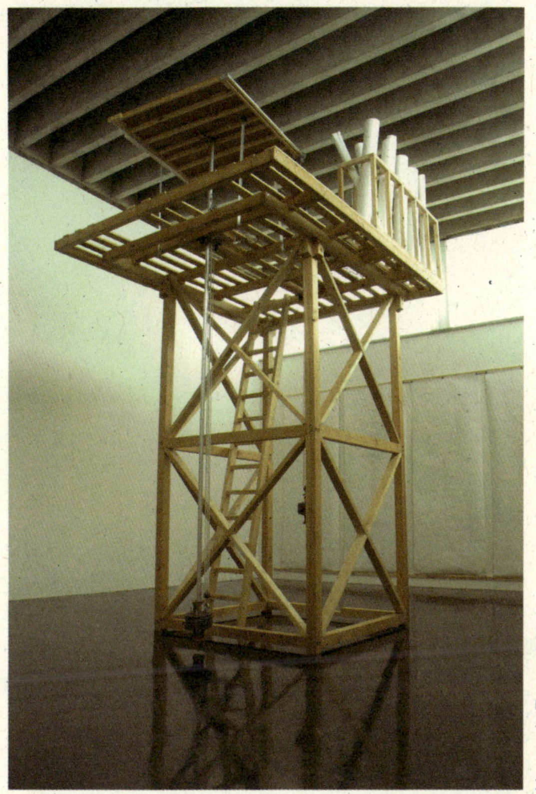

Harmonic Tower, 2005

pendulums, in a shape that once again recalls a Da Vinci machine. The pendulums draw harmonic sketches that in their dynamic equilibrium – their 'steady states' – refer to music and mathematics. A final piece is also influenced by the question of sound. Shawcross was inspired by an acoustic telescope that confirmed the Big Bang theory and the expansion of the universe in 1963, by receiving sound from space. A huge acoustic horn, six metres long and five metres wide is attached to a windowless shed on stilts which the viewer can enter. It looks like an old gramophone but it also brings to mind the image of a giant human ear that can listen to the remotest secrets of the universe. Shawcross's horizon is once again that of the cosmos and its mysteries.

The substantial, ontological nature of his work, the interest in research combining philosophical, scientific, metaphysical and even mystical motives, associate the British artist with certain interesting artists spread across the globe. The American Tim Hawkinson, the German Björn Dhalem, and the Italian Gianni Caravaggio come to mind. Through very diverse practices, these artists share with Shawcross a fascination with the cosmos and its dynamic, and an art capable of bringing to light territories inaccessible to rational thought. Their attitude towards science is thus for the most part anecdotal, metaphorical and literary. In a world such as ours, conditioned by the disciplined experience of a language that inclines towards a univocal objectivity, the metaphorical and literary principles of their works can be seen as an authentic means of understanding connections and relations: an imperfect procedure, but one that nonetheless is cable of discerning the richness of meanings precisely where the concept appears insufficient.

Loop System Quintet

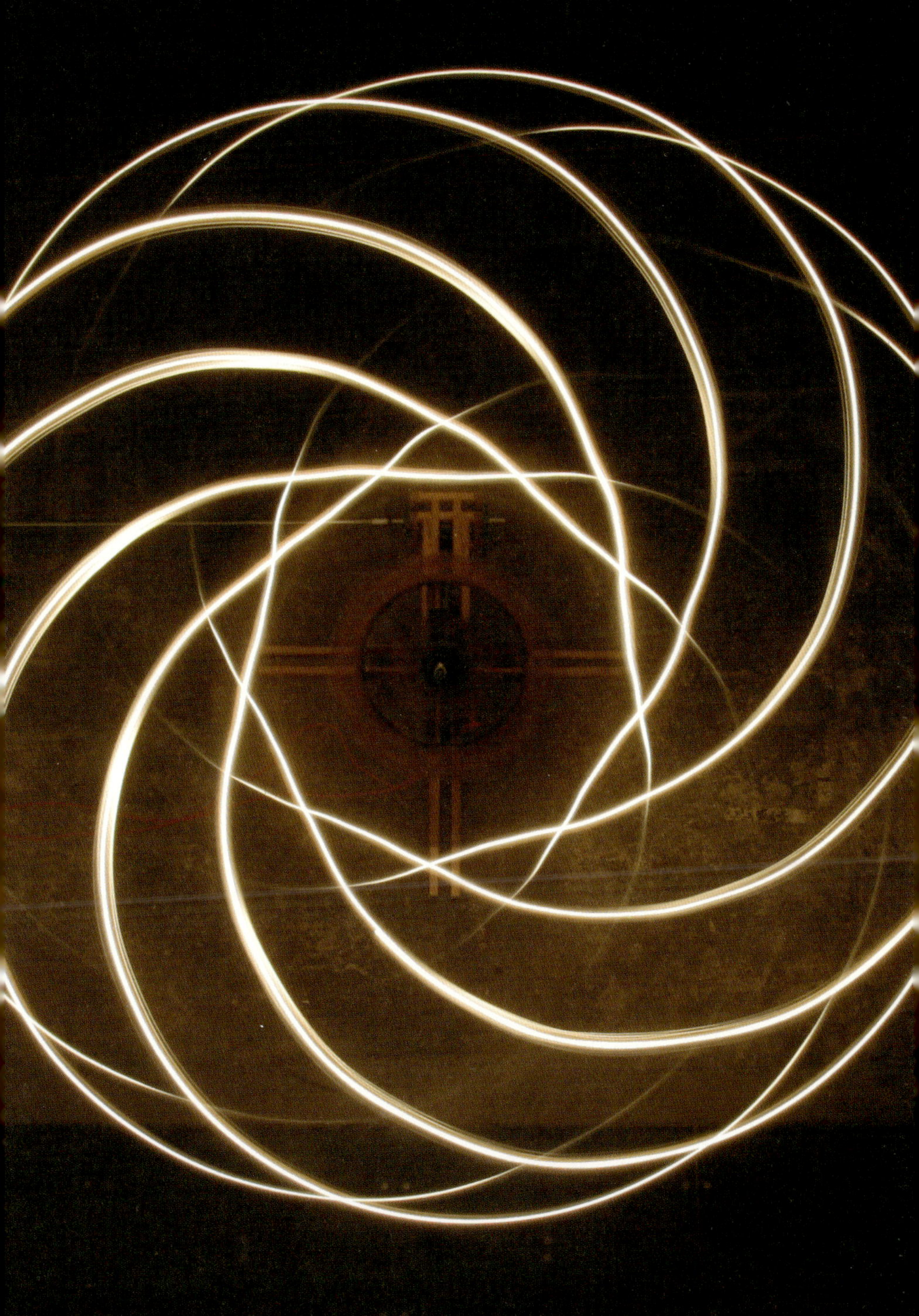

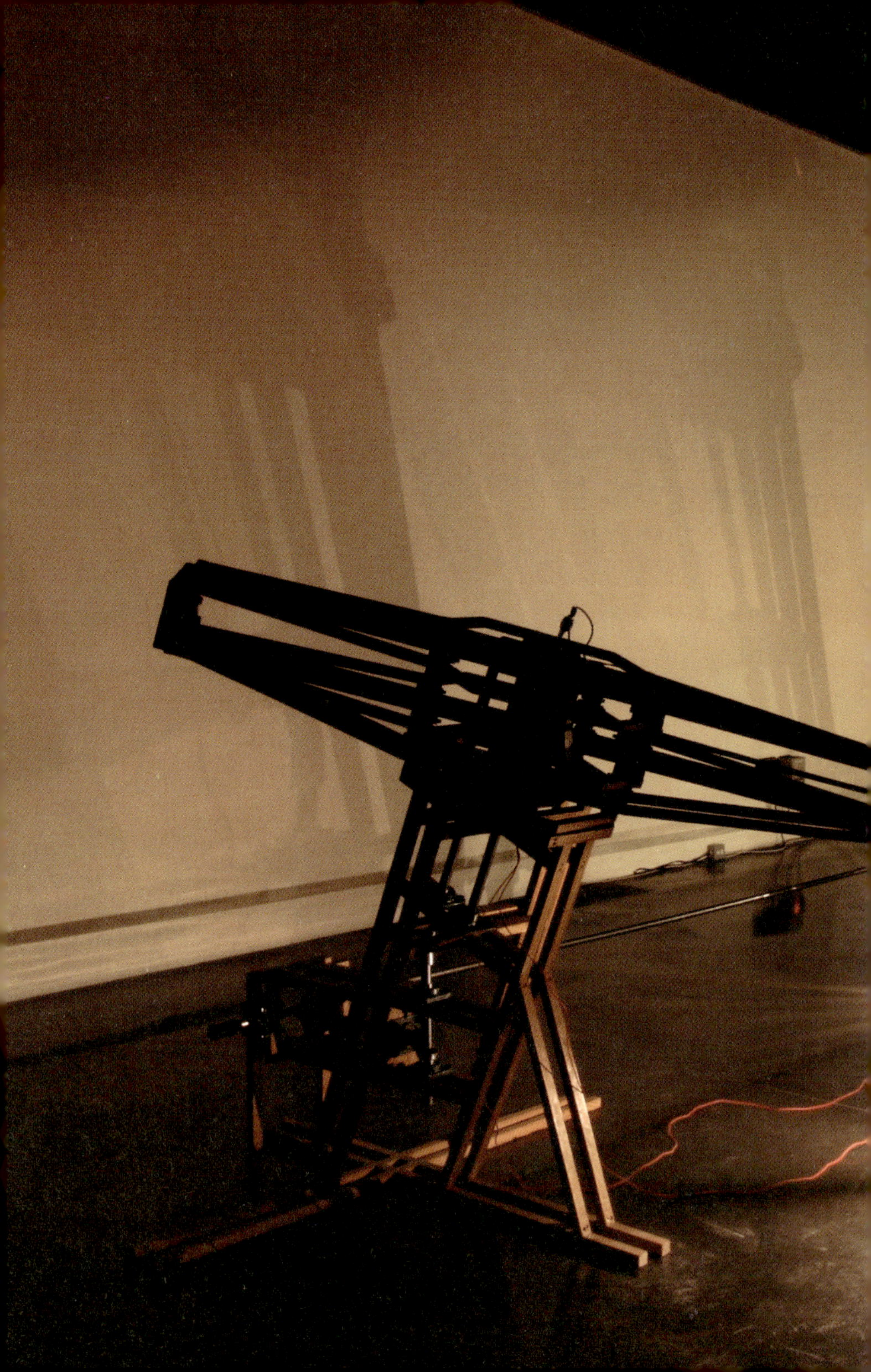

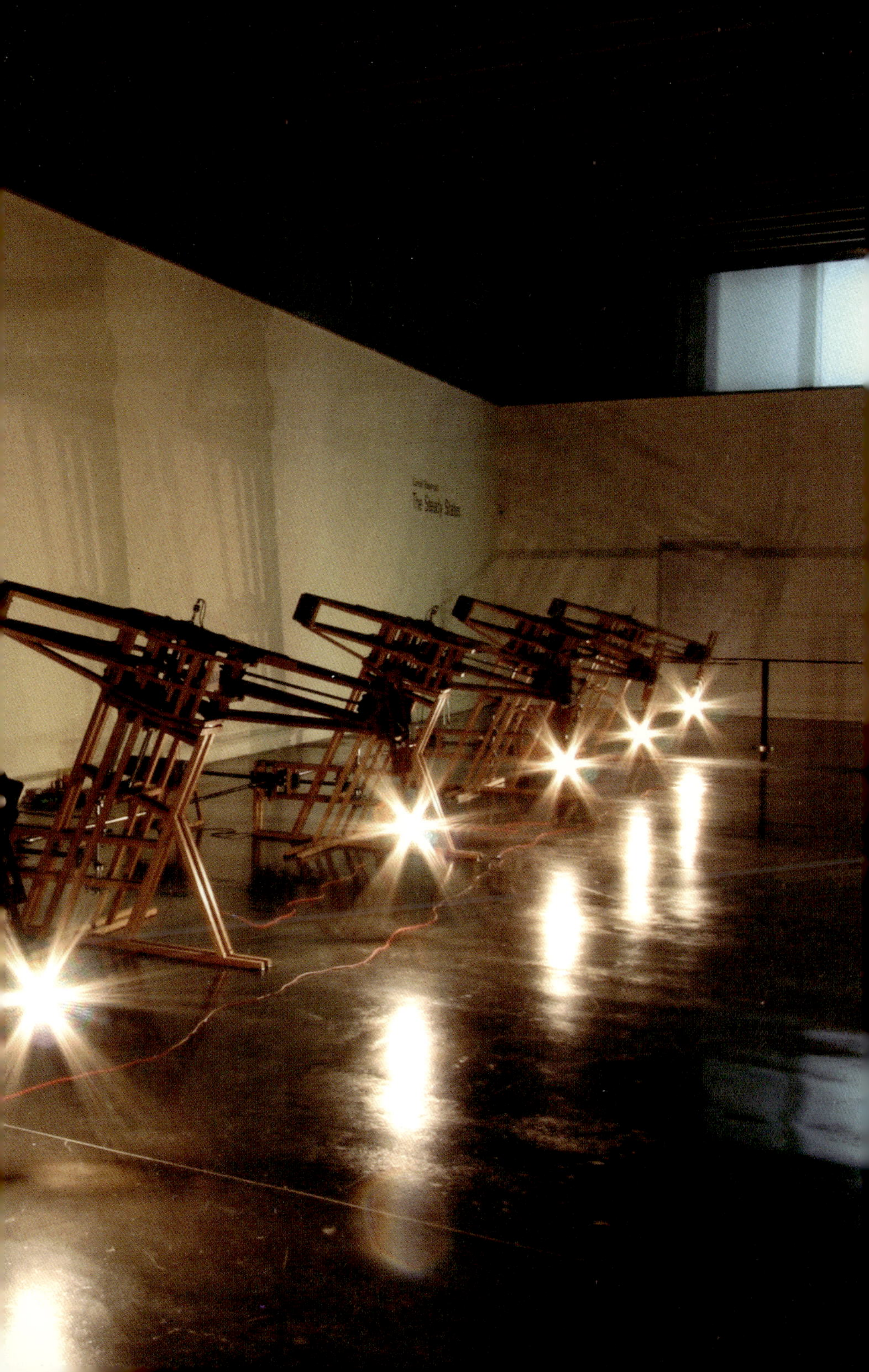

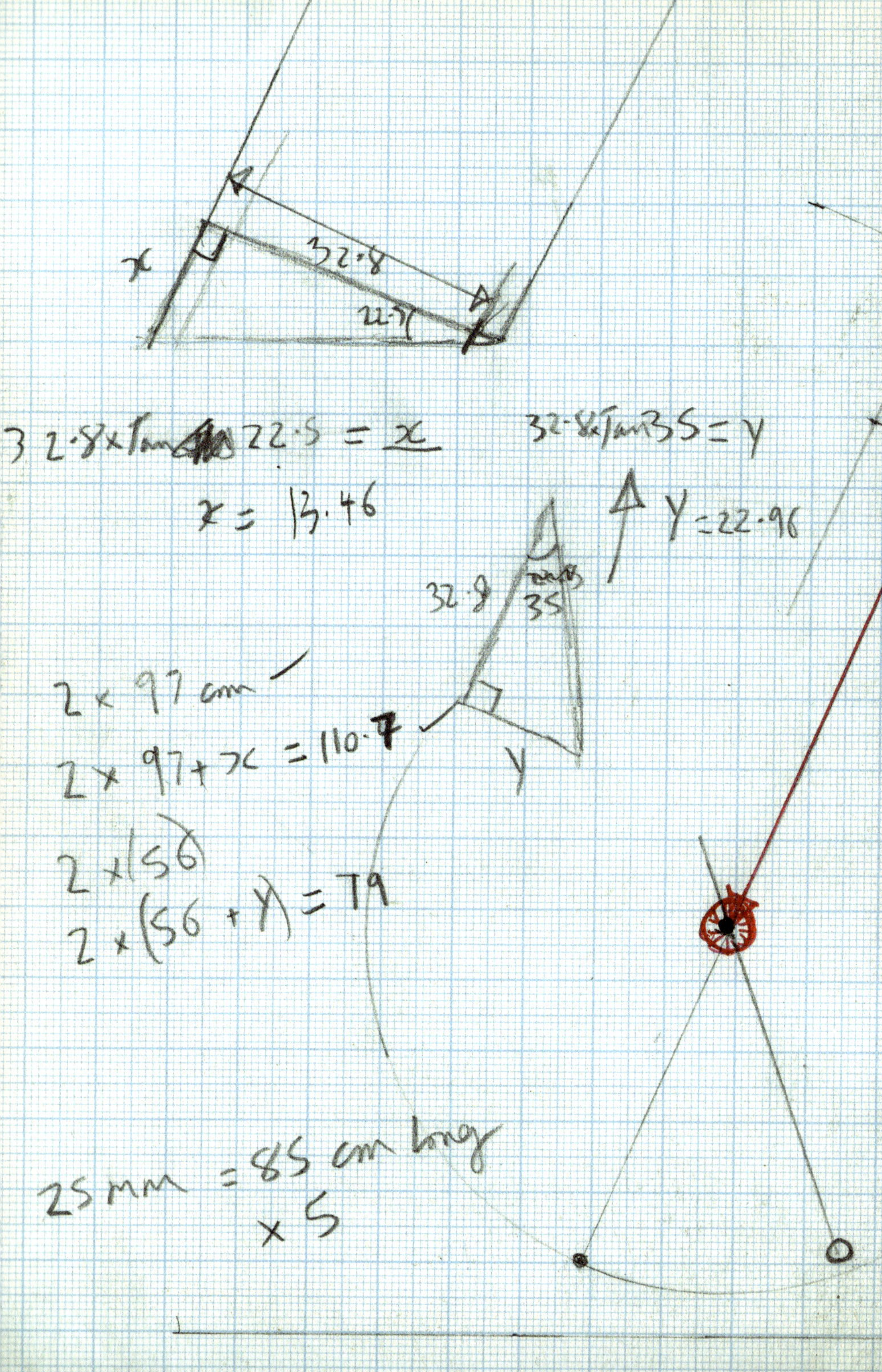

x
32.8
22.5
32.8 x Tan 22.5 = x
x = 13.46
32.8 x Tan 35 = y
y = 22.96
32.8
35
y
2 x 97 cm
2 x 97 + x = 110.7
2 x (56)
2 x (56 + y) = 79
25 mm = 85 cm long
x 5

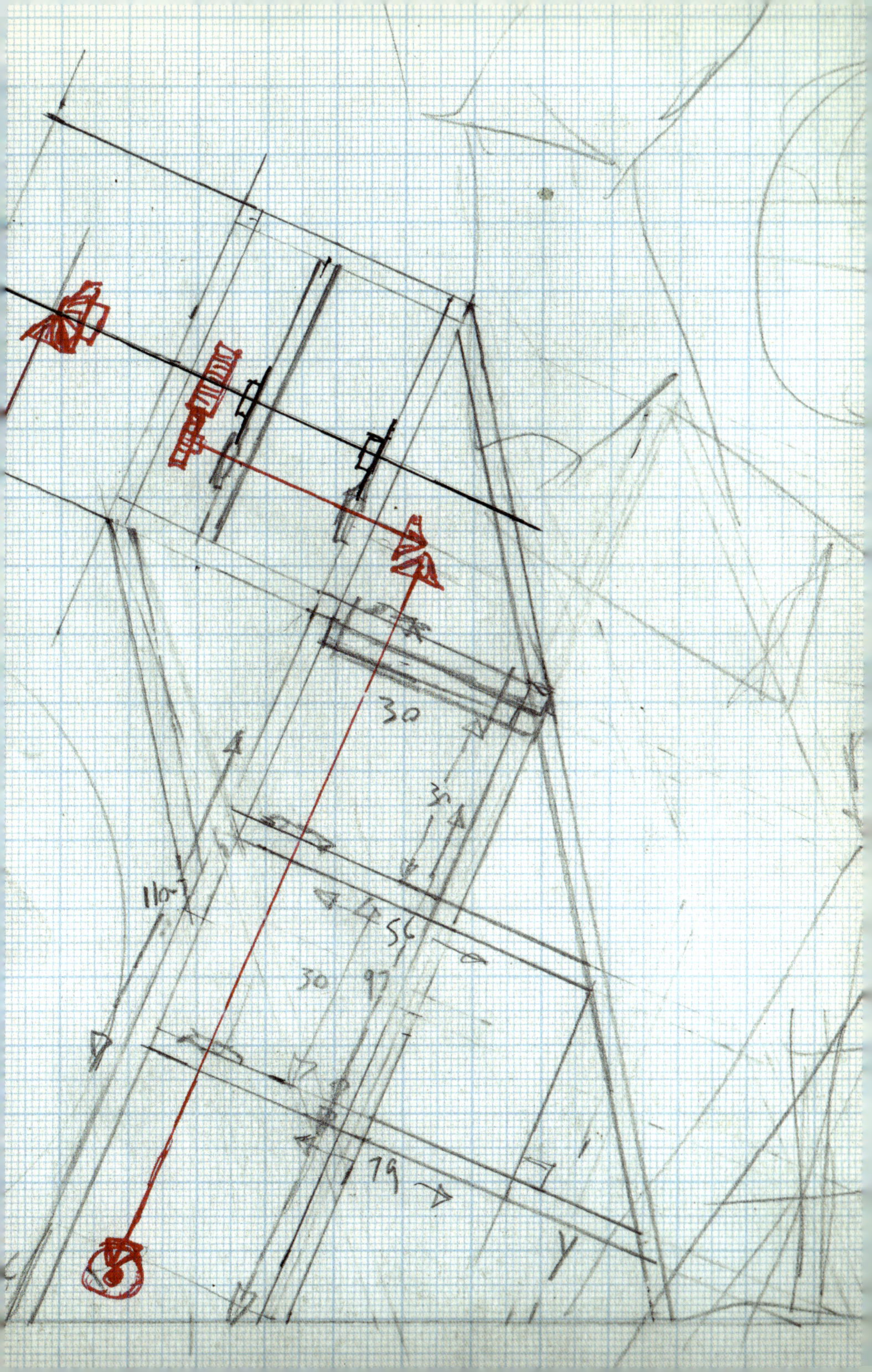

30
35
110
56
30
97
79

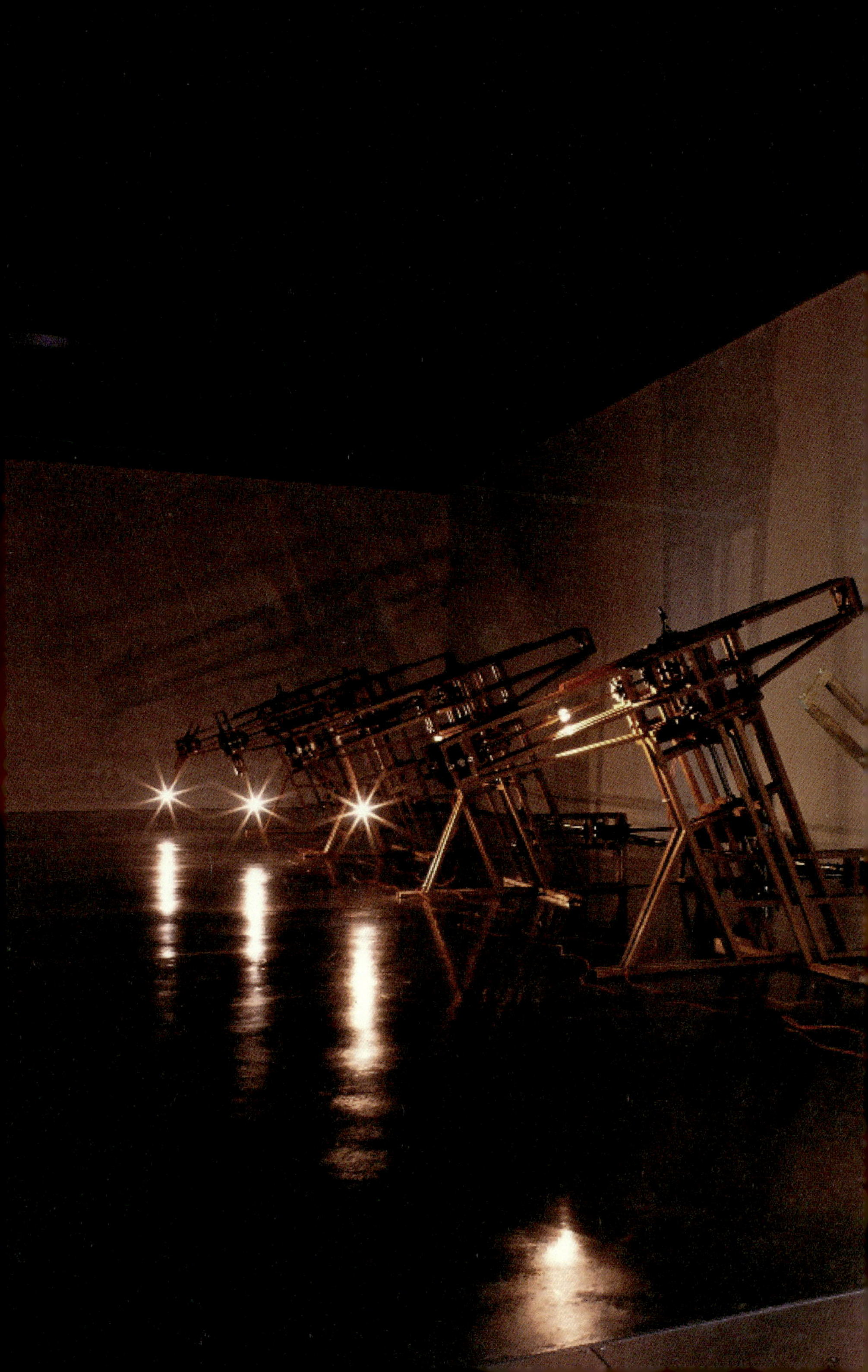

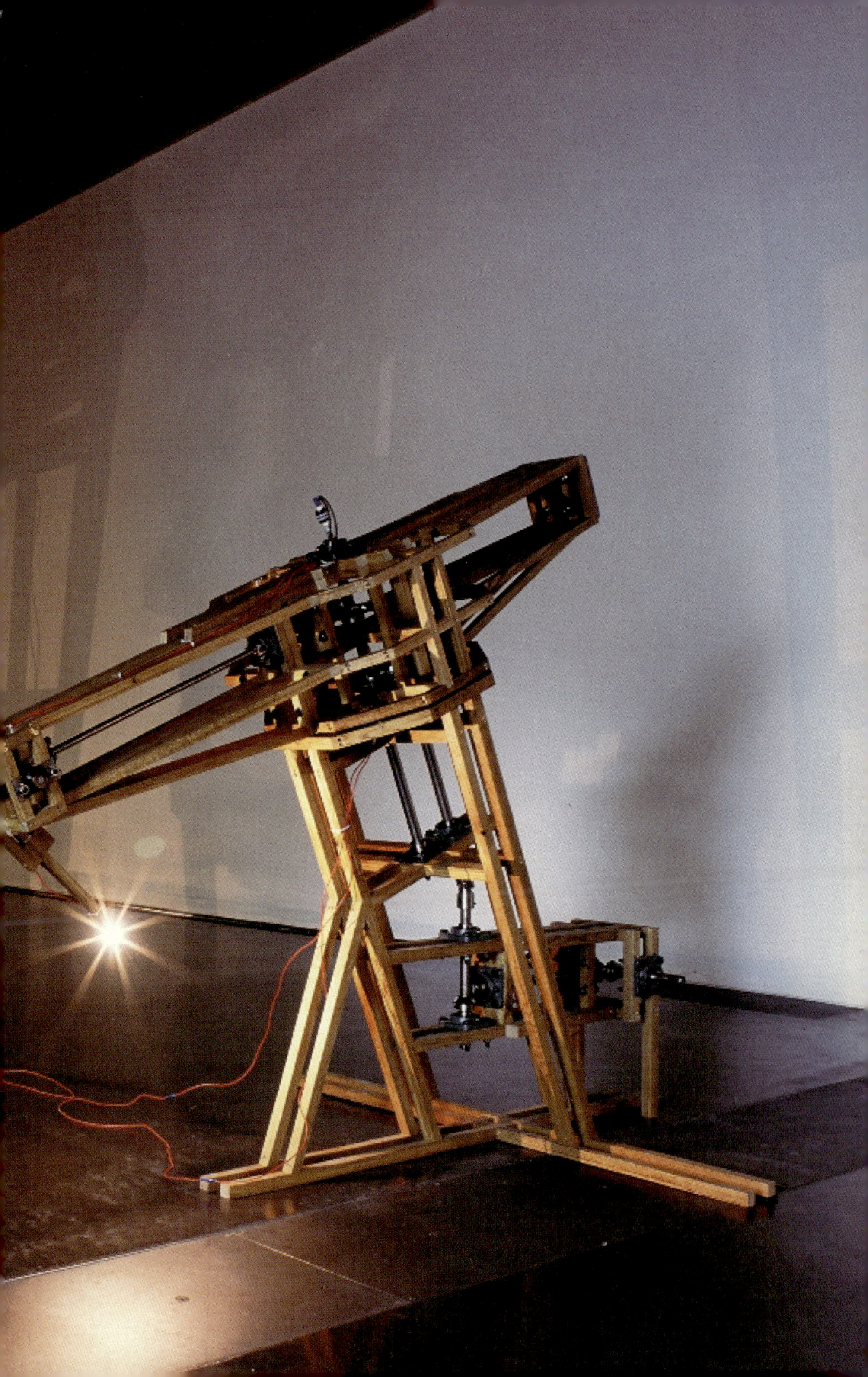

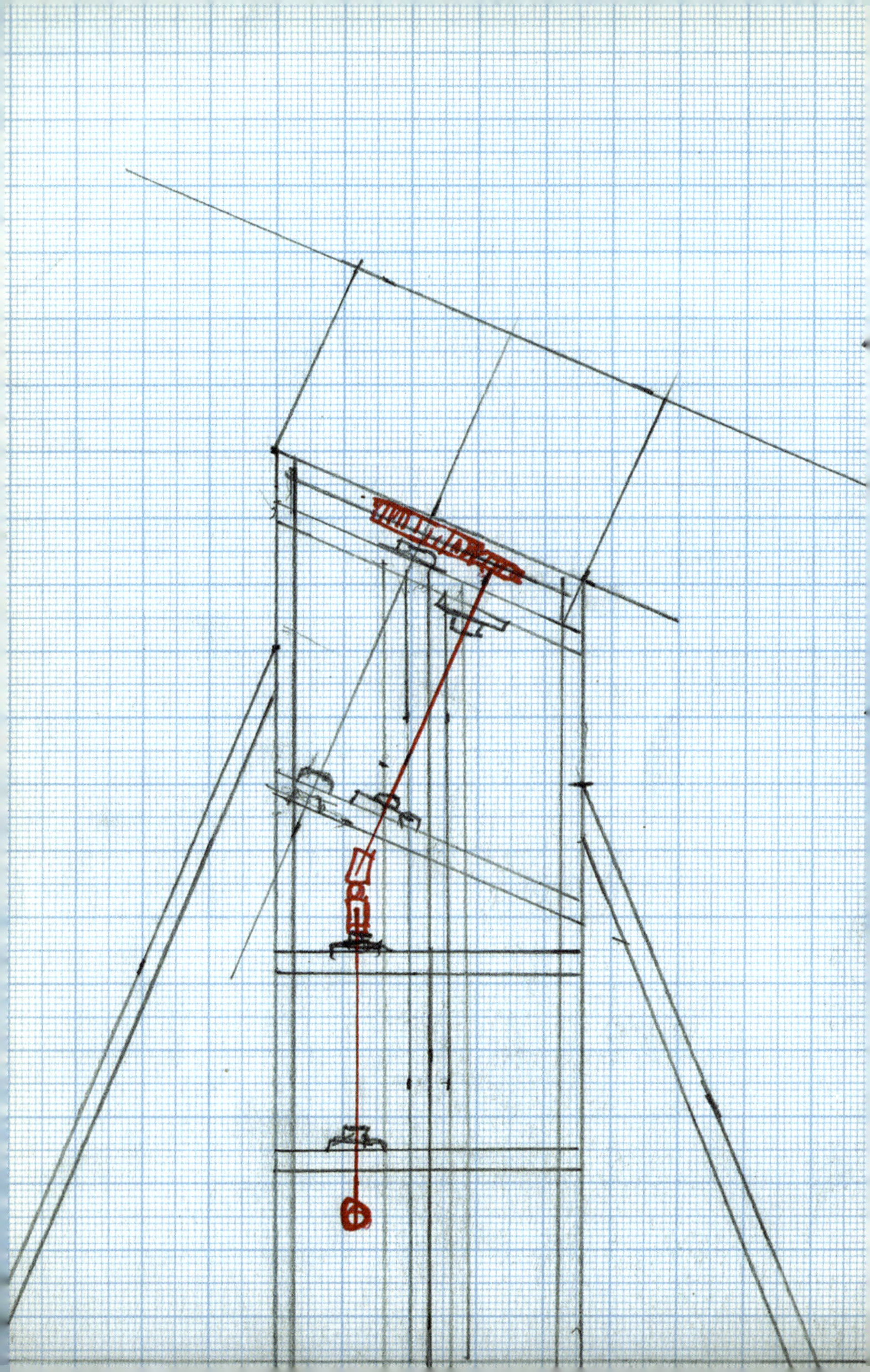

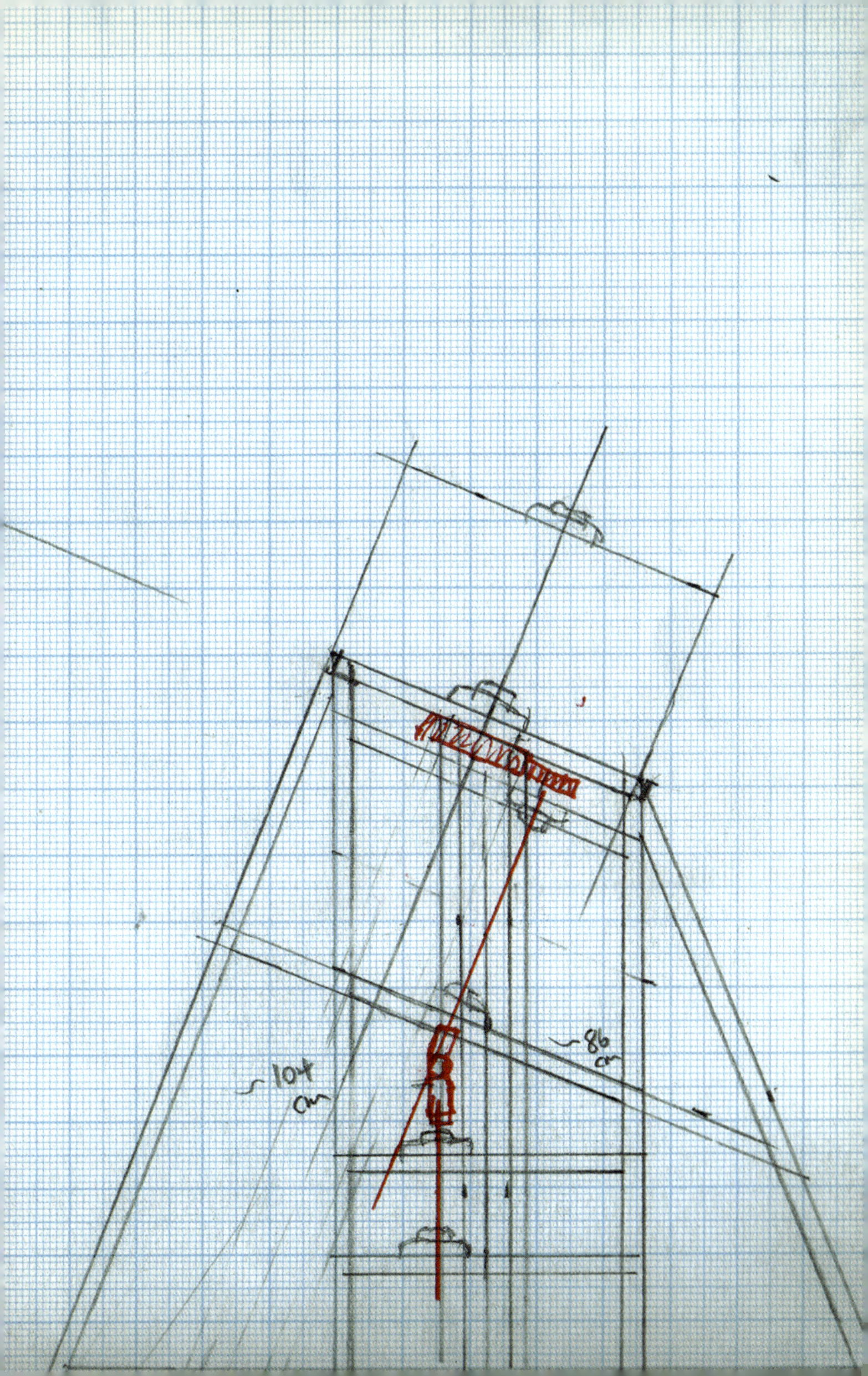
104 cm
86 cm

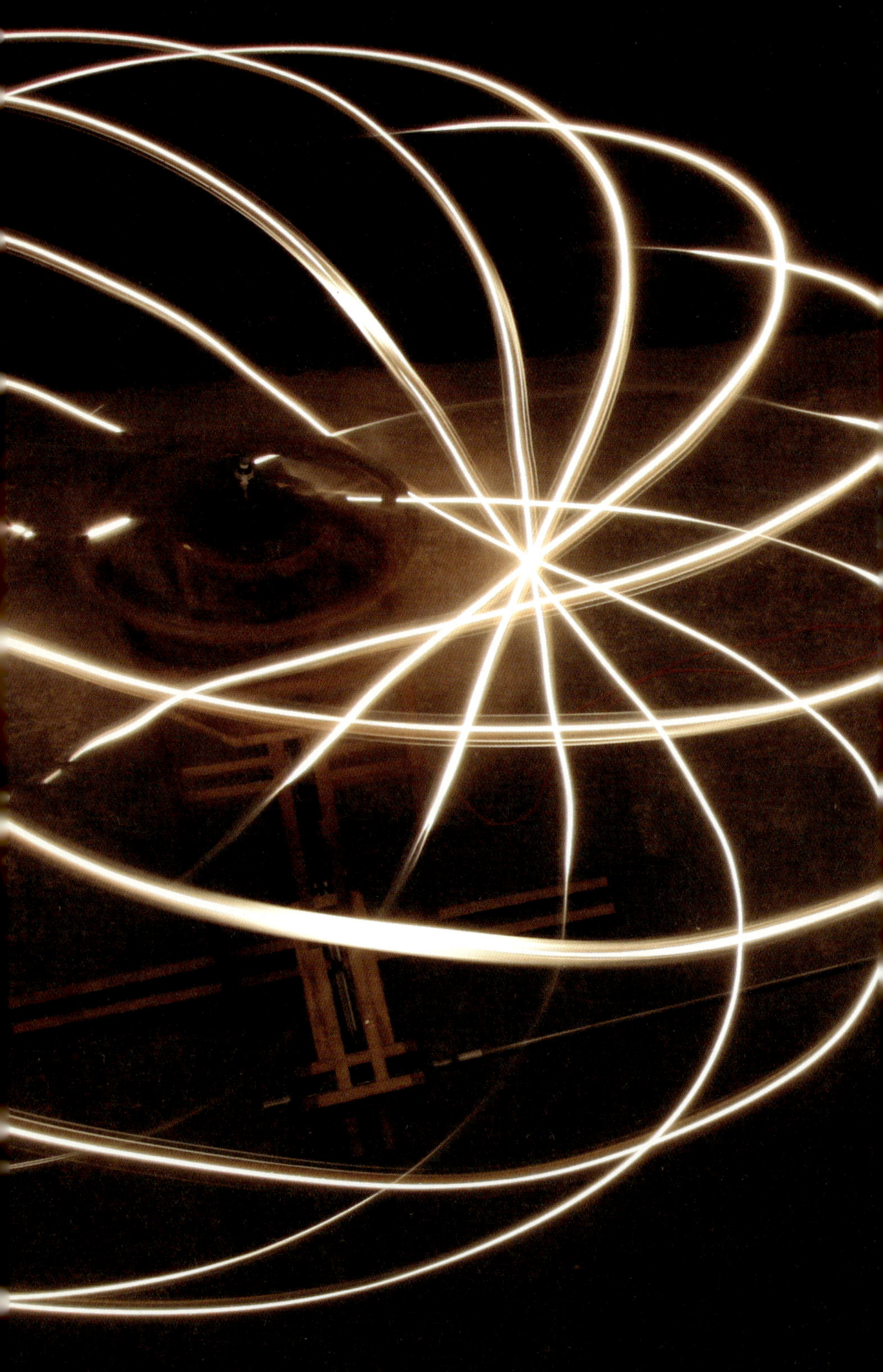

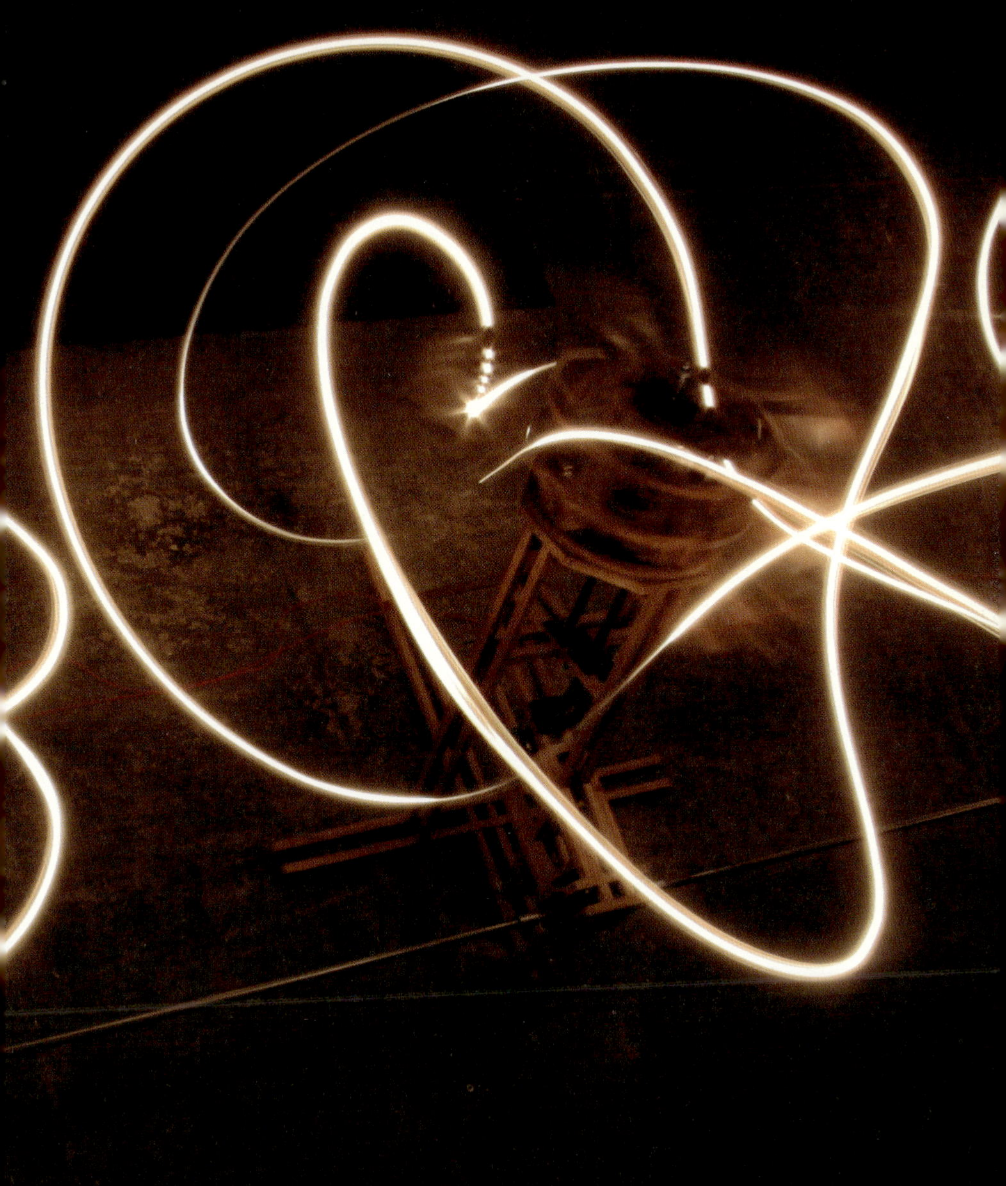

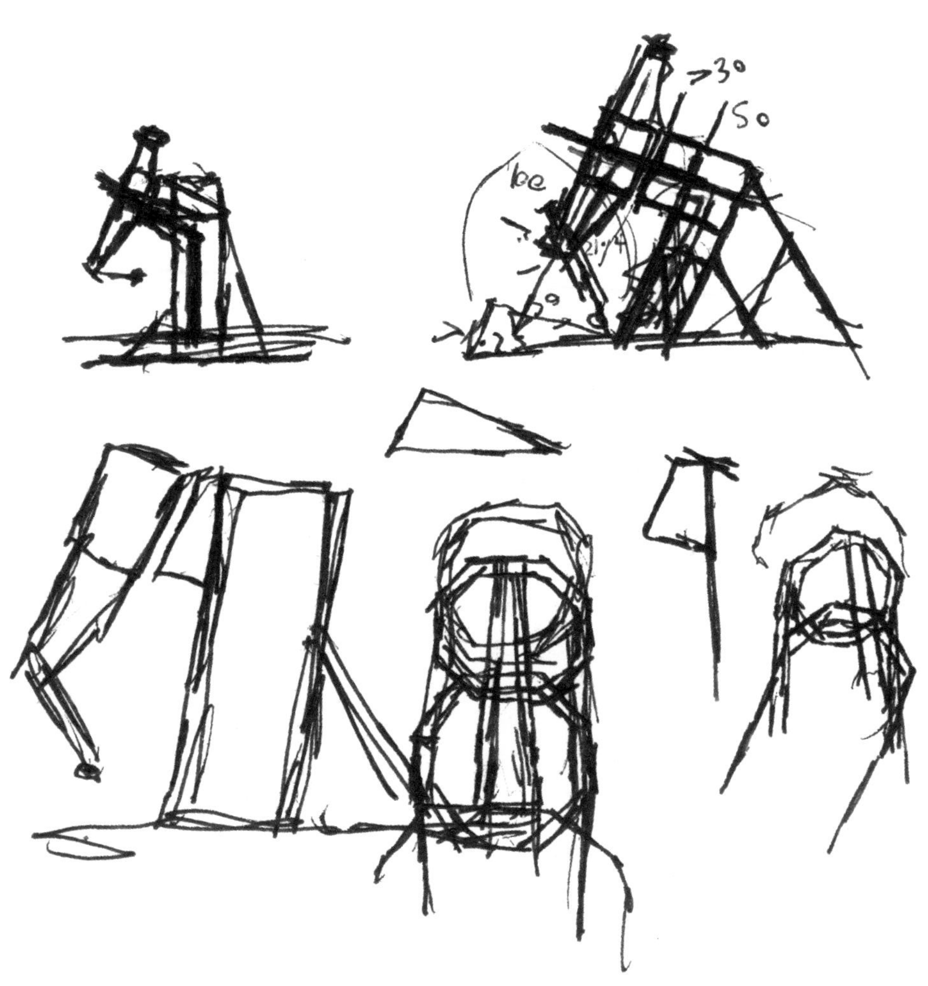

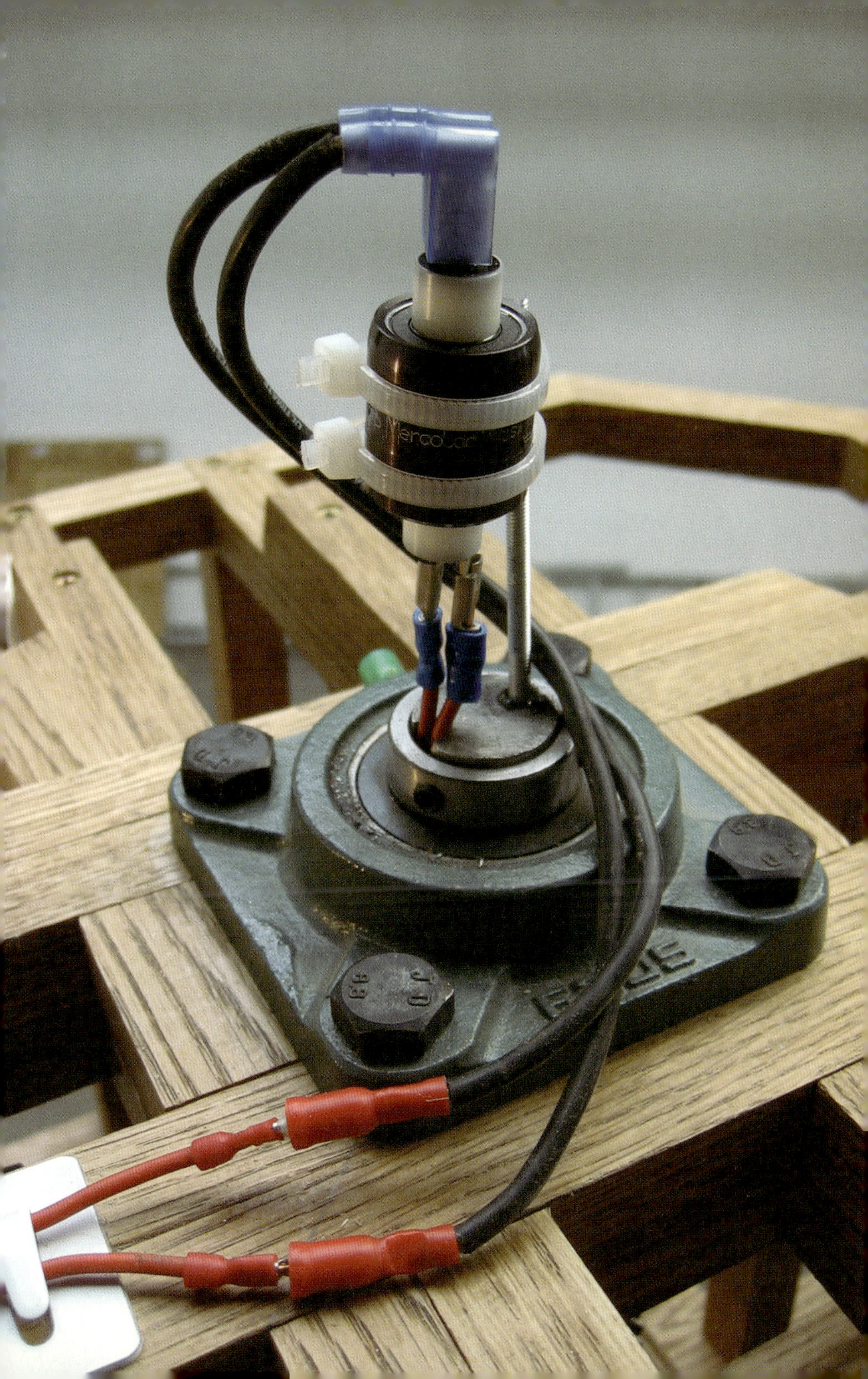
Mercotac

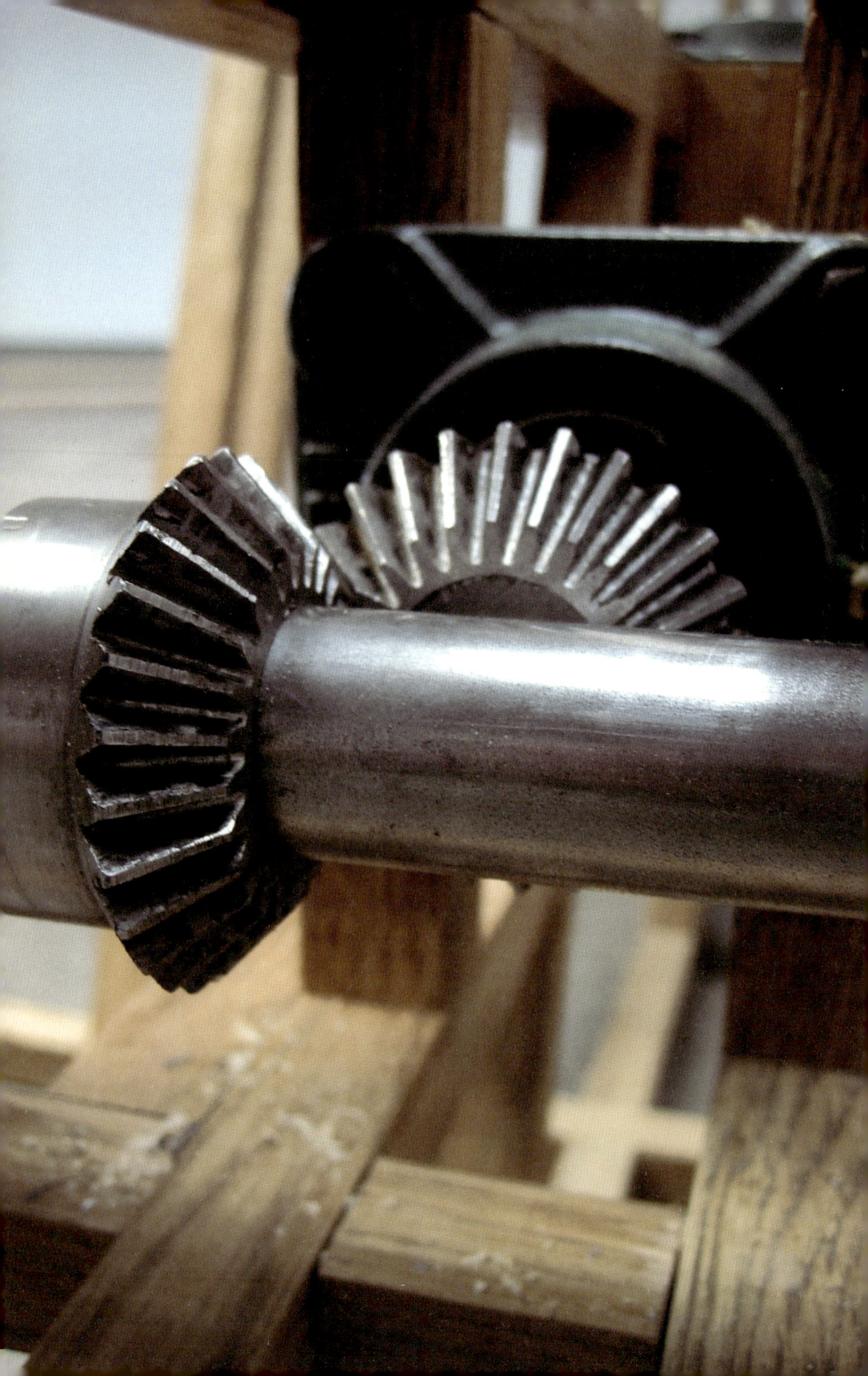

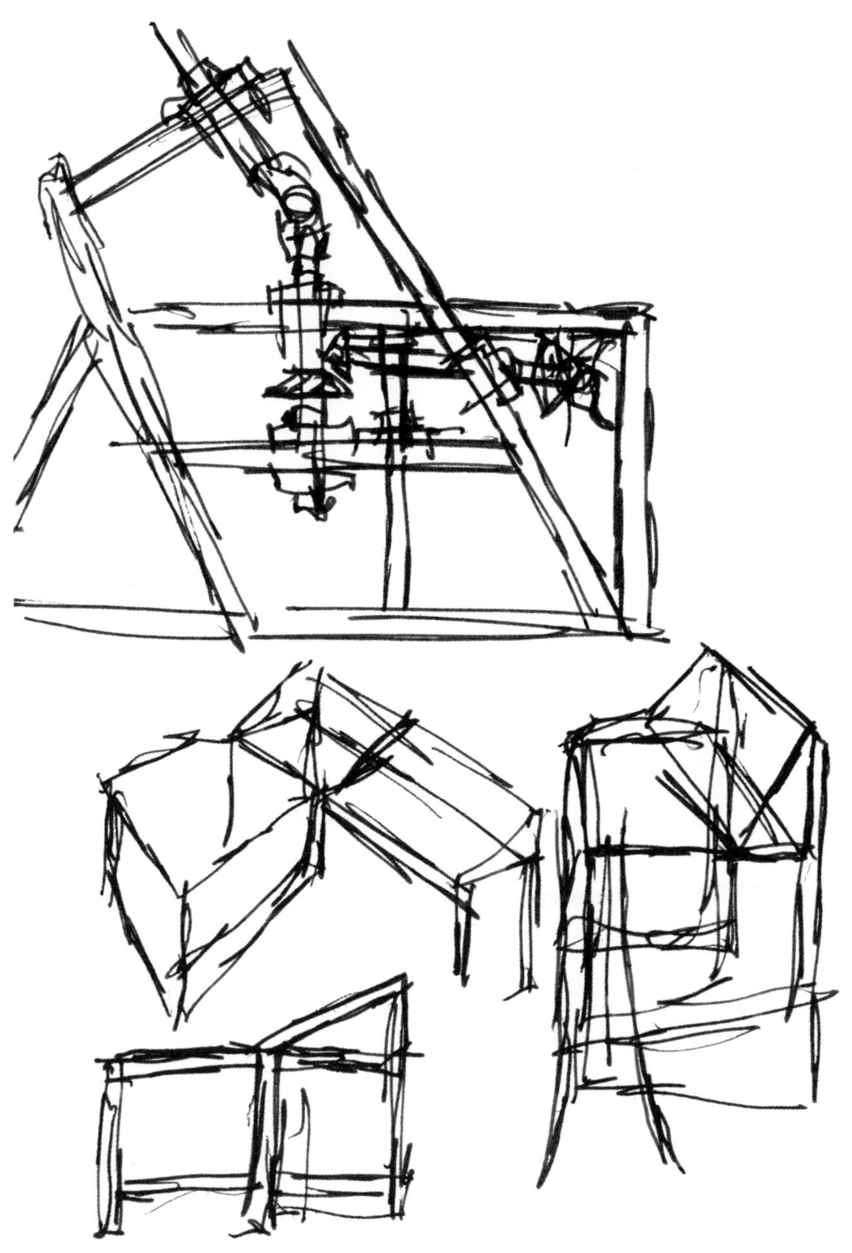

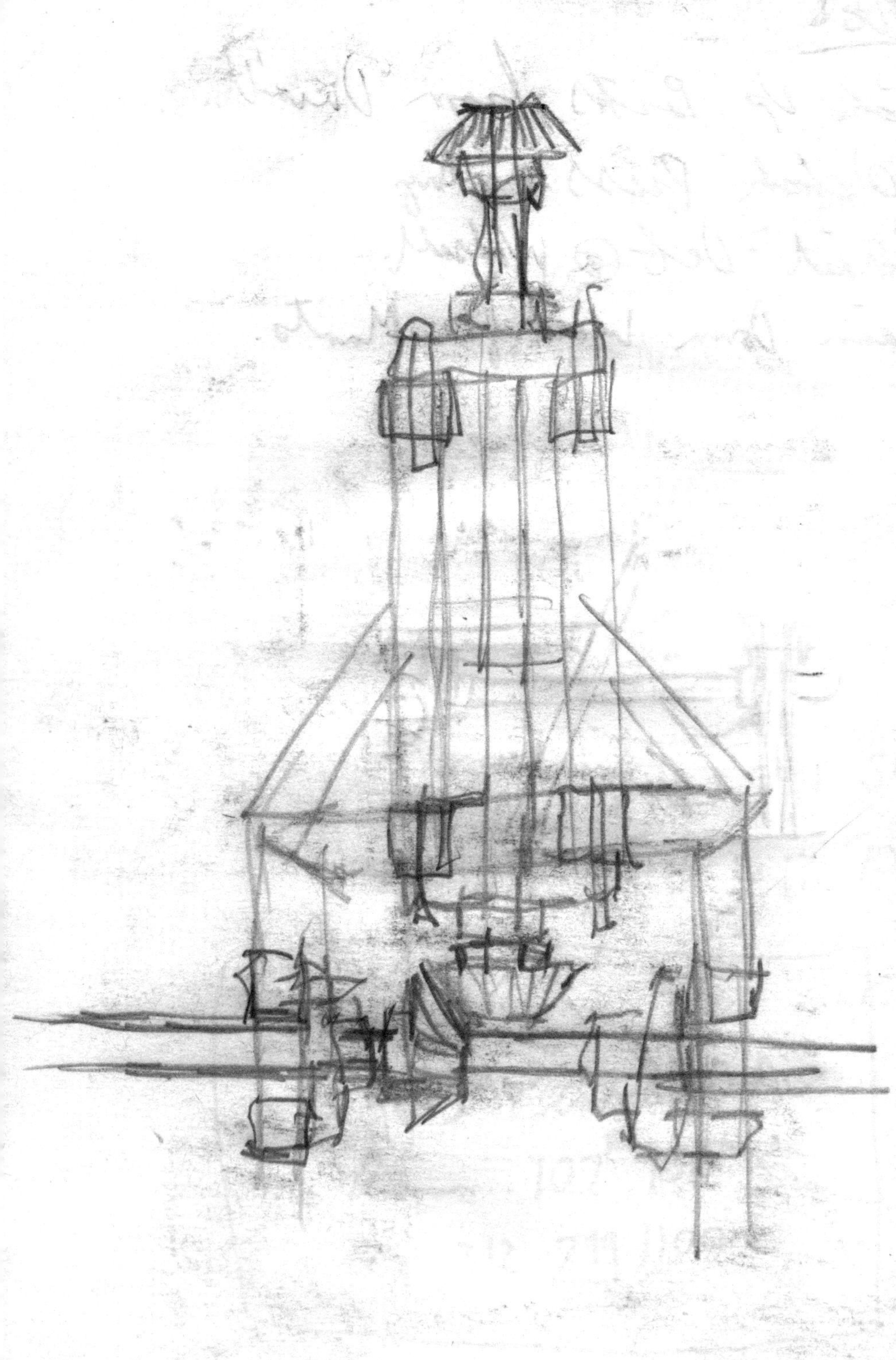

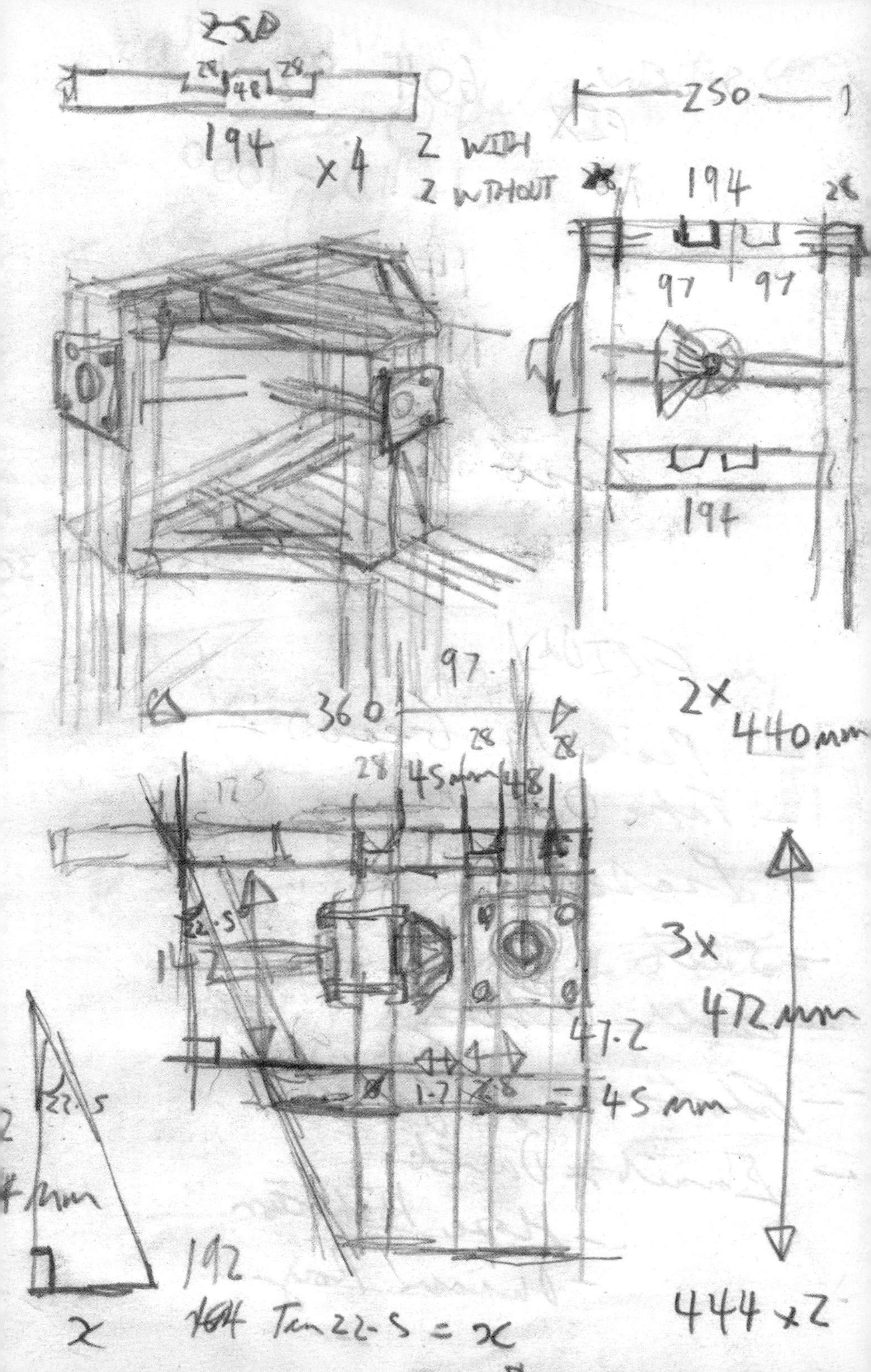

250
28
48
28
194
x 4
2 WITH
2 WITHOUT
250
194
28
97
97
194
97
360
2x
440mm
28
28
28
45mm
48
22.5
142
3x
472mm
47.2
1.7
28
45mm
22.5
192
Tan 22.5 = x
444 x 2

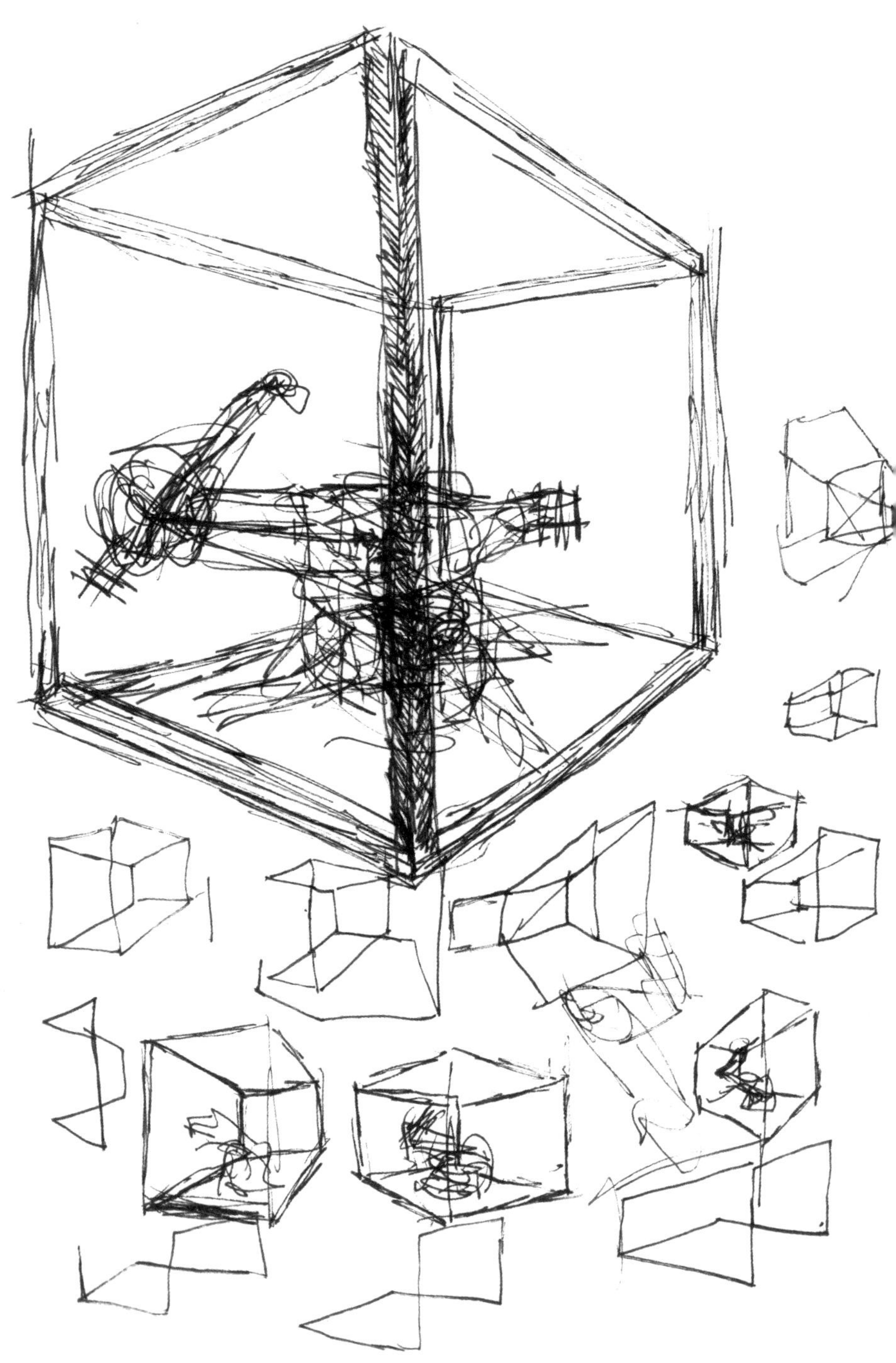

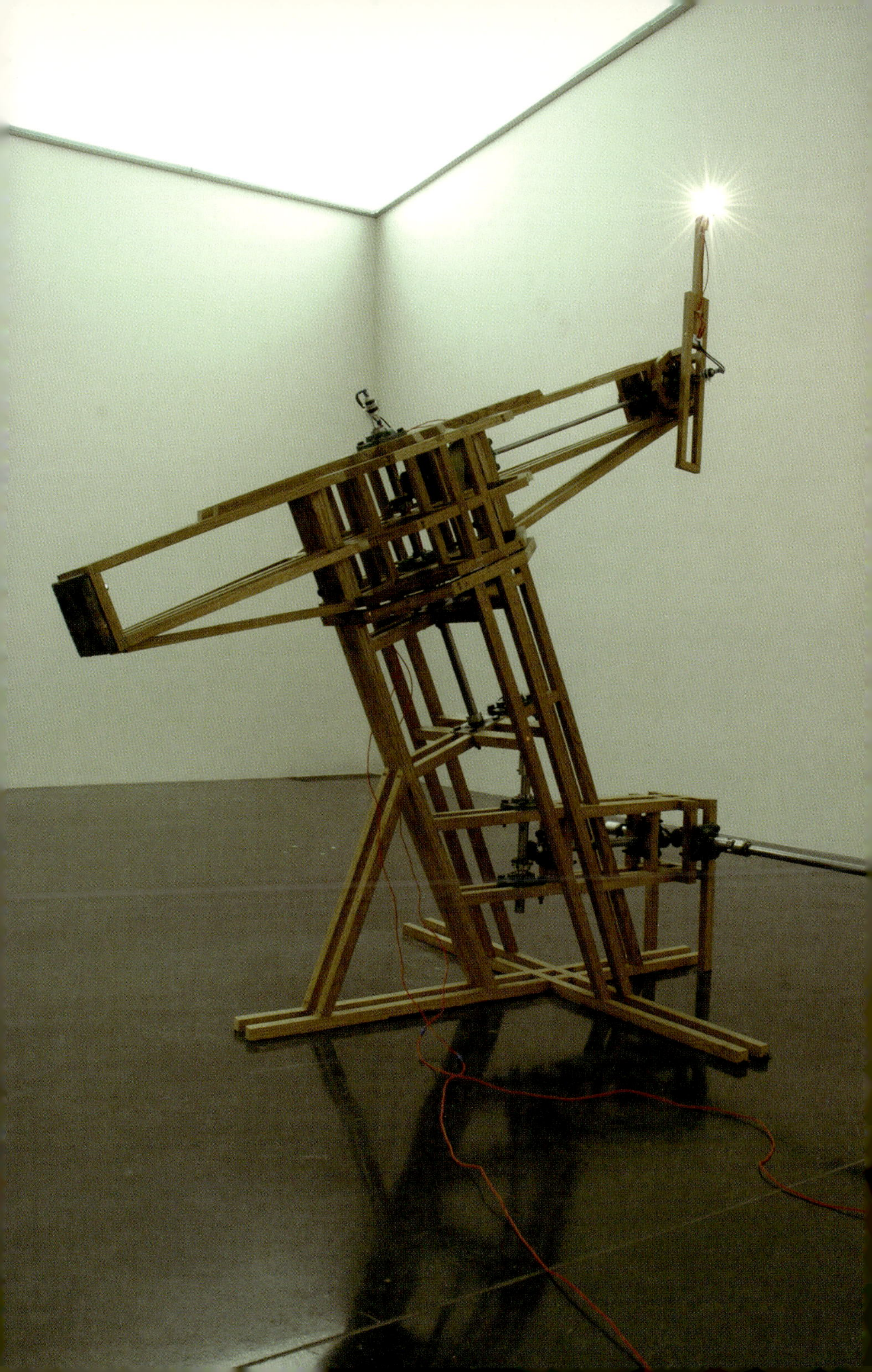

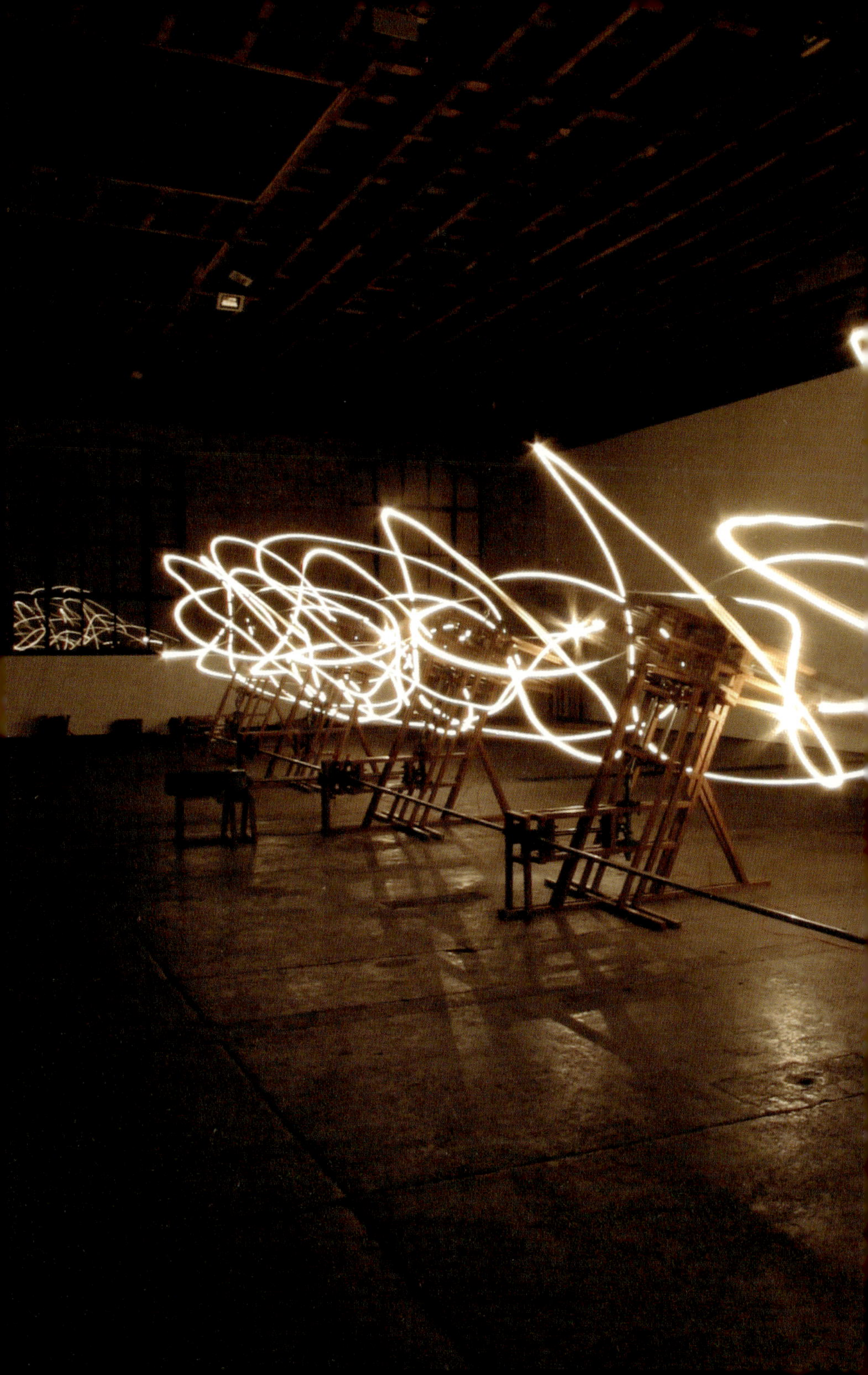

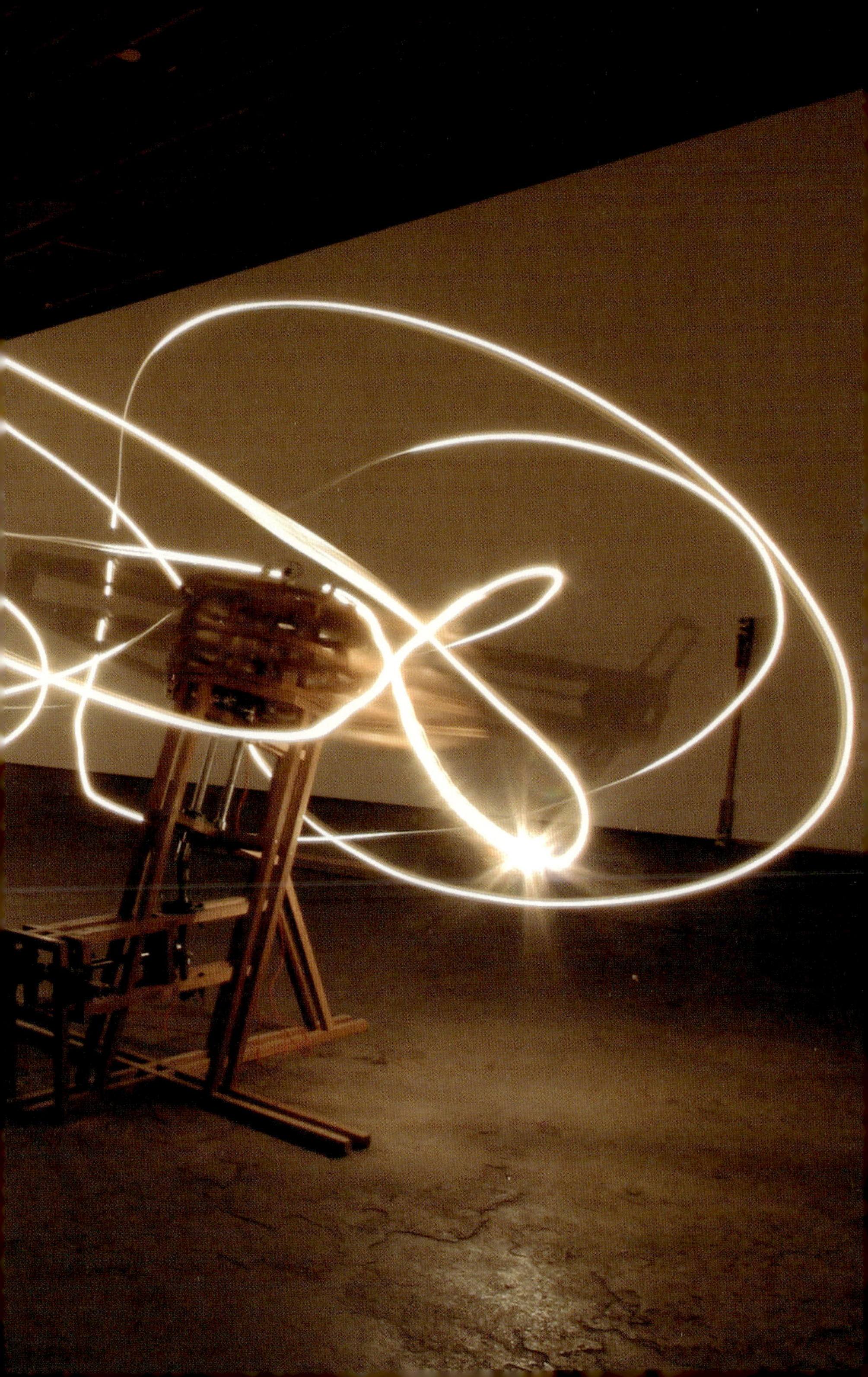

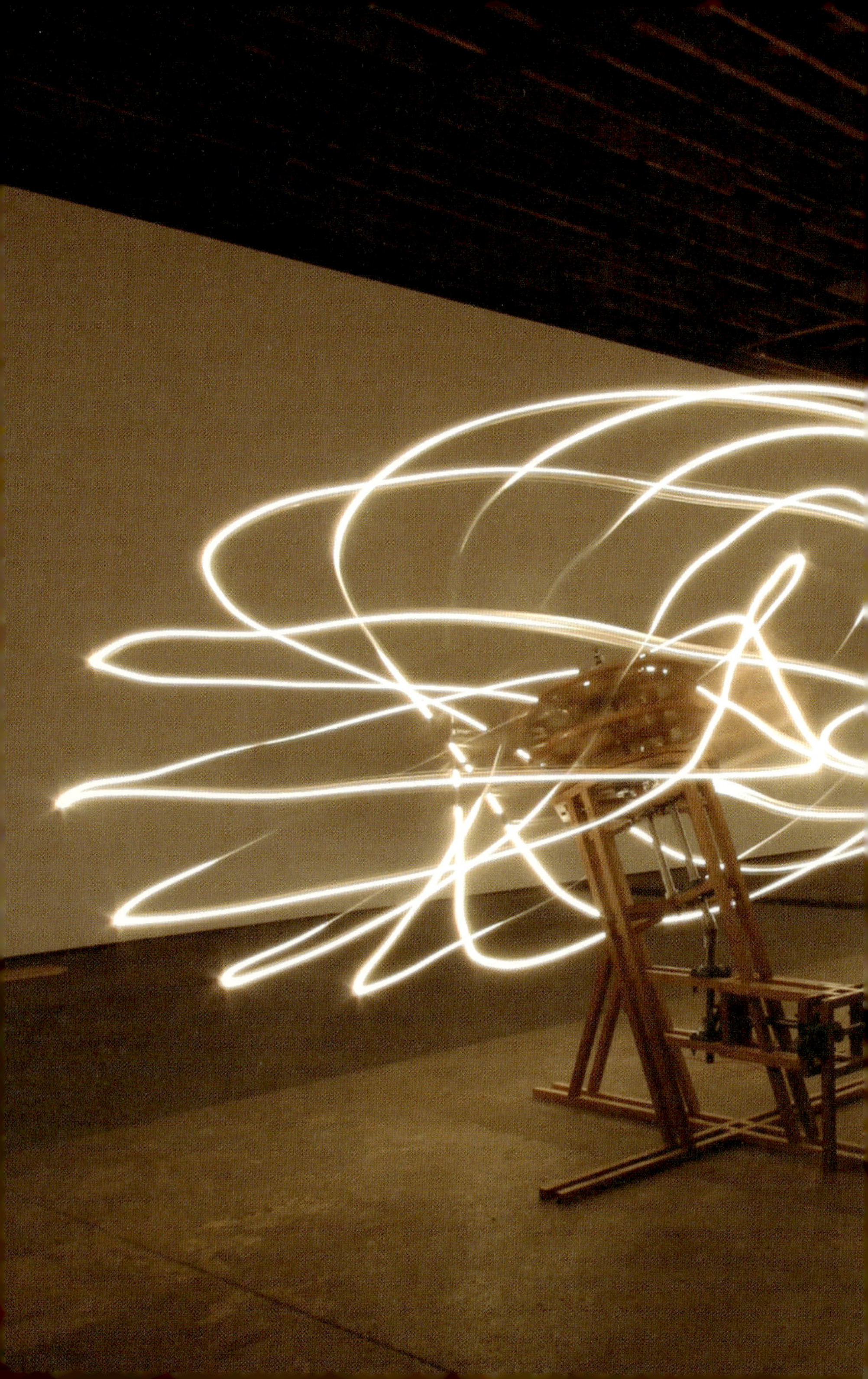

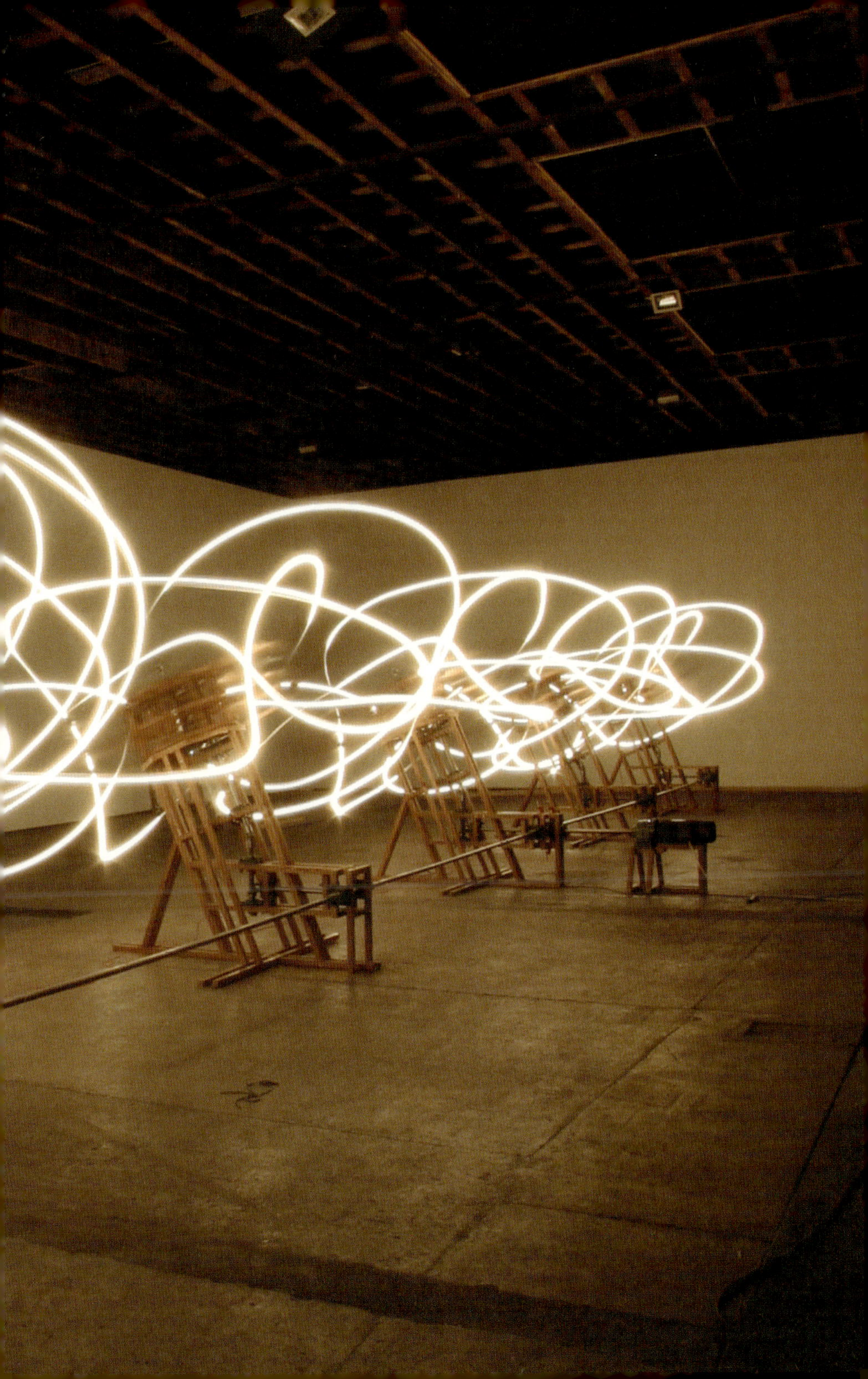

RATIOS

TEETH

2 : 1 OCTAVE	40 : 20	x 12
5 : 3 MAJOR 6th	50 : 30	x 12
8 : 5 MINOR SIXTH	40 : 25	x 12
3 : 2 FIFTH	45 : 30	x 12
4 : 3 FOURTH	40 : 30	x 12
5 : 4 MAJOR 3RD	50 : 40	x 12
6 : 5 MINOR 3RD	~~60 : 25~~ 30 : 25	x 12
9 : 8 SECOND	45 : 40	x 12

BEYOND

3 : 1 OCTAVE + A 5th

4 : 1 TWO OCTAVES

5 : 3

600 x 3 = 1800   360 x = 1080

3000   1800

1020   1080

3600 1800 Big 360 small

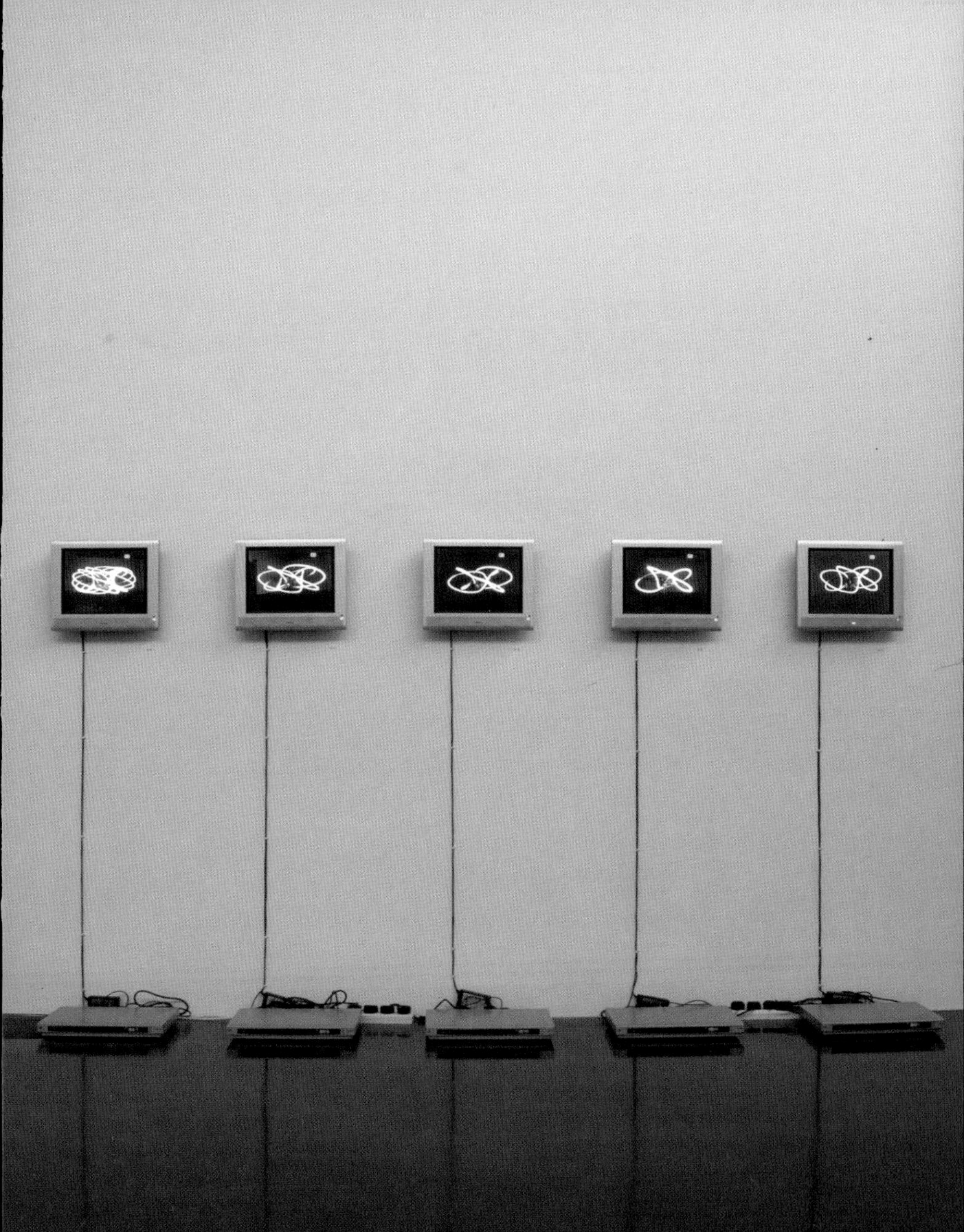

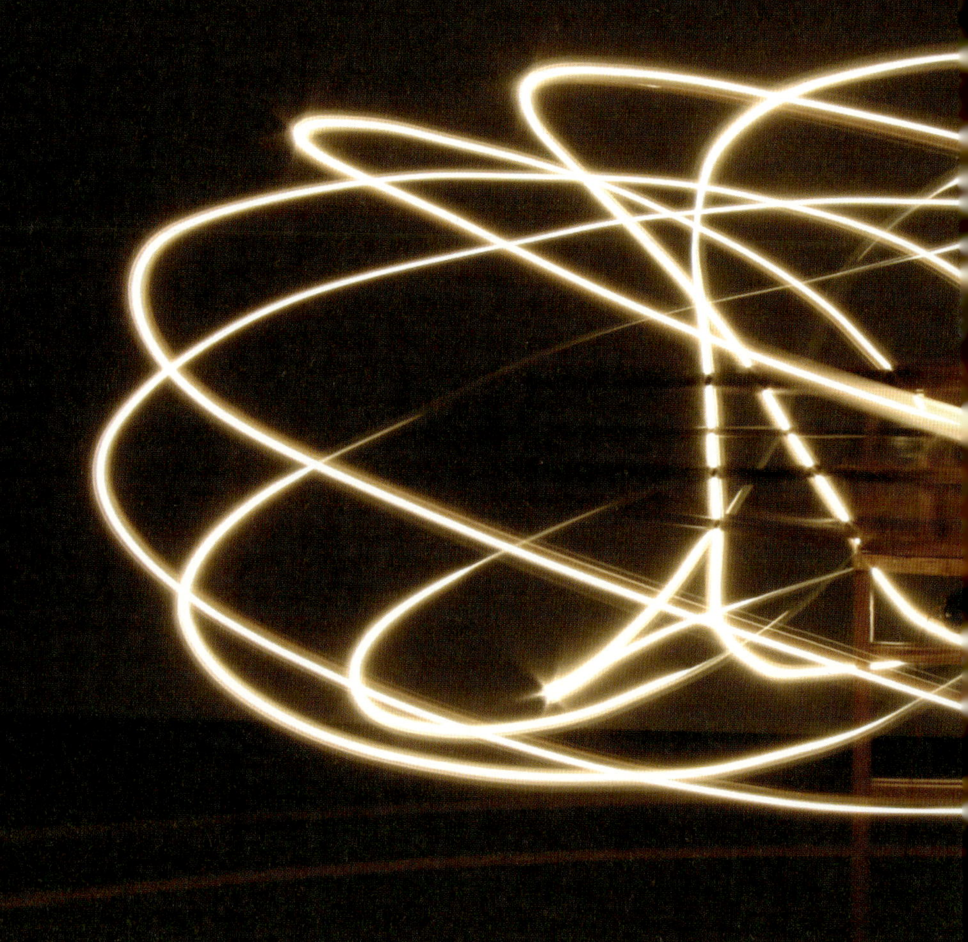

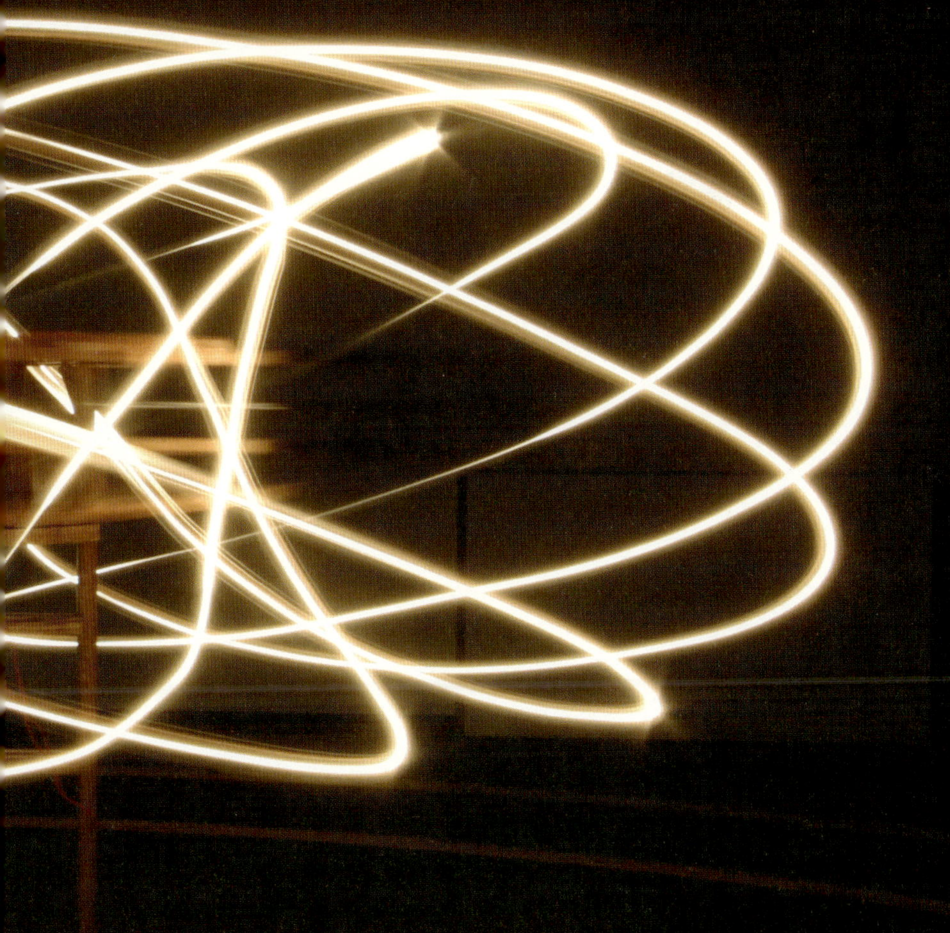

The Second, 9:8 ratio, 40:30 teeth

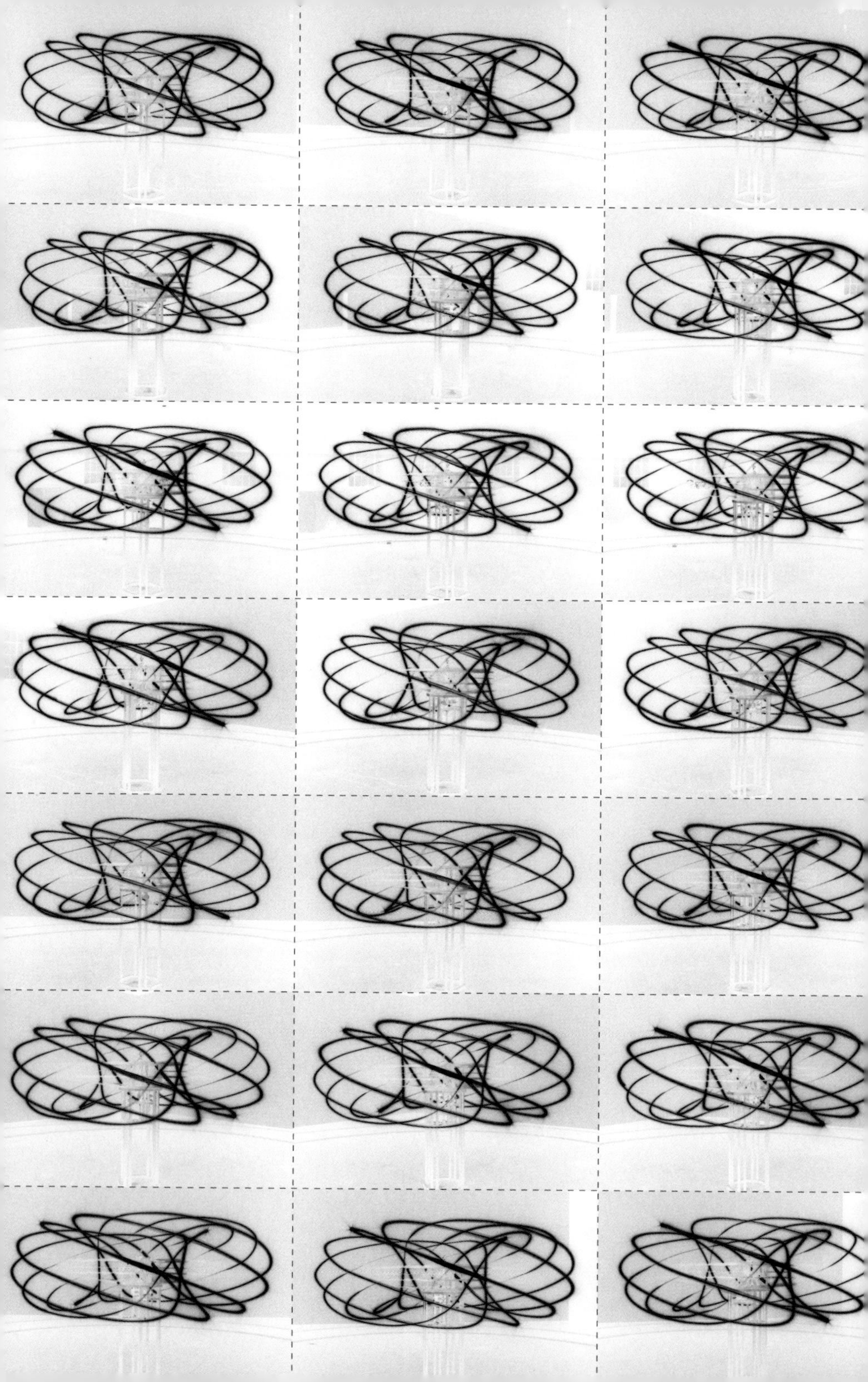

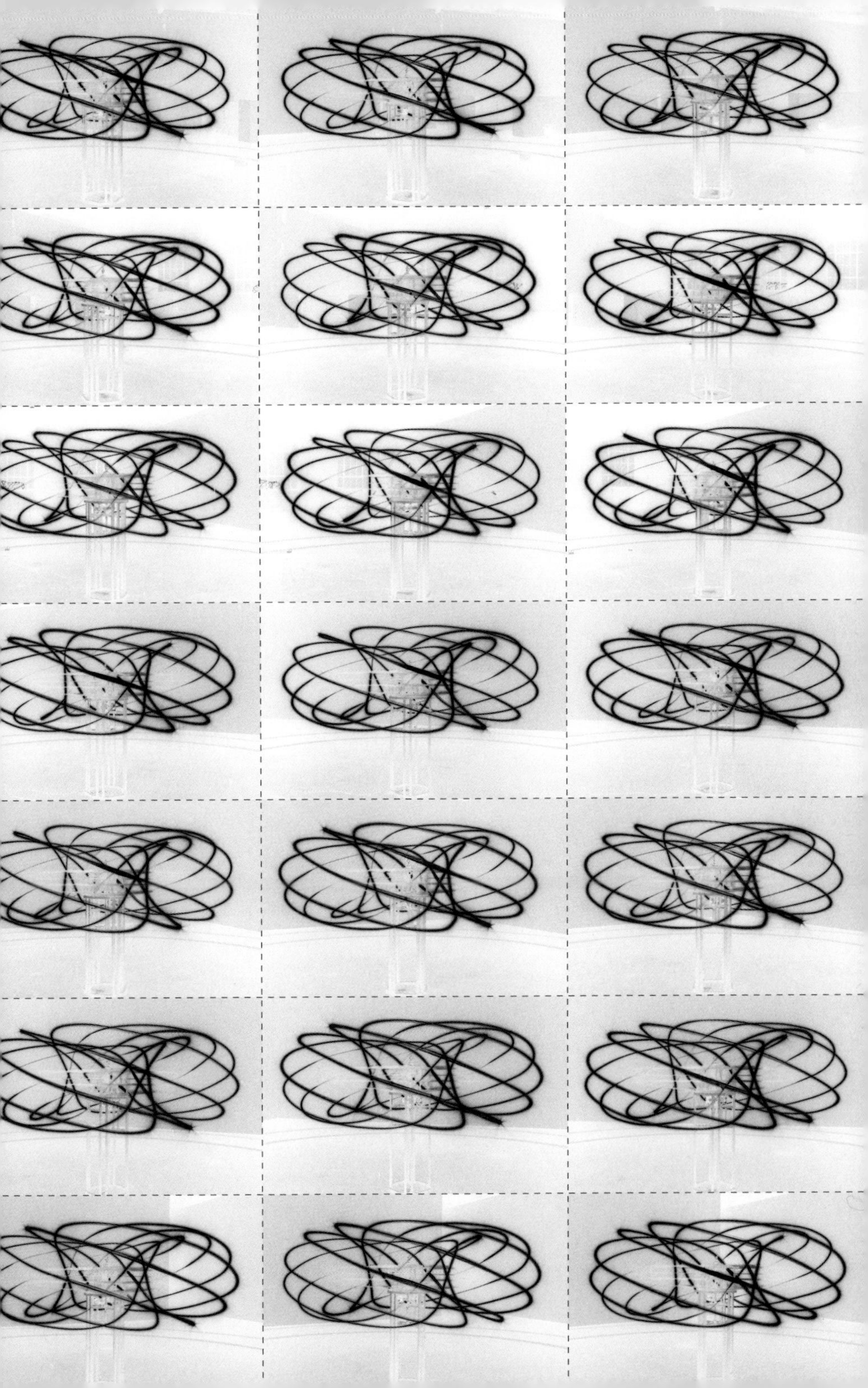

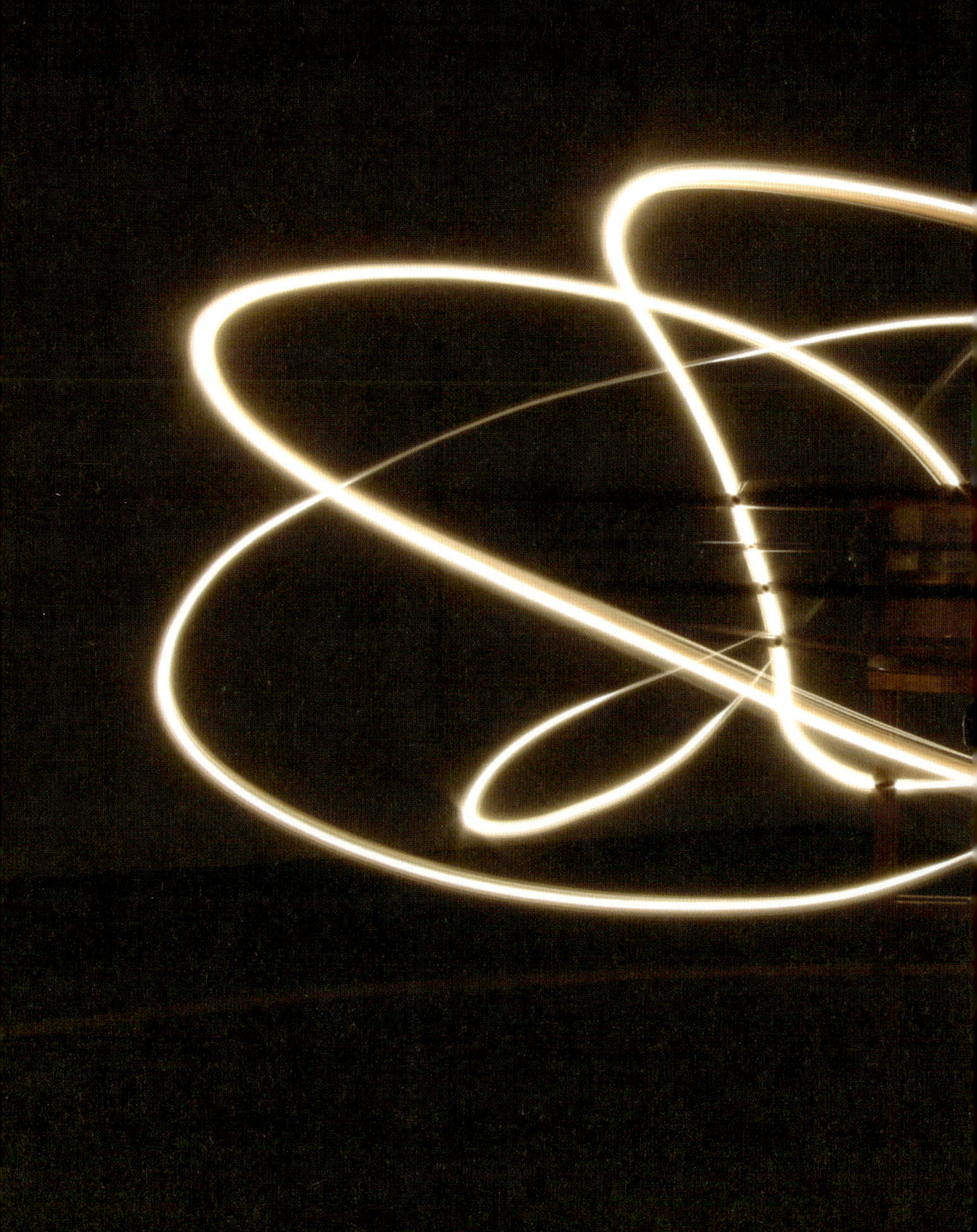

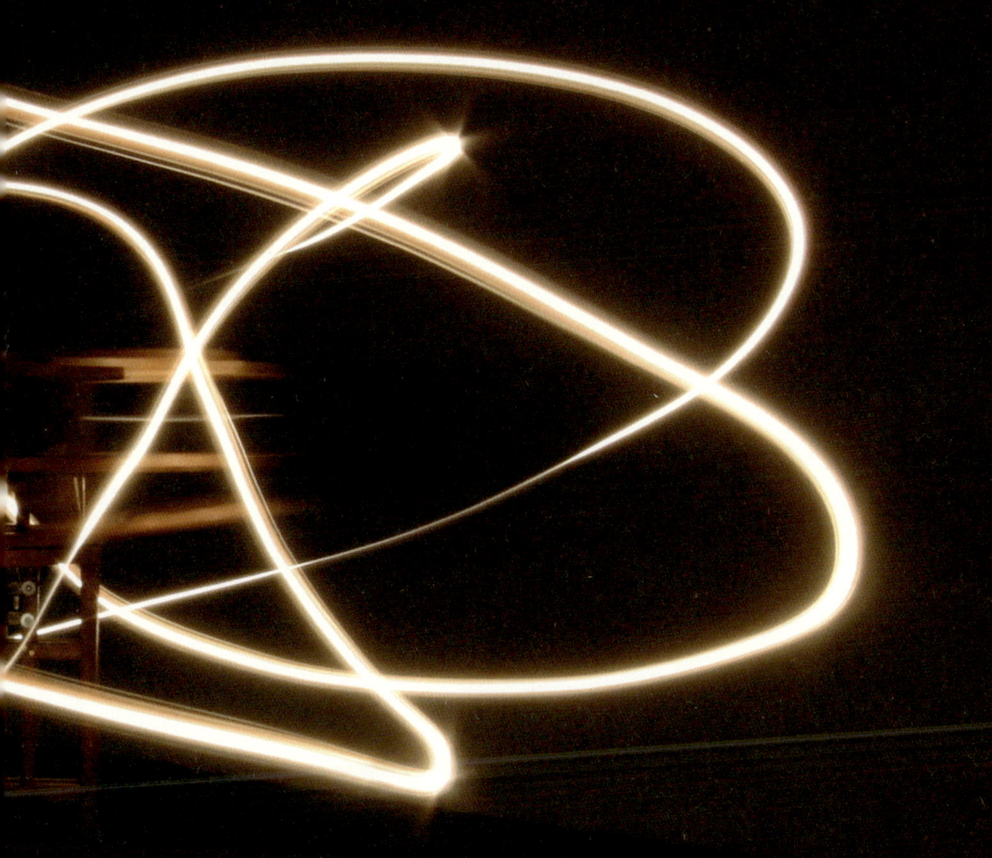

The Third, 5:4 ratio, 50:40 teeth

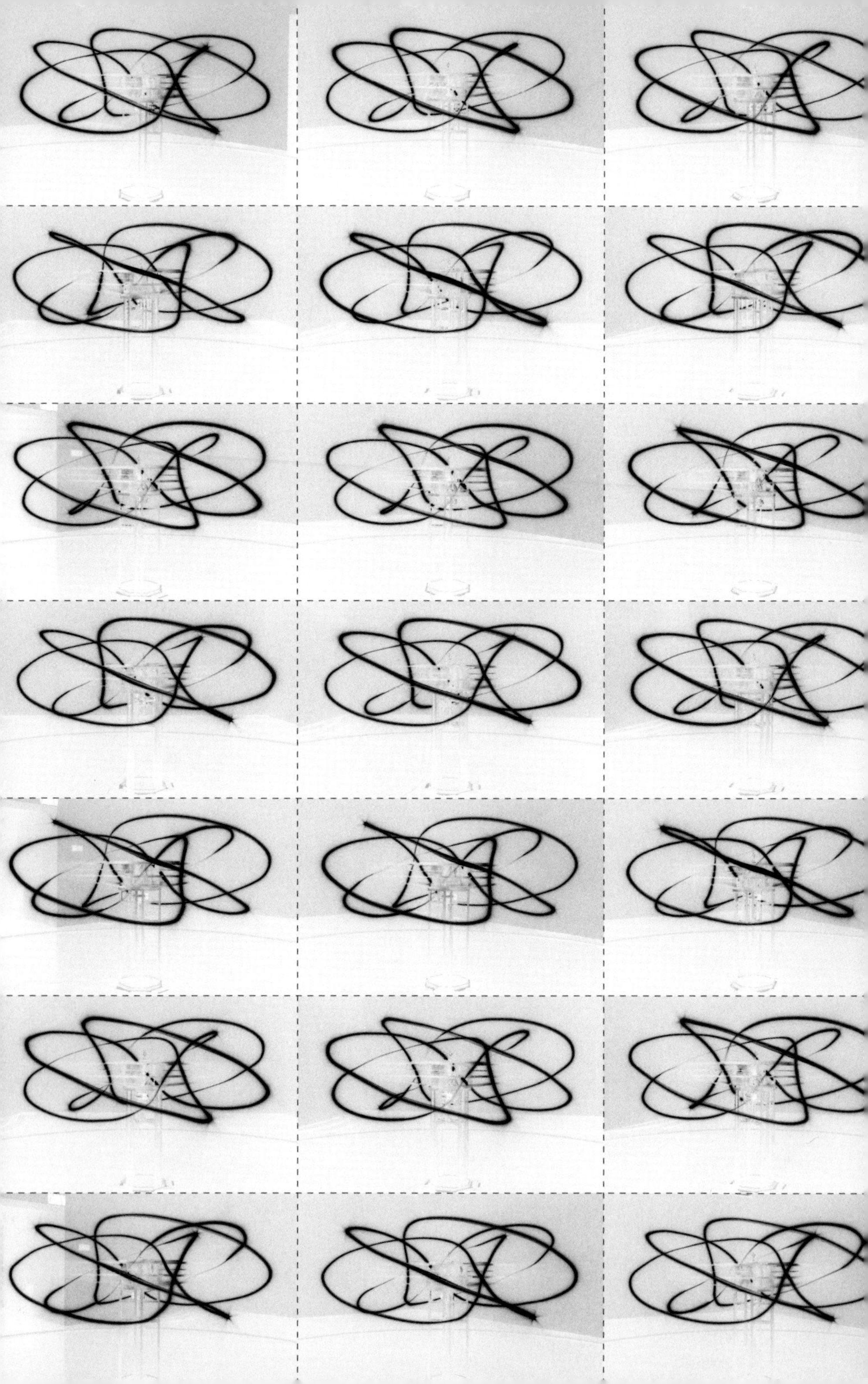

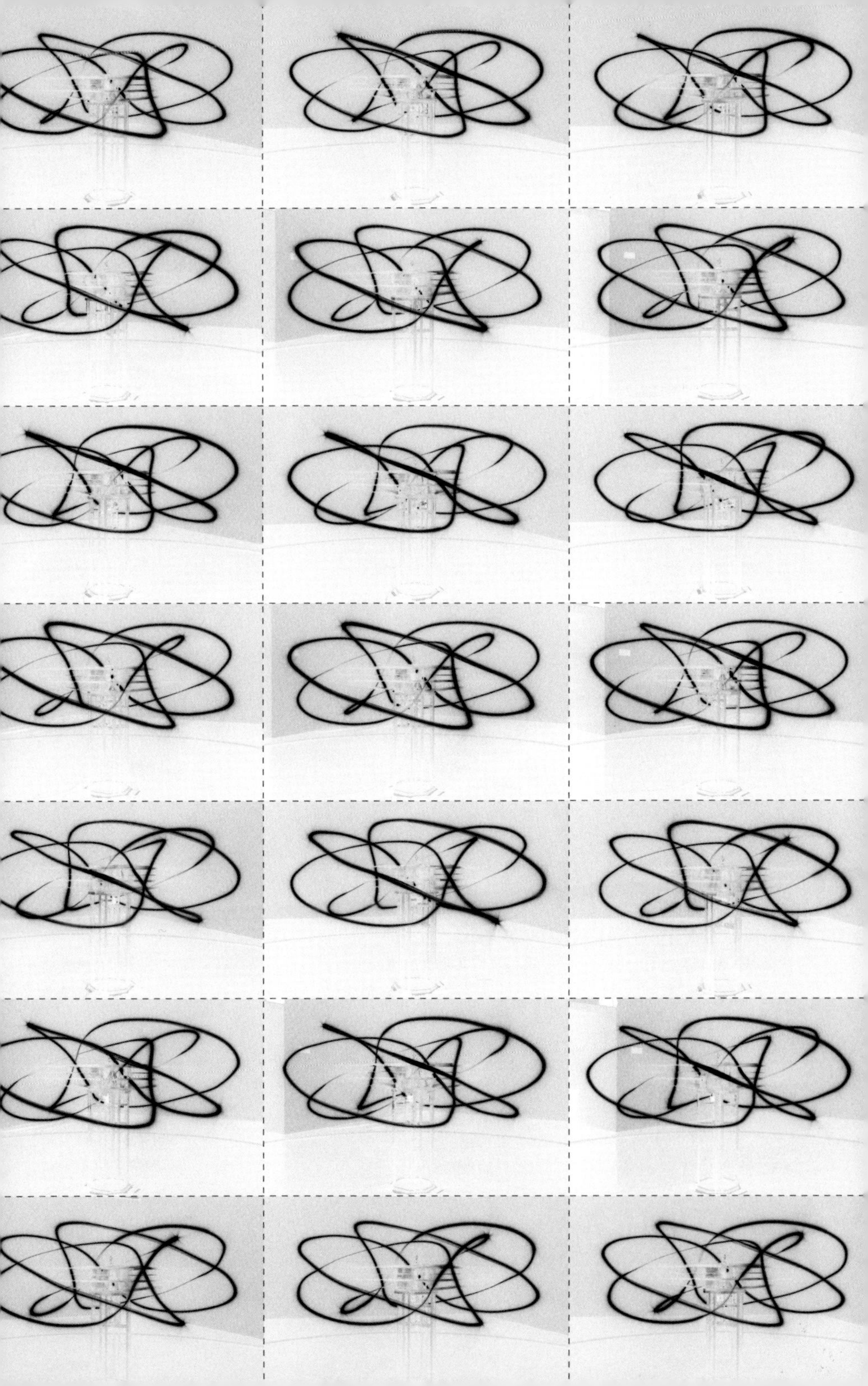

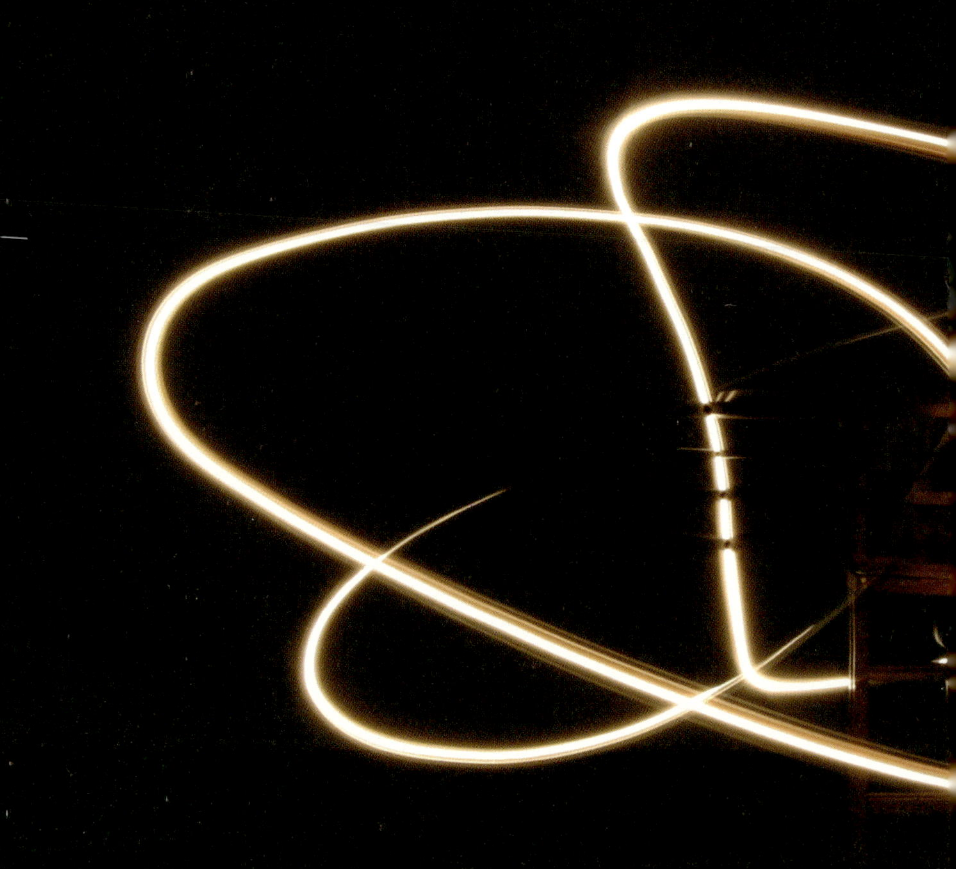

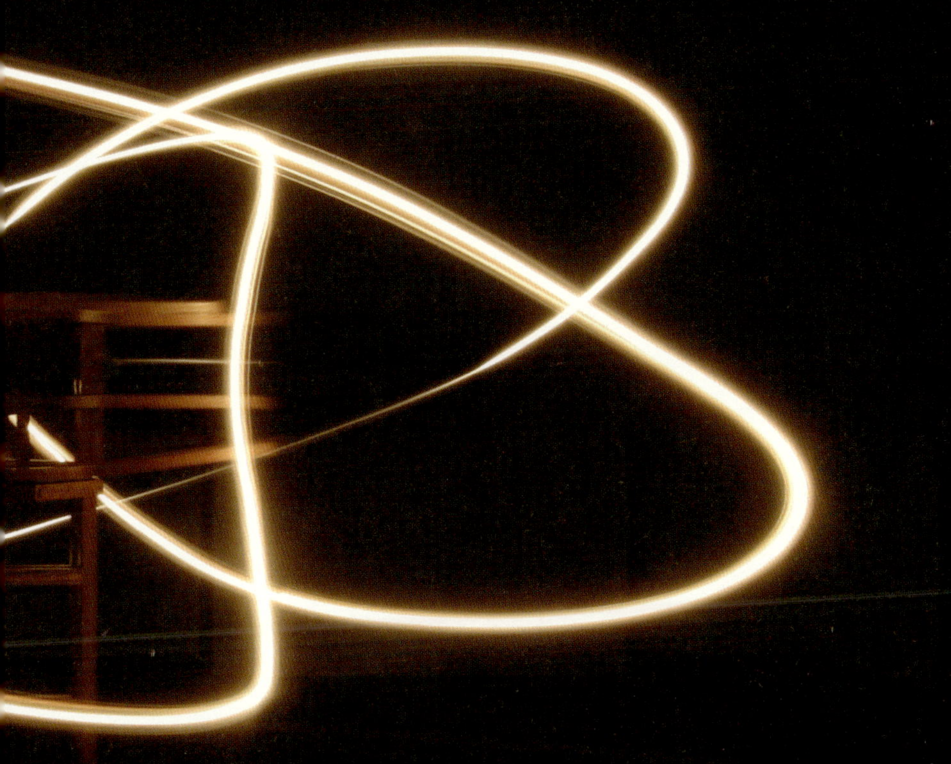

The Fourth, 4:3 ratio, 40:30 teeth

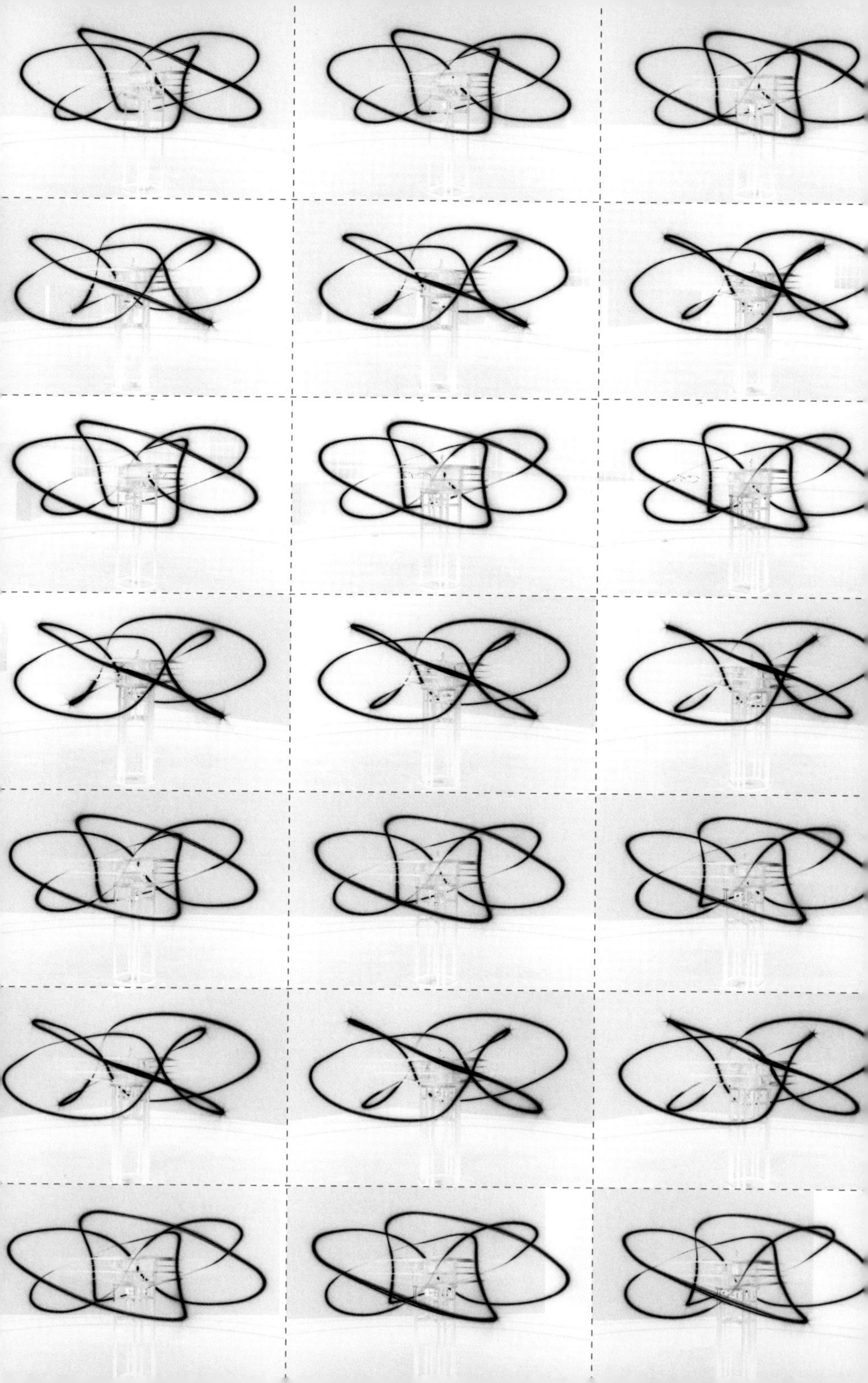

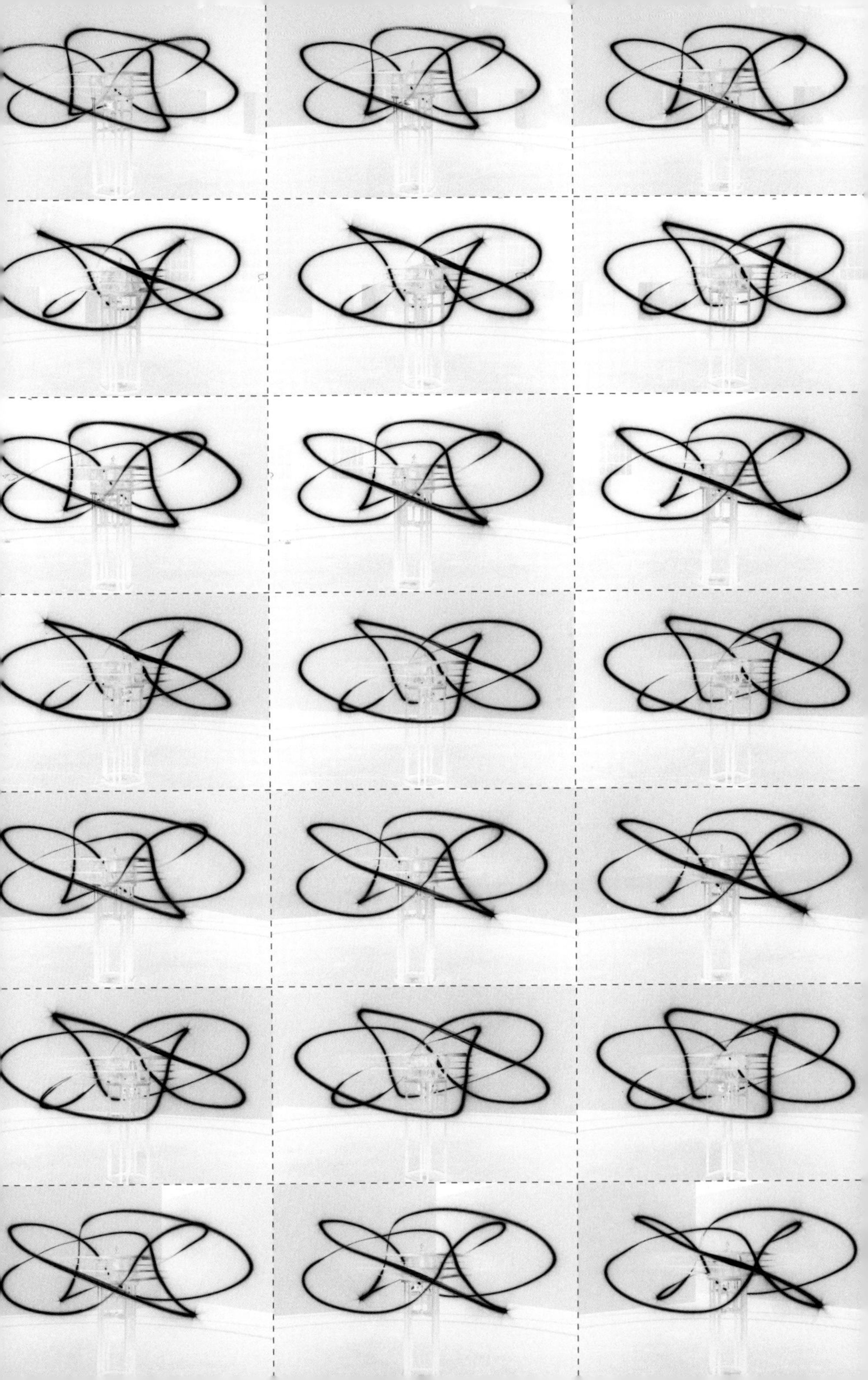

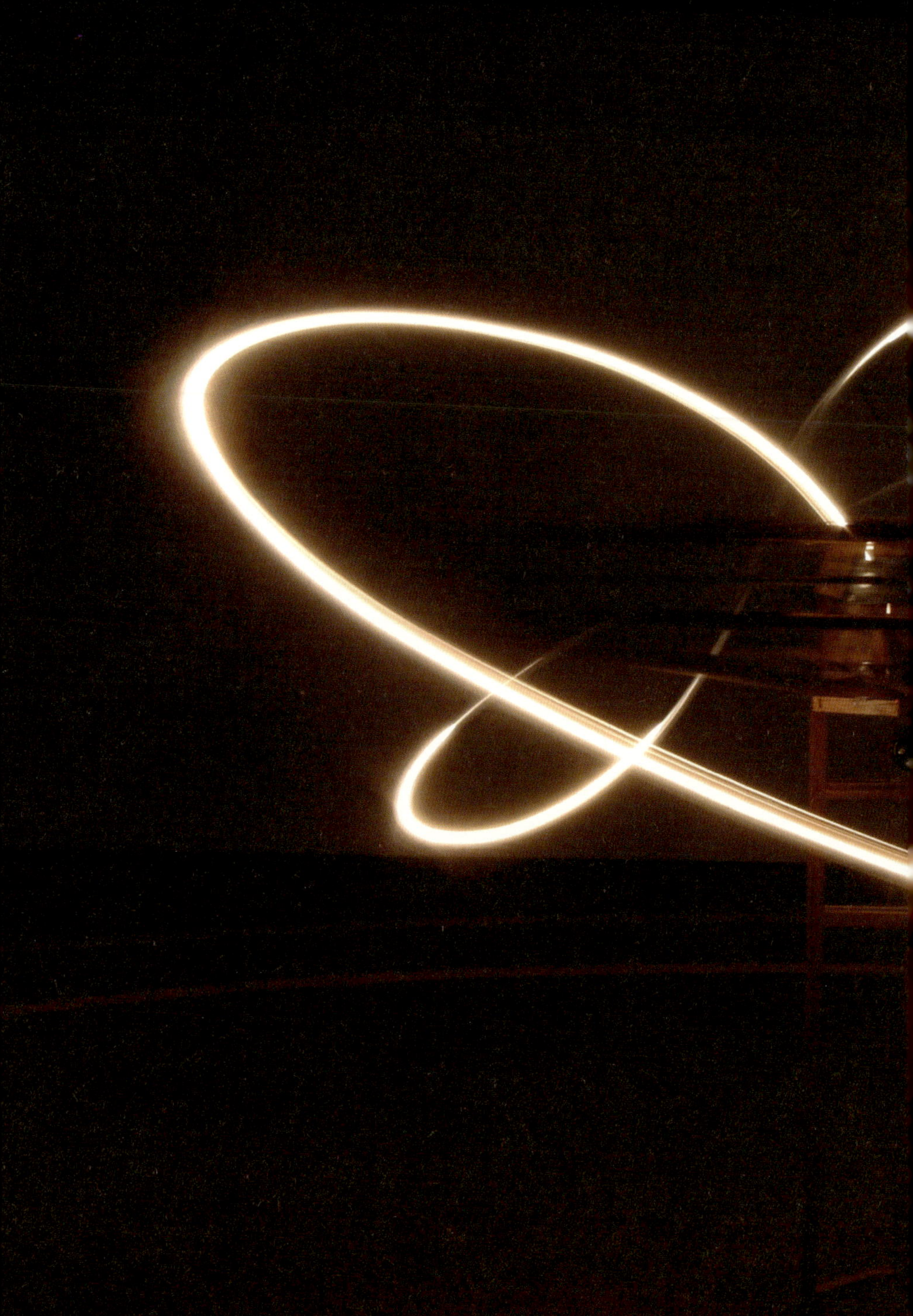

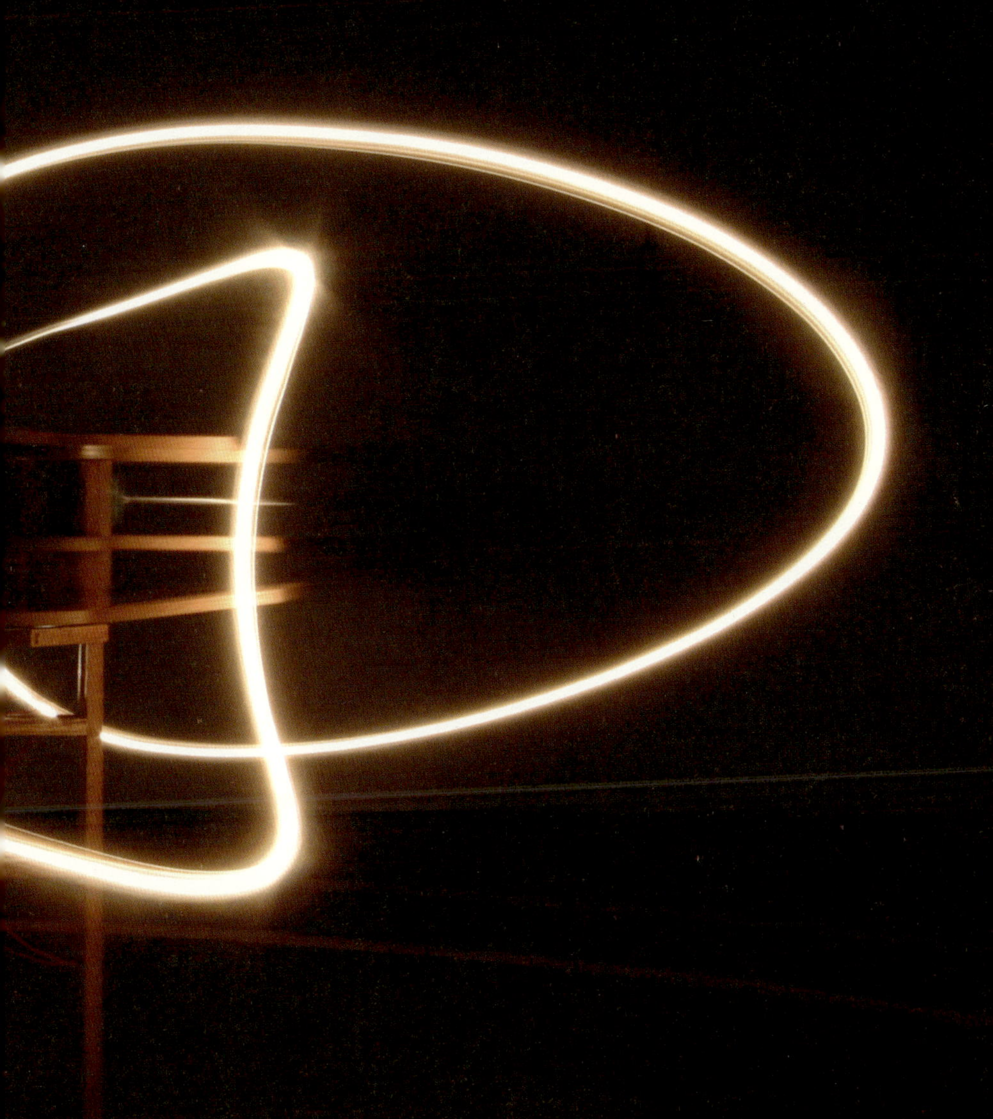

The Fifth, 3:2 ratio, 45:30 teeth

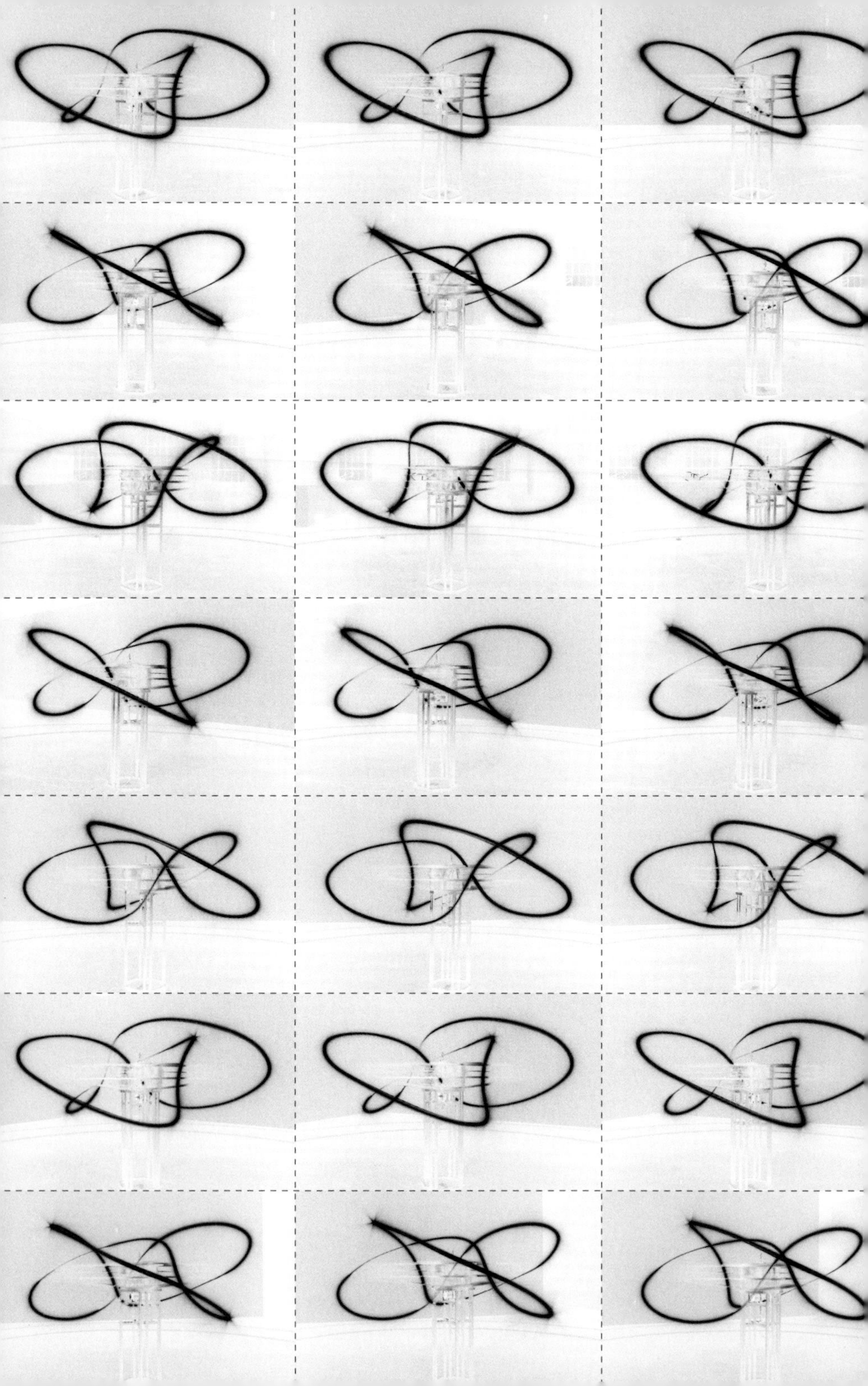

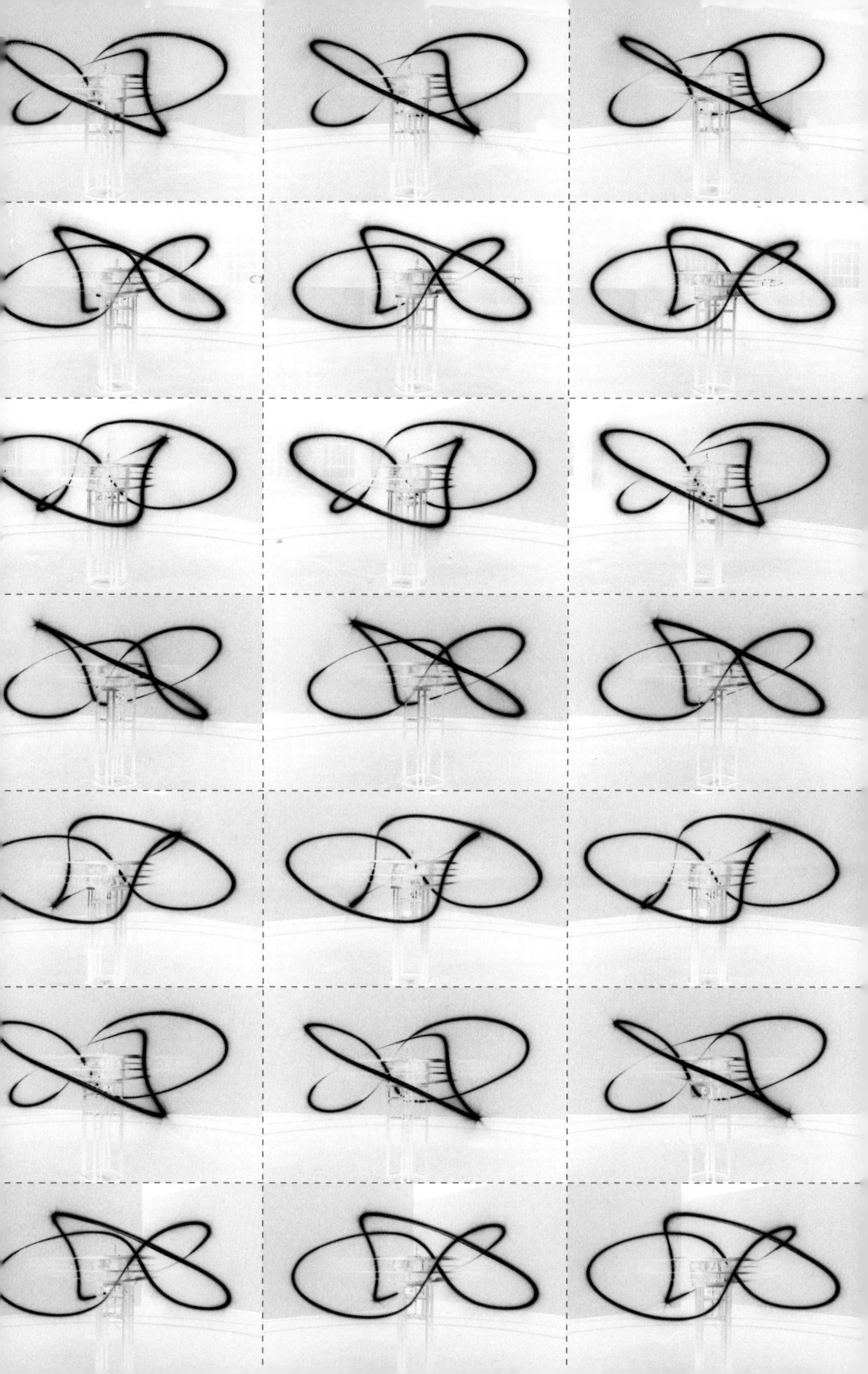

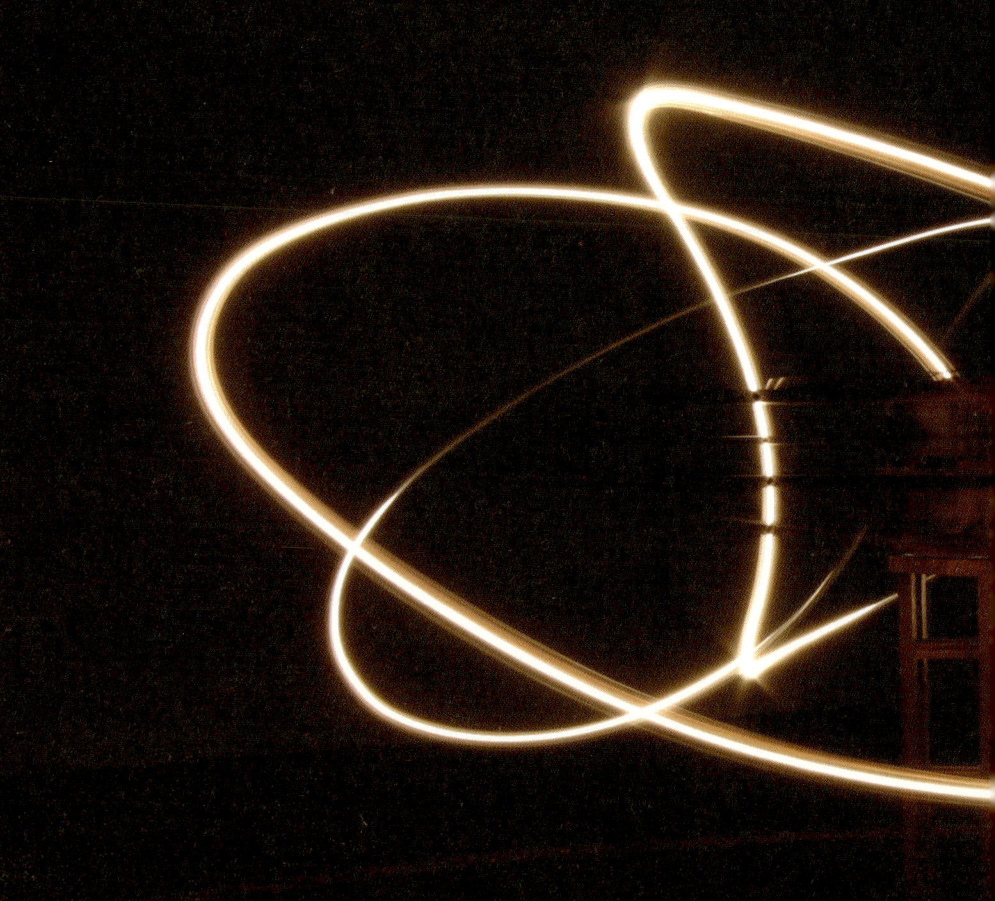

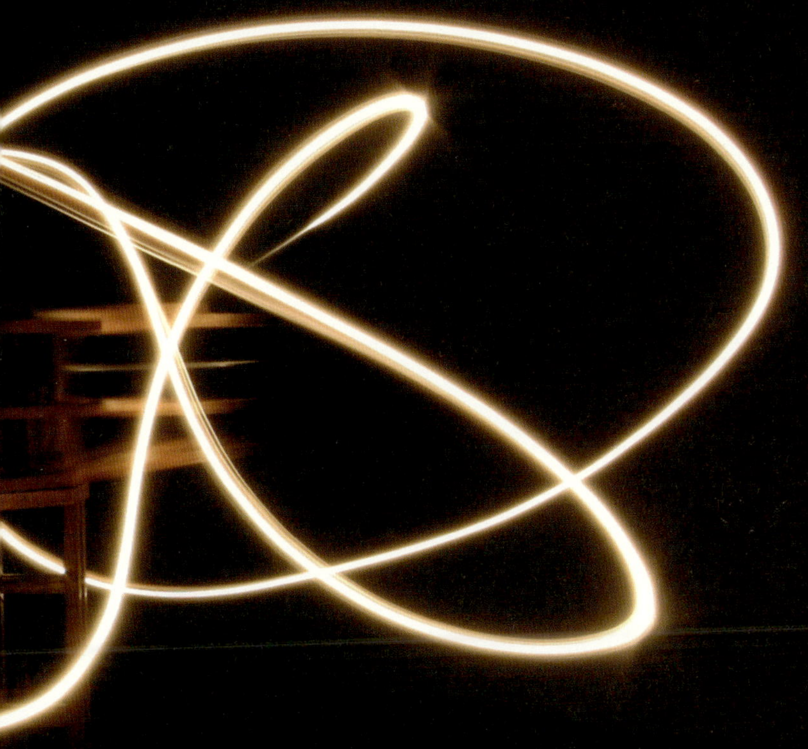

The Sixth, 5:3 ratio, 50:30 teeth

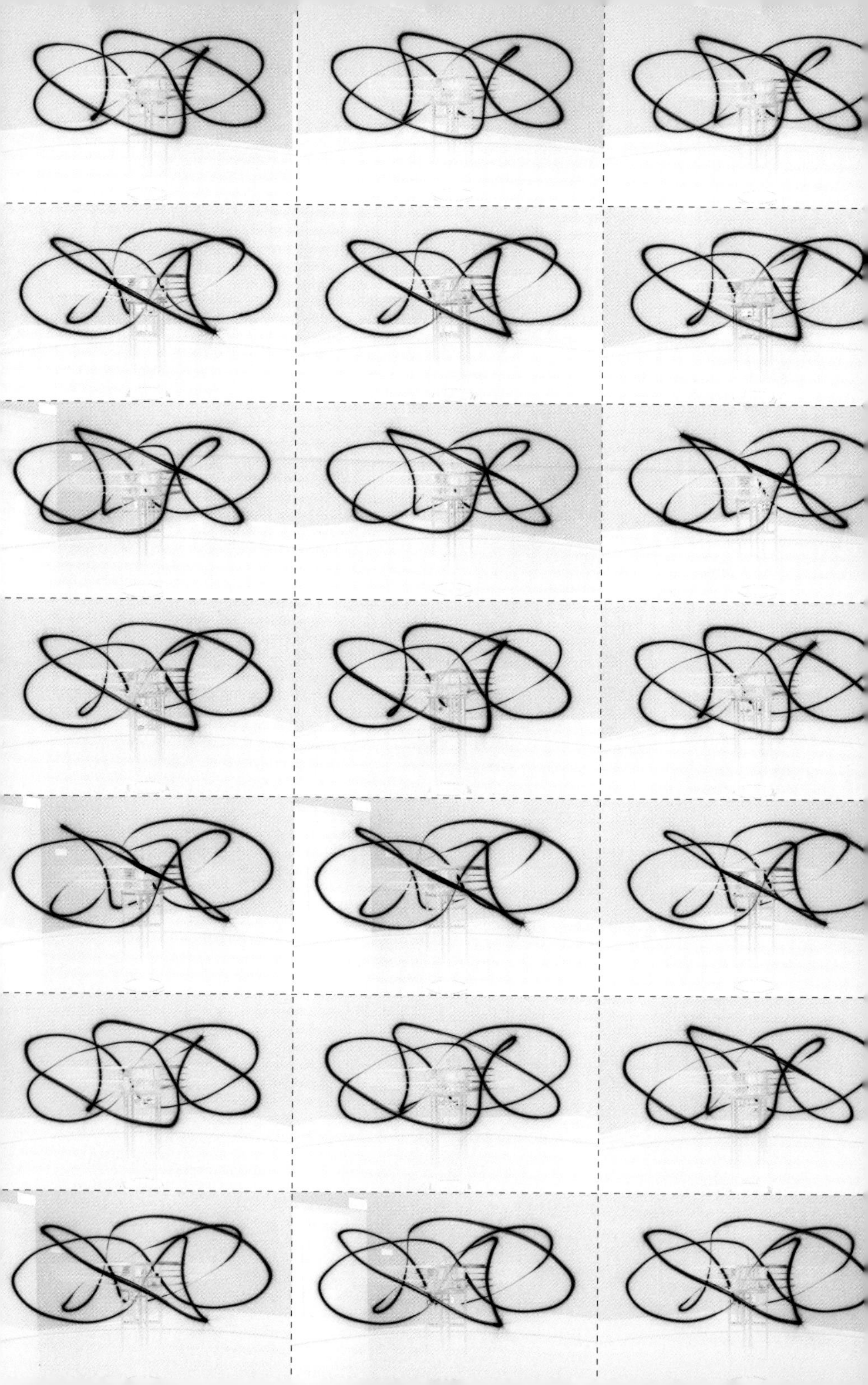

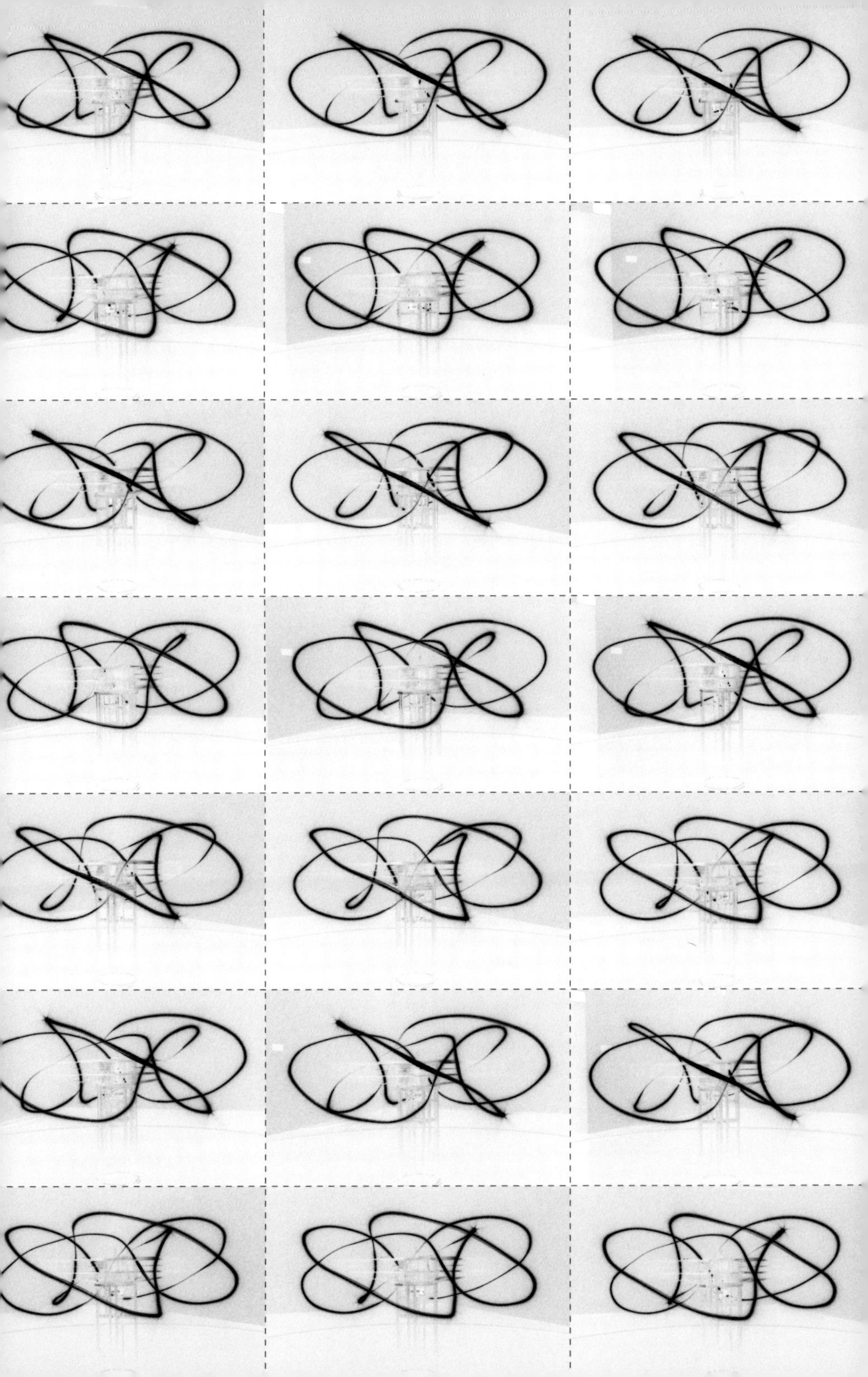

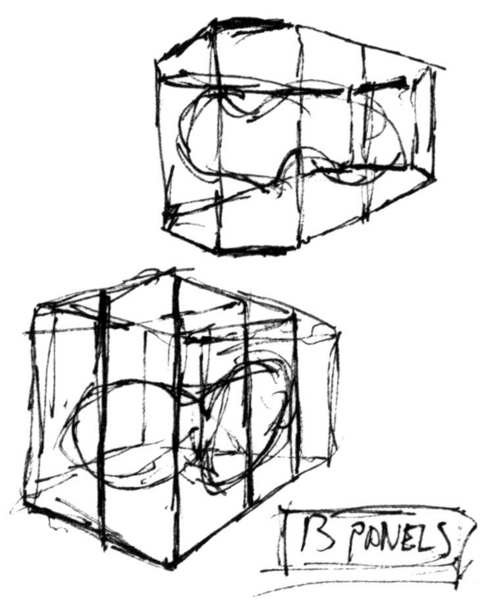
13 PANELS

Space Trumpet

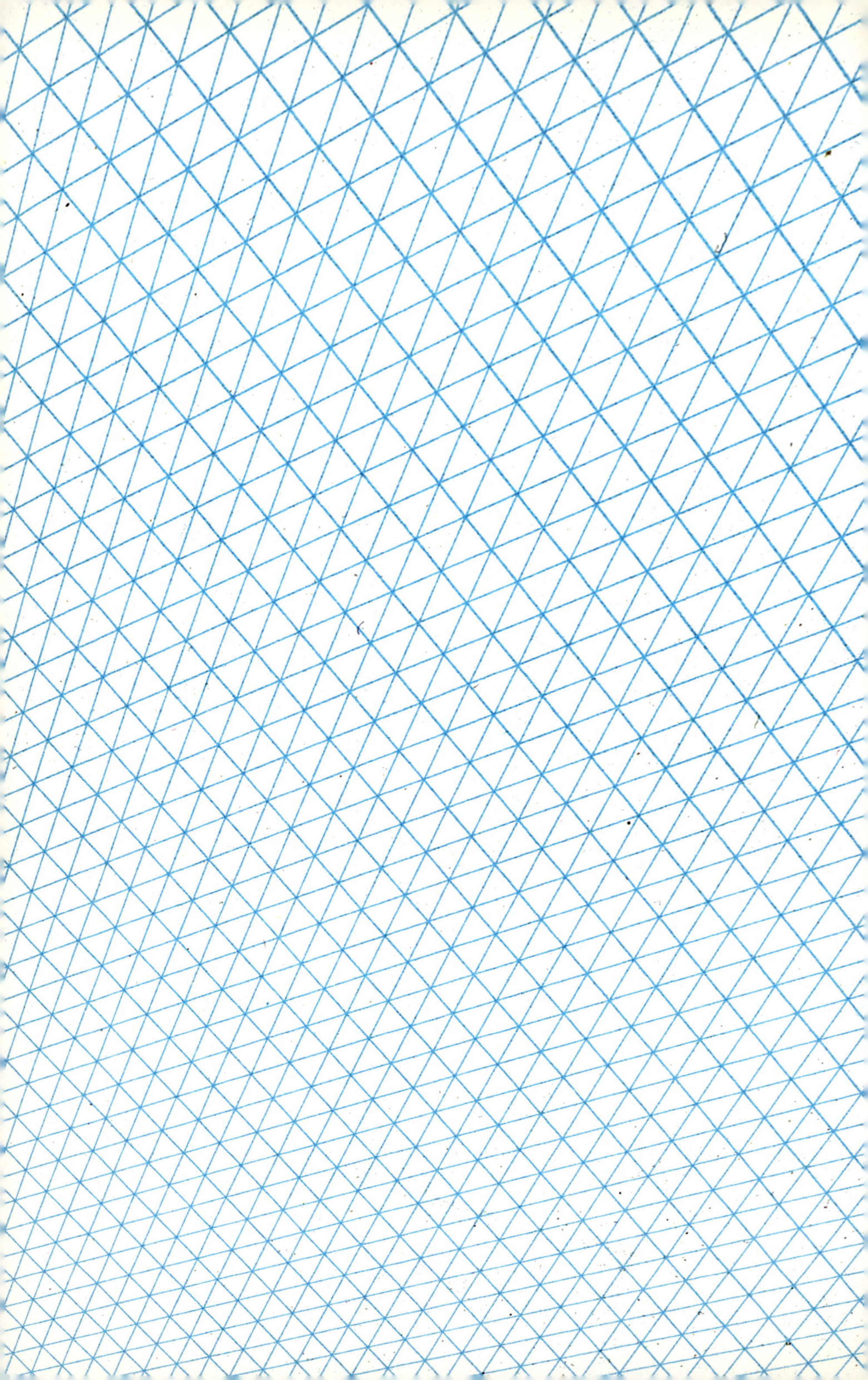

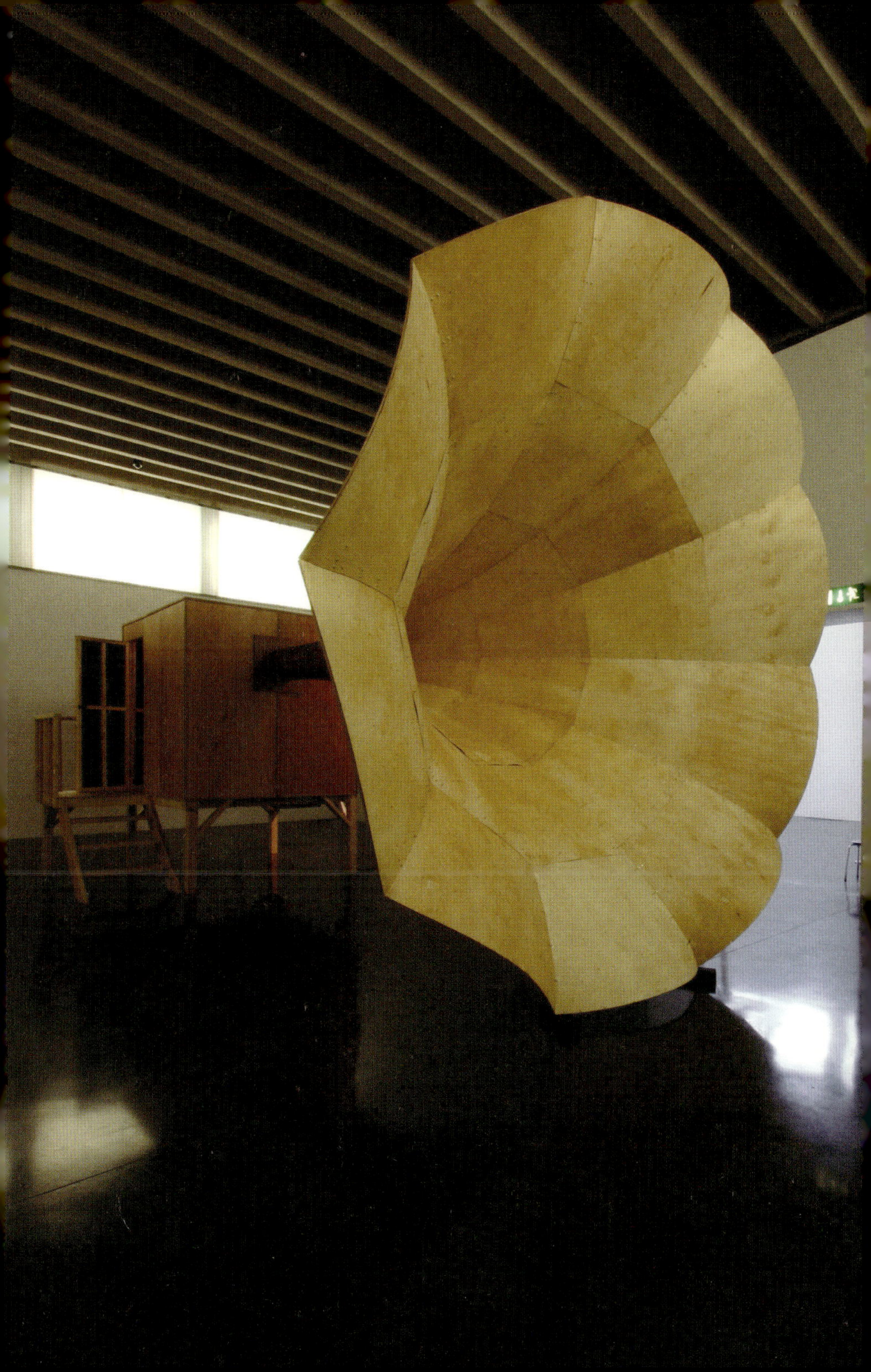

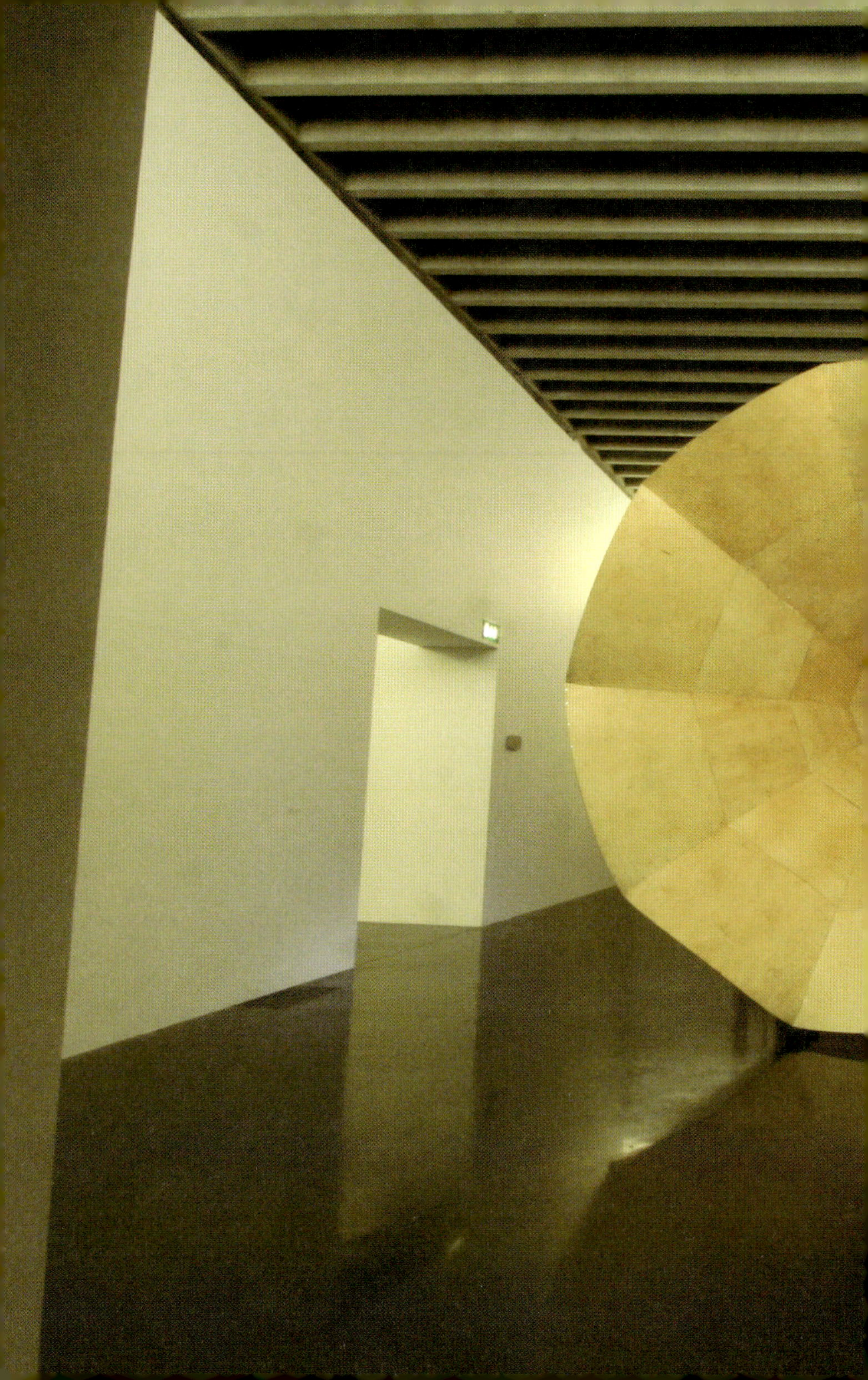

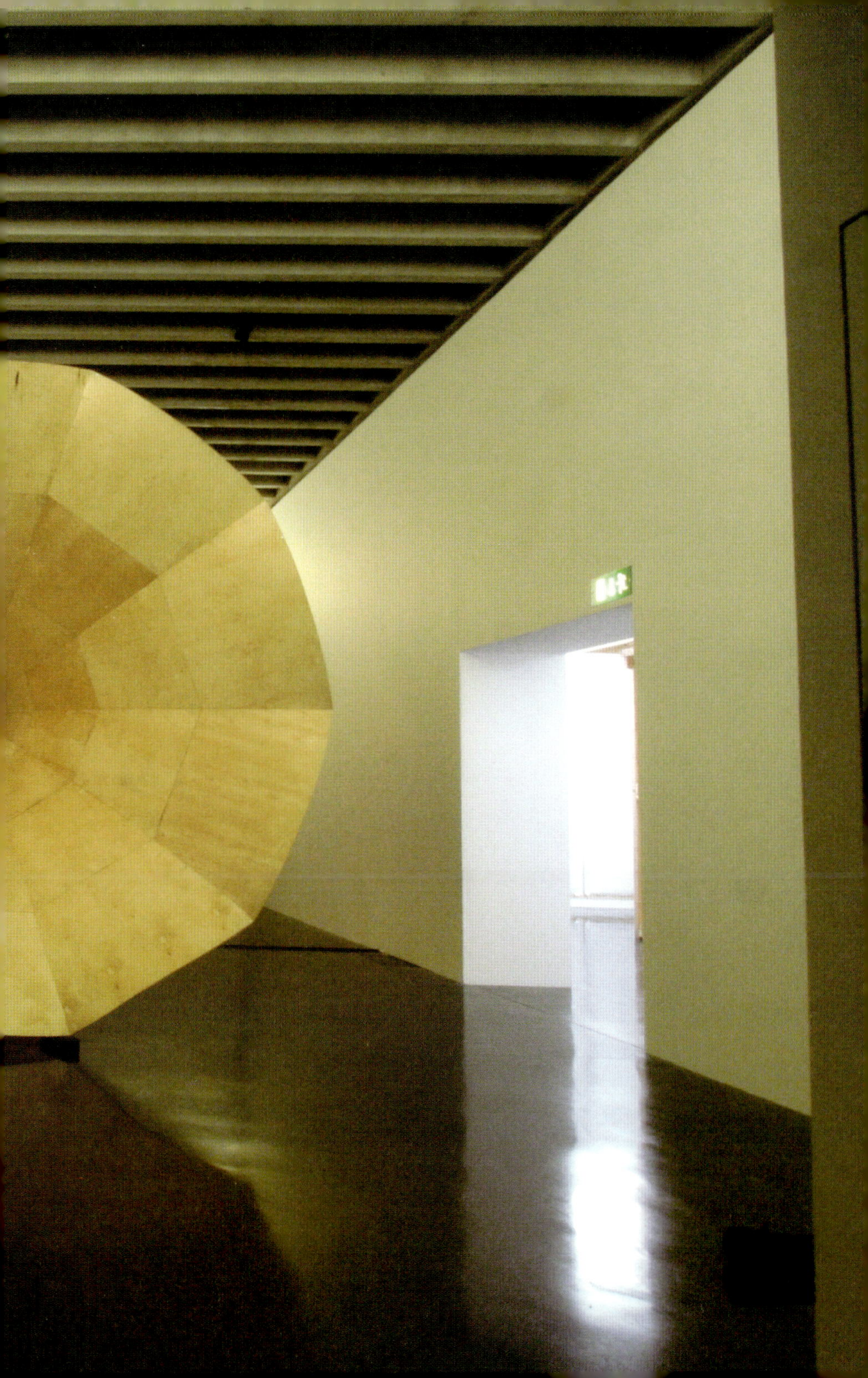

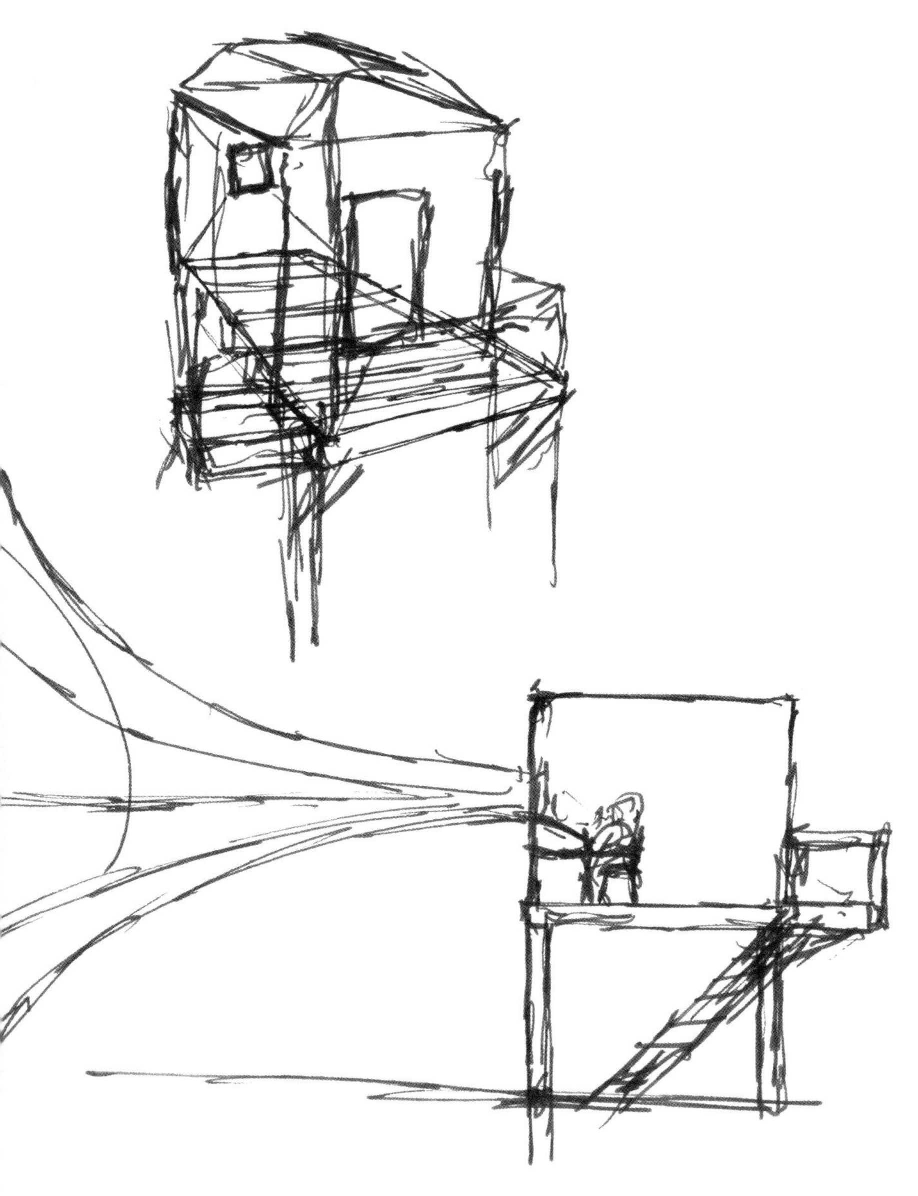

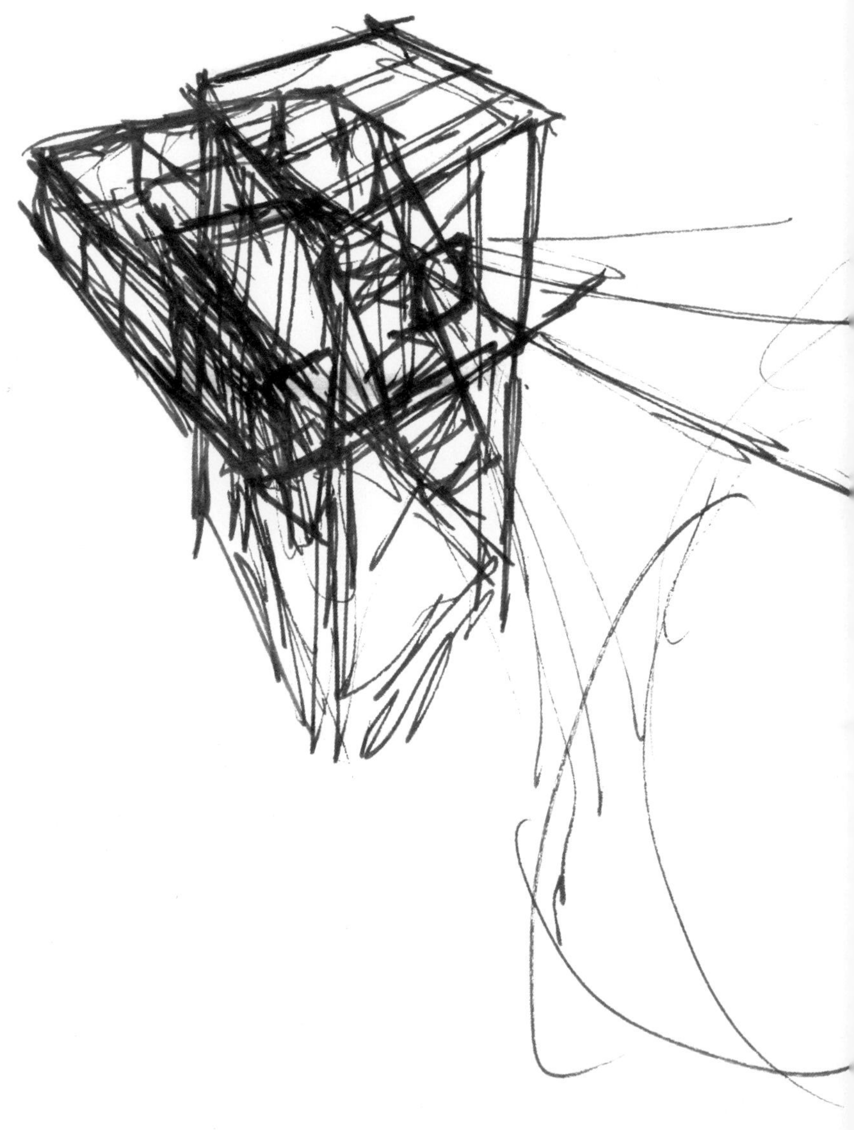

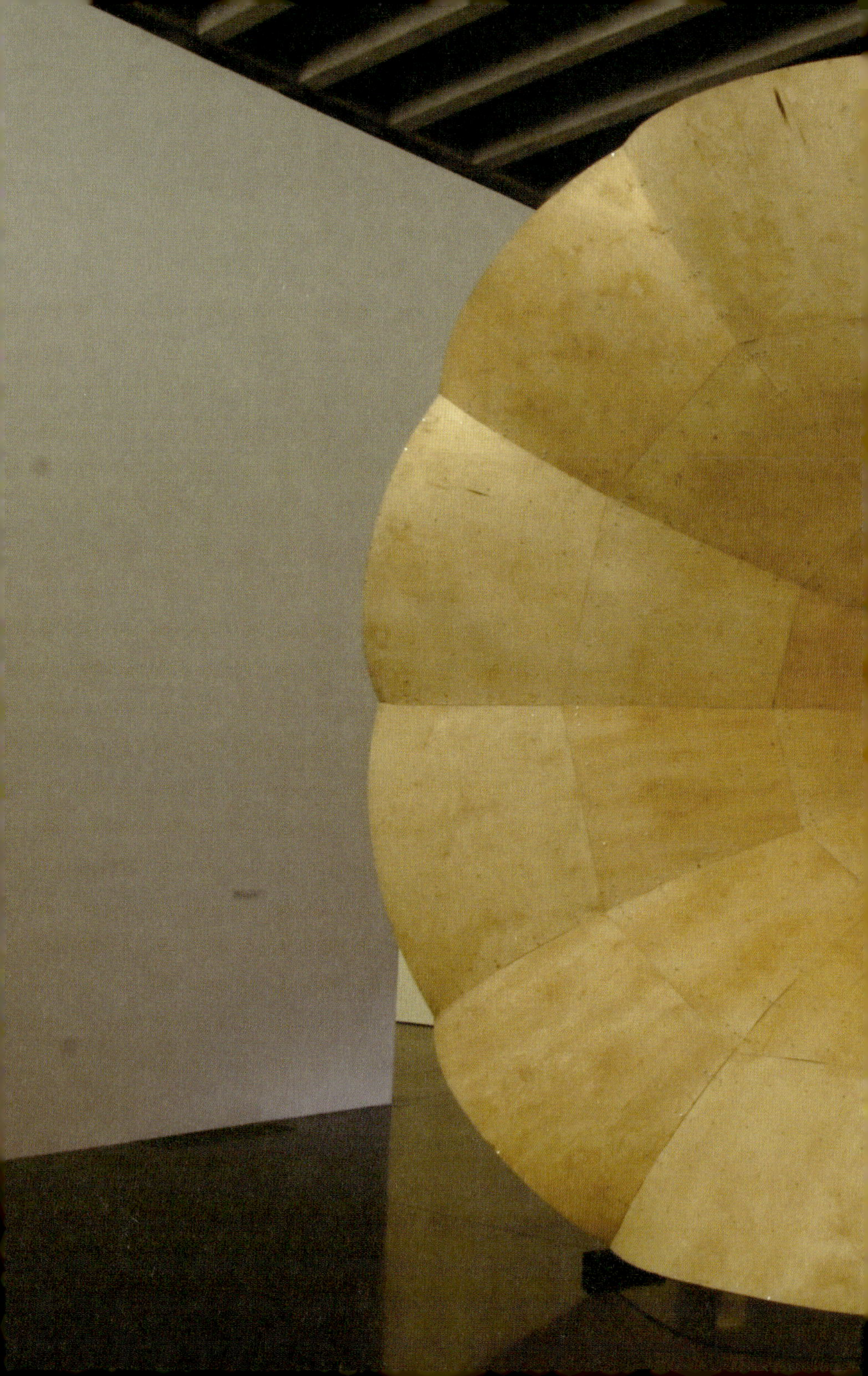

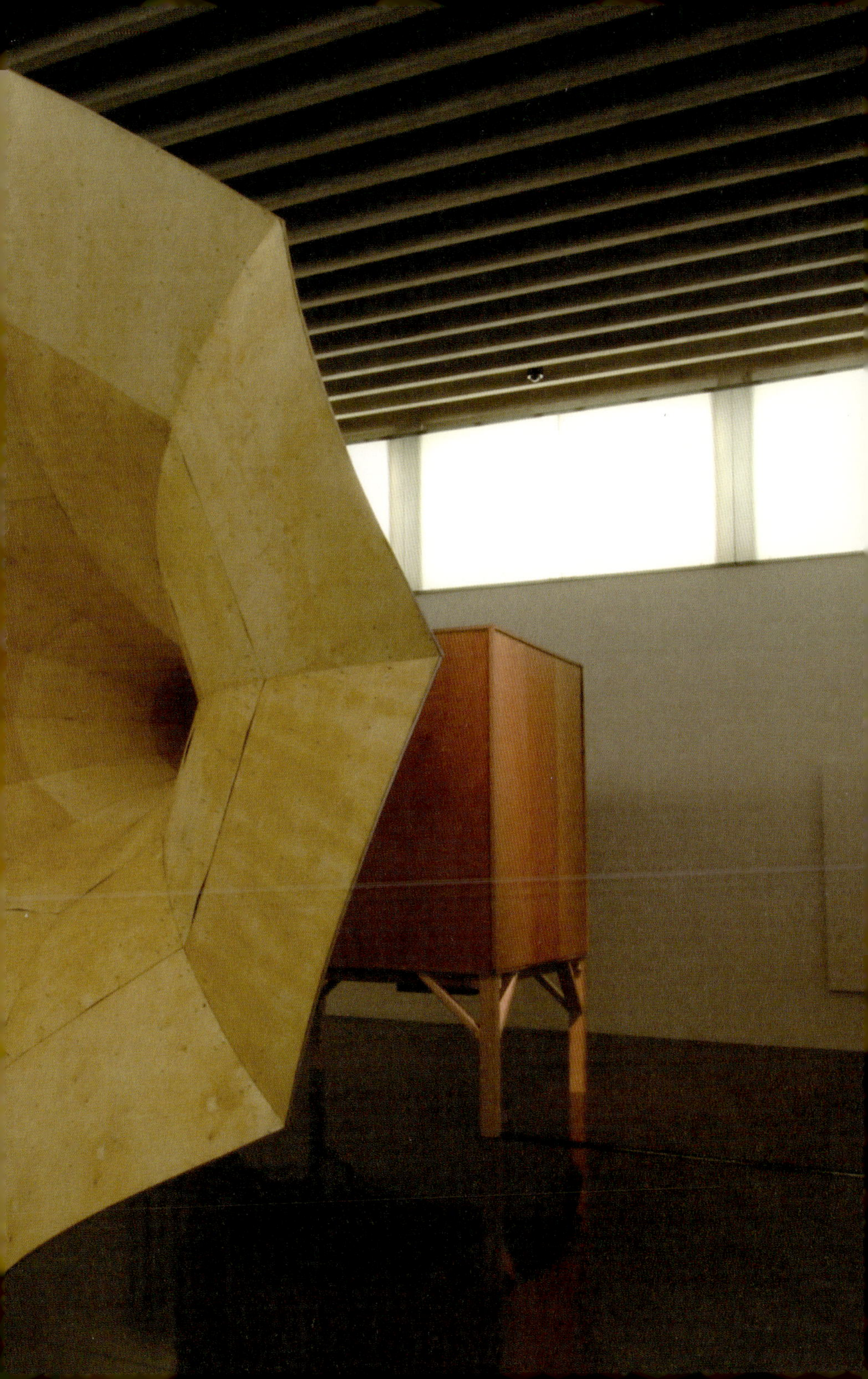

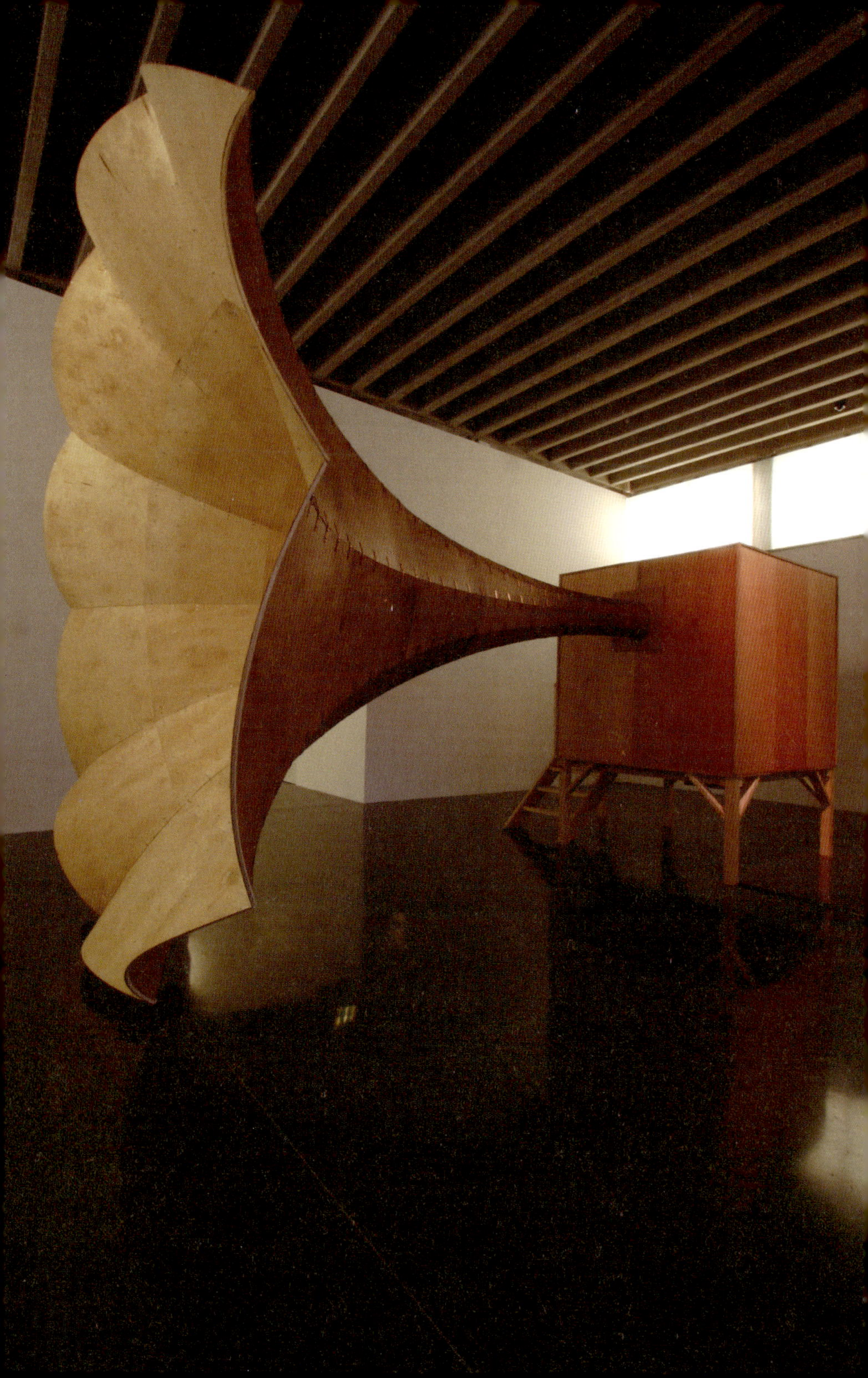

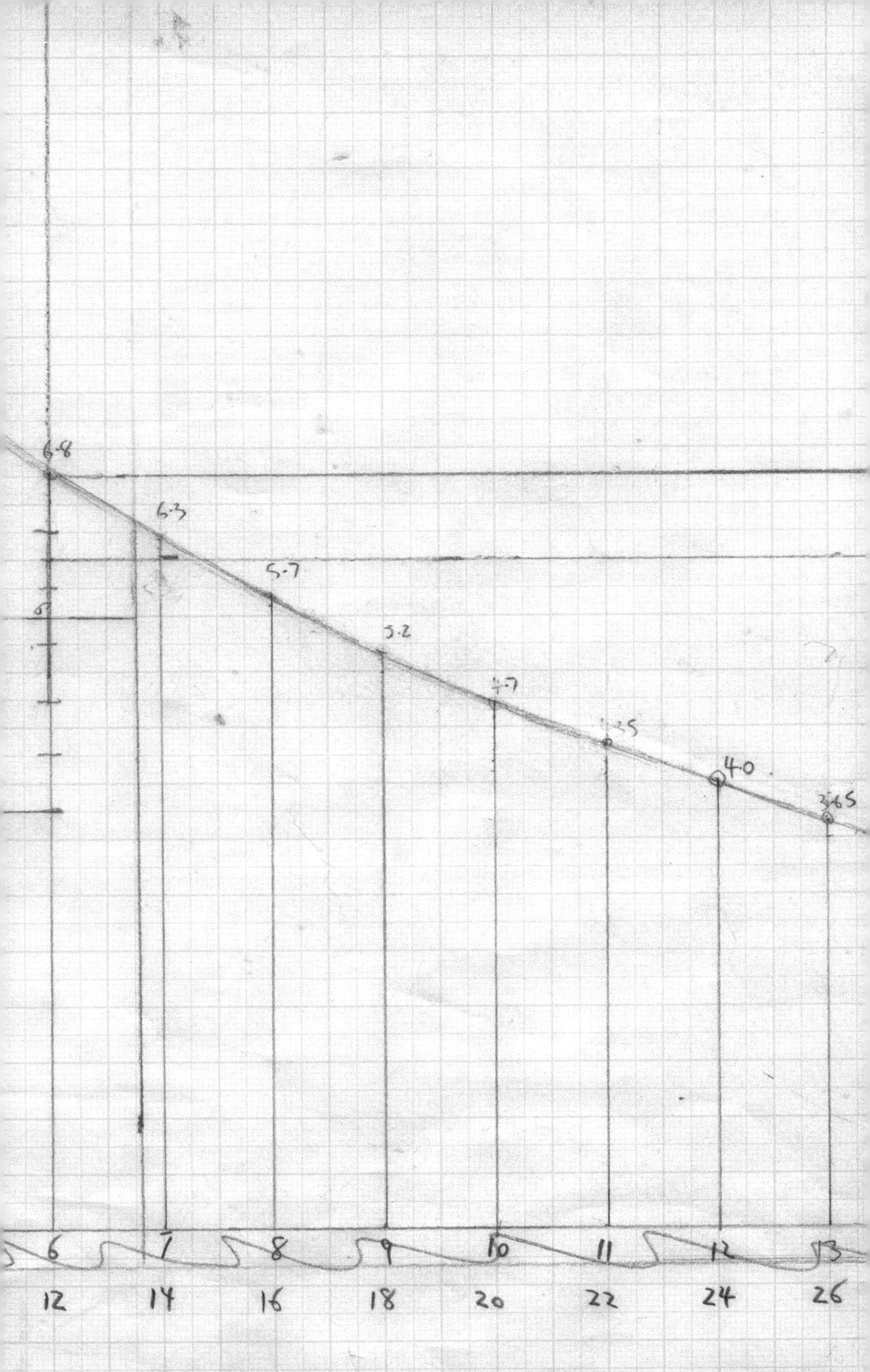
6·8
6·3
5·7
5·2
4·7
4·0
6
7
8
9
10
11
12
13
12
14
16
18
20
22
24
26

ARNO PENZIOSE
ROBERT WILSON

Within Cabin is the dwelling of a Scientist. Lonely and blind. A pair of head phones are his way of mapping space. 3-D drawings ~~of the un~~ interpretations of the universe adorn the ~~space~~ interior, plaster models from god's eye view. Implication of a bat-like exhistance; the 3-D mapping of space through sound.

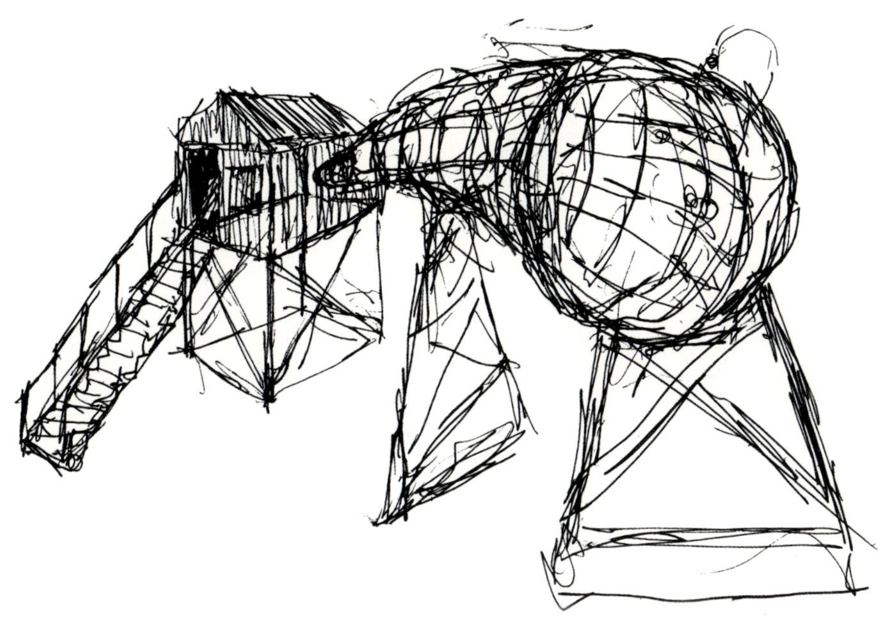

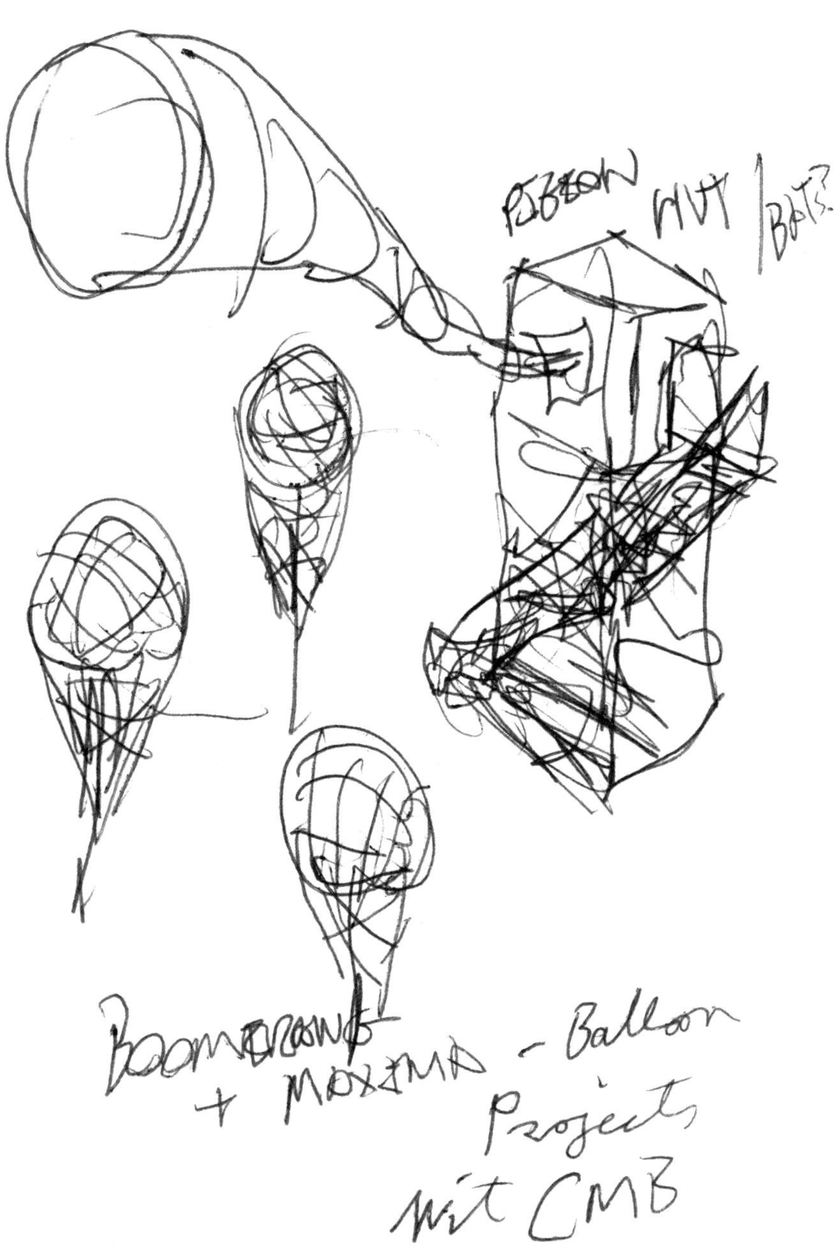
PIGEON HUT / BATS?
BOOMERANG + MAXIMA - Balloon Projects mit CMB

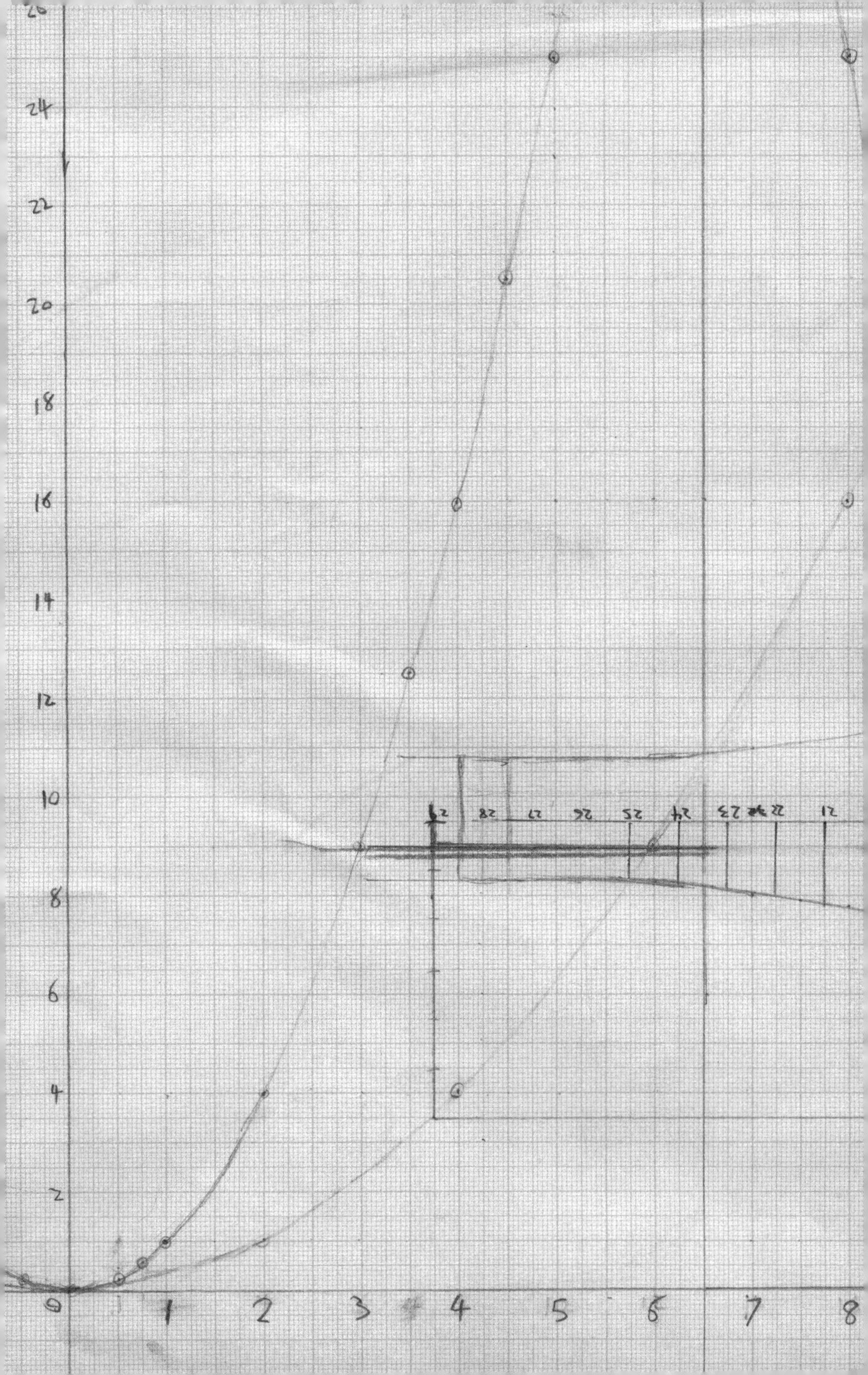

24
22
20
18
16
14
12
10
8
6
4
2
0
1
2
3
4
5
6
7
8

1:1 SCALE

	Length From End * CM	r DIAR *	C = 2πr *	1/12 → 1/10
1	20	290	1822	151
2	40	25.8	1621	135
3	60	23.4	1470	122.5
4	80	211	1325	110.4
5	100	191	1200	100
6	120	171	1074	89.5
7	140	158	992	82.7
8	160	143	898	74.87
9	180	131	823	68.6
10	200	118	741	61.8
11	220	109	684	57
12	240	101	634	52.8
13	260	92	578	48
14	280	83	521	43.5
15	300	75	471	39.3
16	320	68	427	35.6
17	340	63	395	33.0
18	360	55	345	28.8
19	380	50	314	26.2
20	400	45	282	23.6
21	420	40	251	20.9
22	440	38	238	19.9
23	460	34	213	17.8
24	480	31	194	16.2
25	500	30	188	15.7
26	520	30		〃
27	540	30	〃	〃
28	560	30	〃	〃
29	580	30		〃
30	600	30	〃	

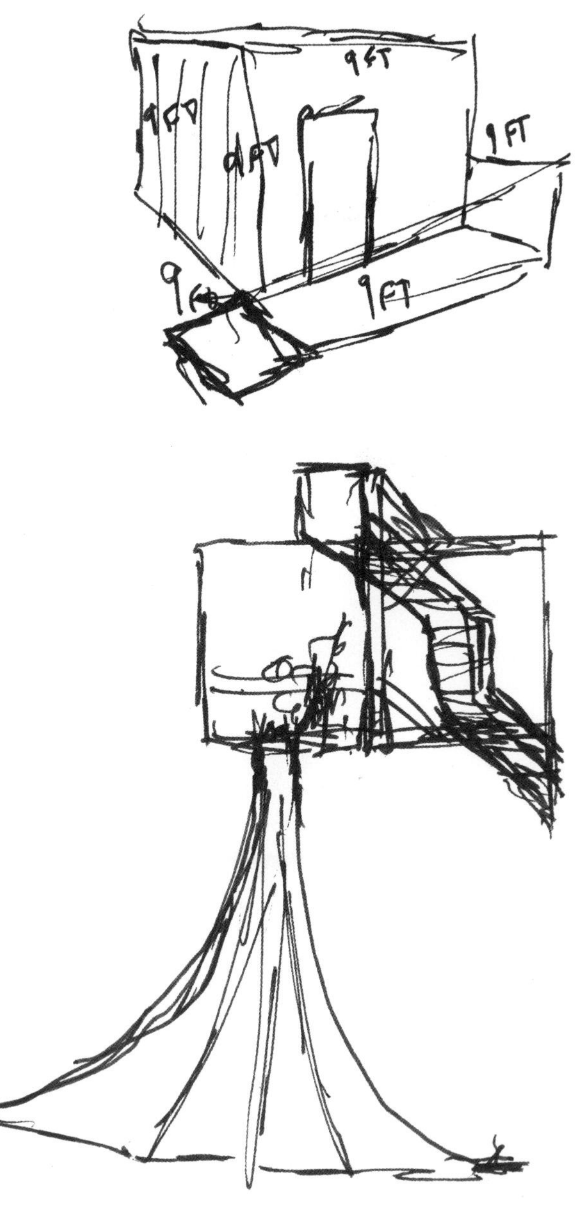
9FT
9FT
9FT
9FT
9FT

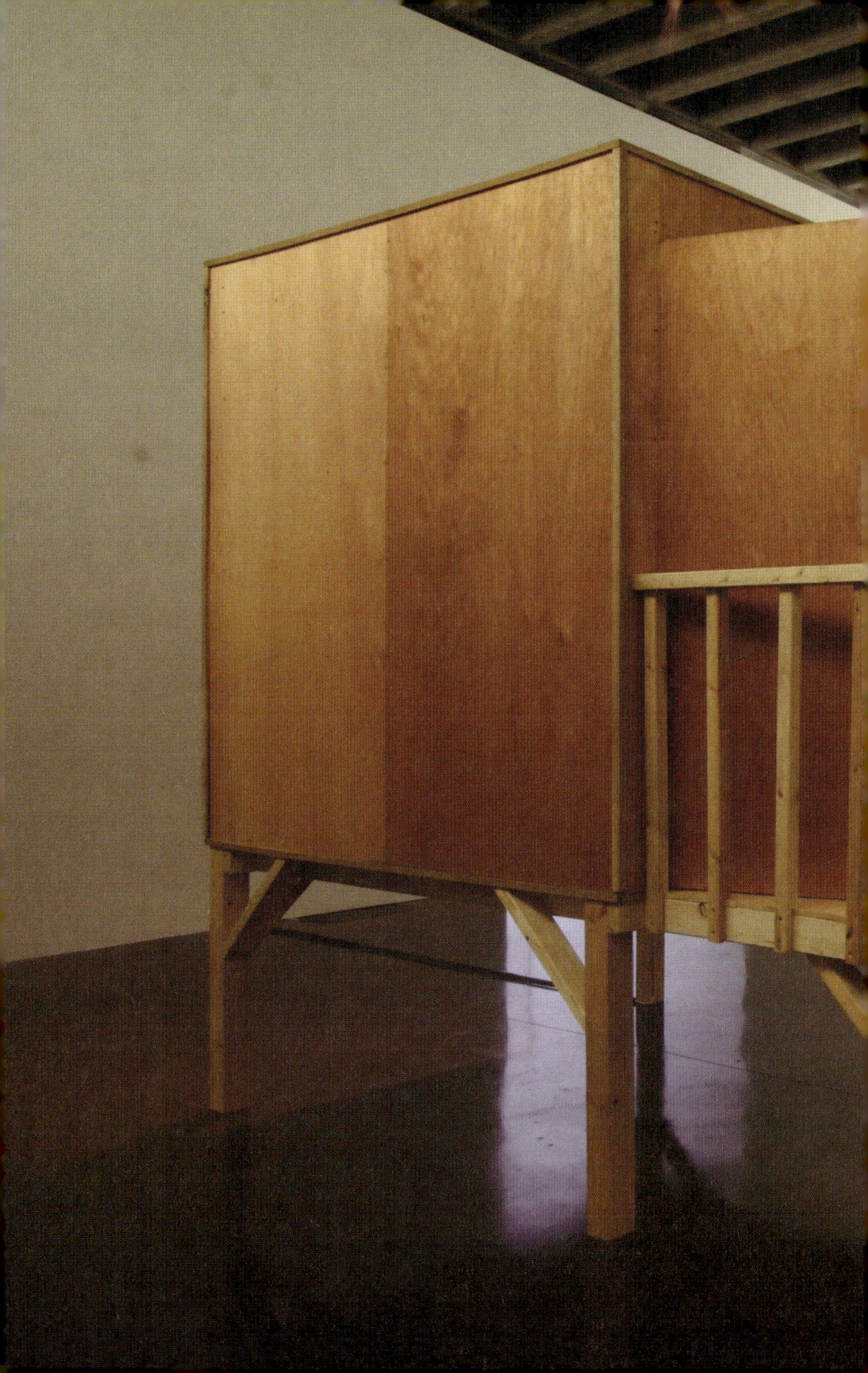

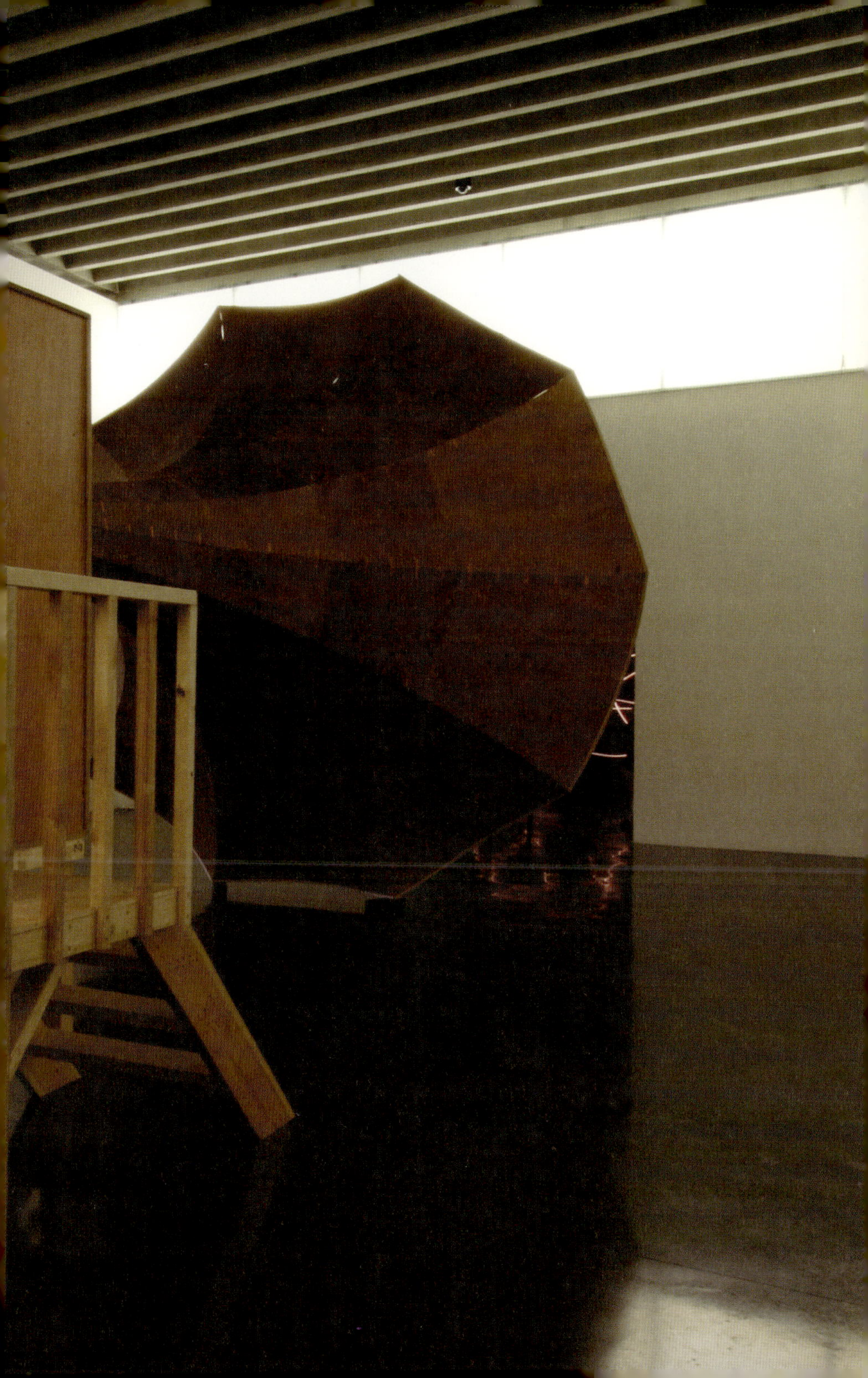

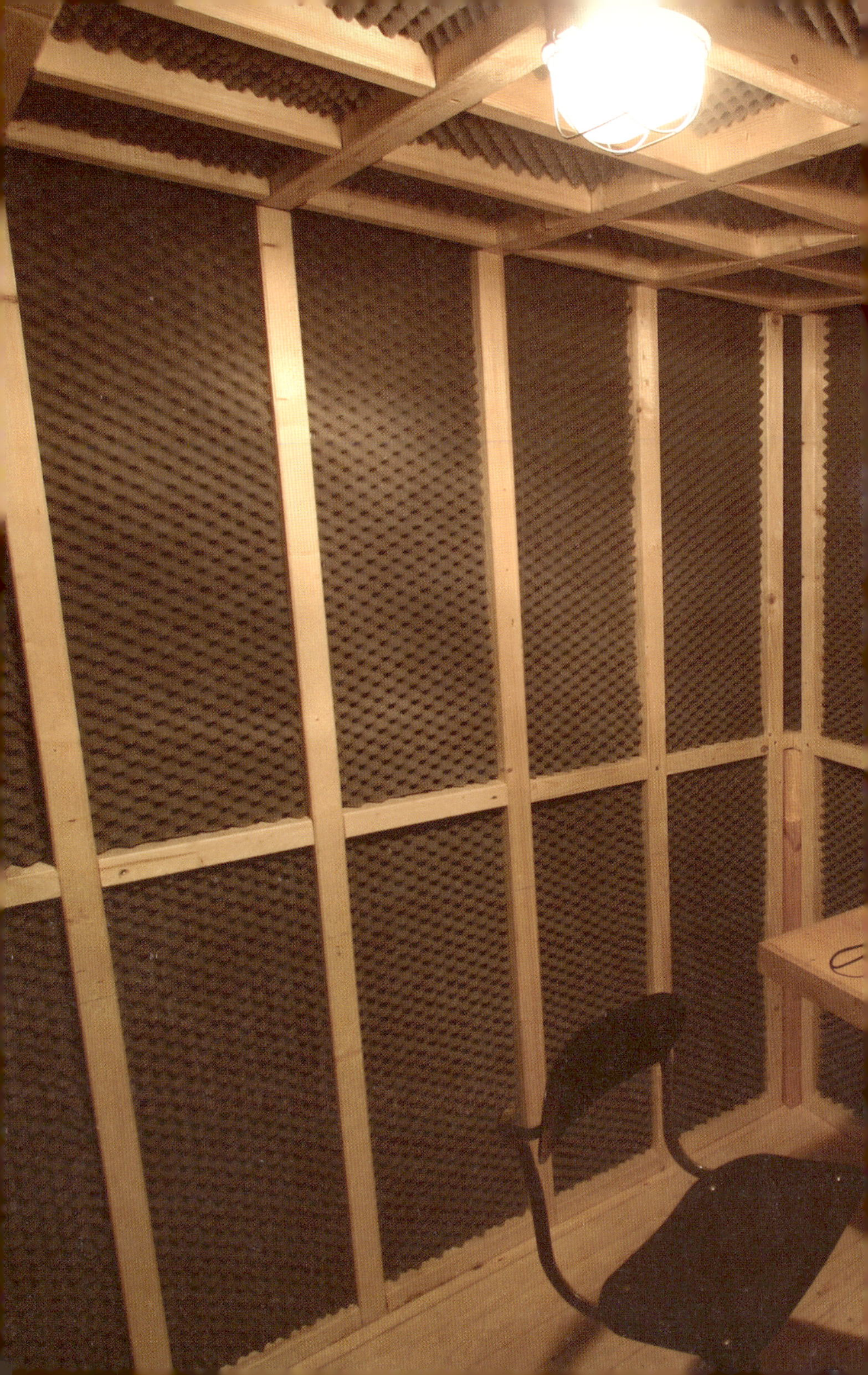

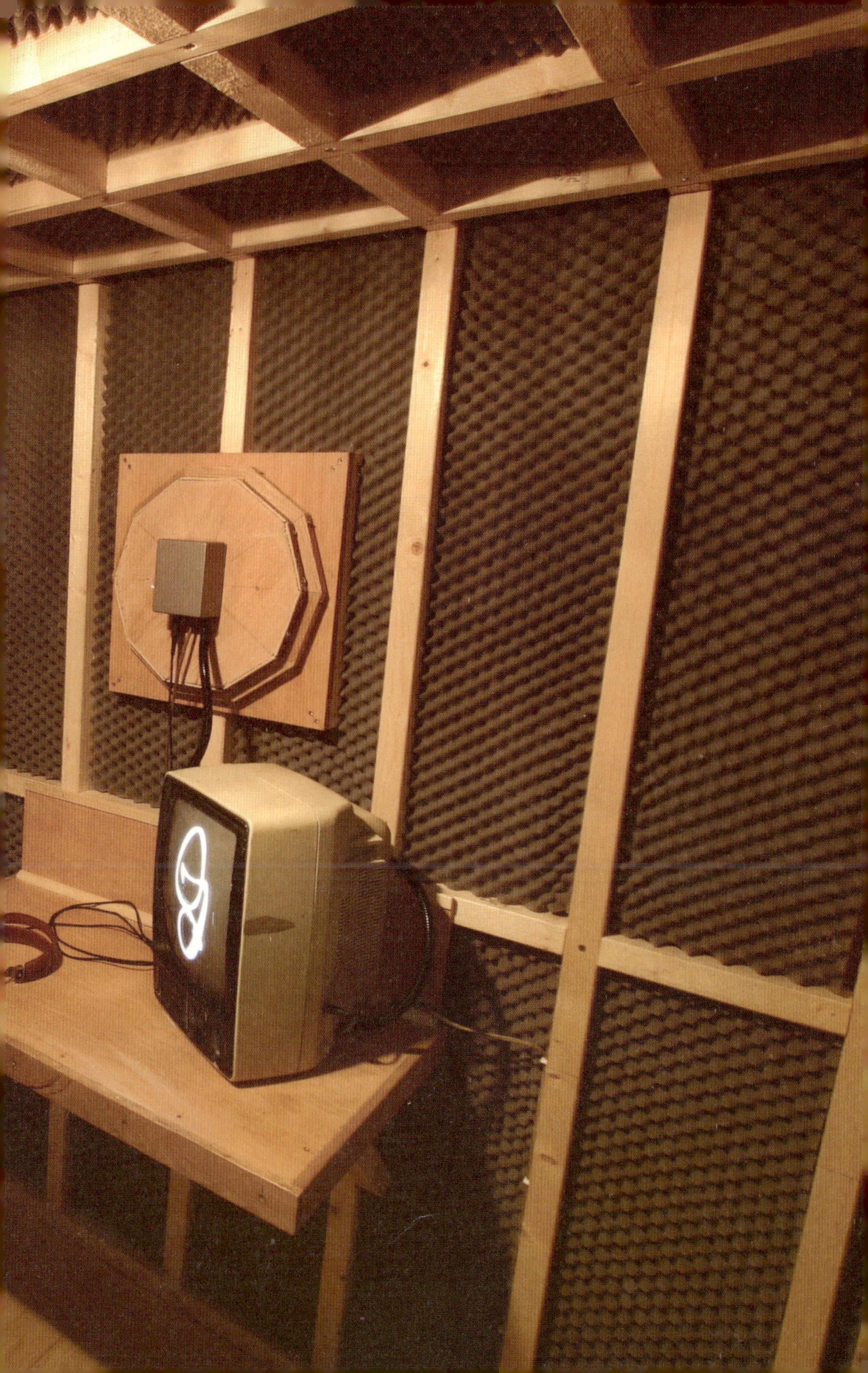

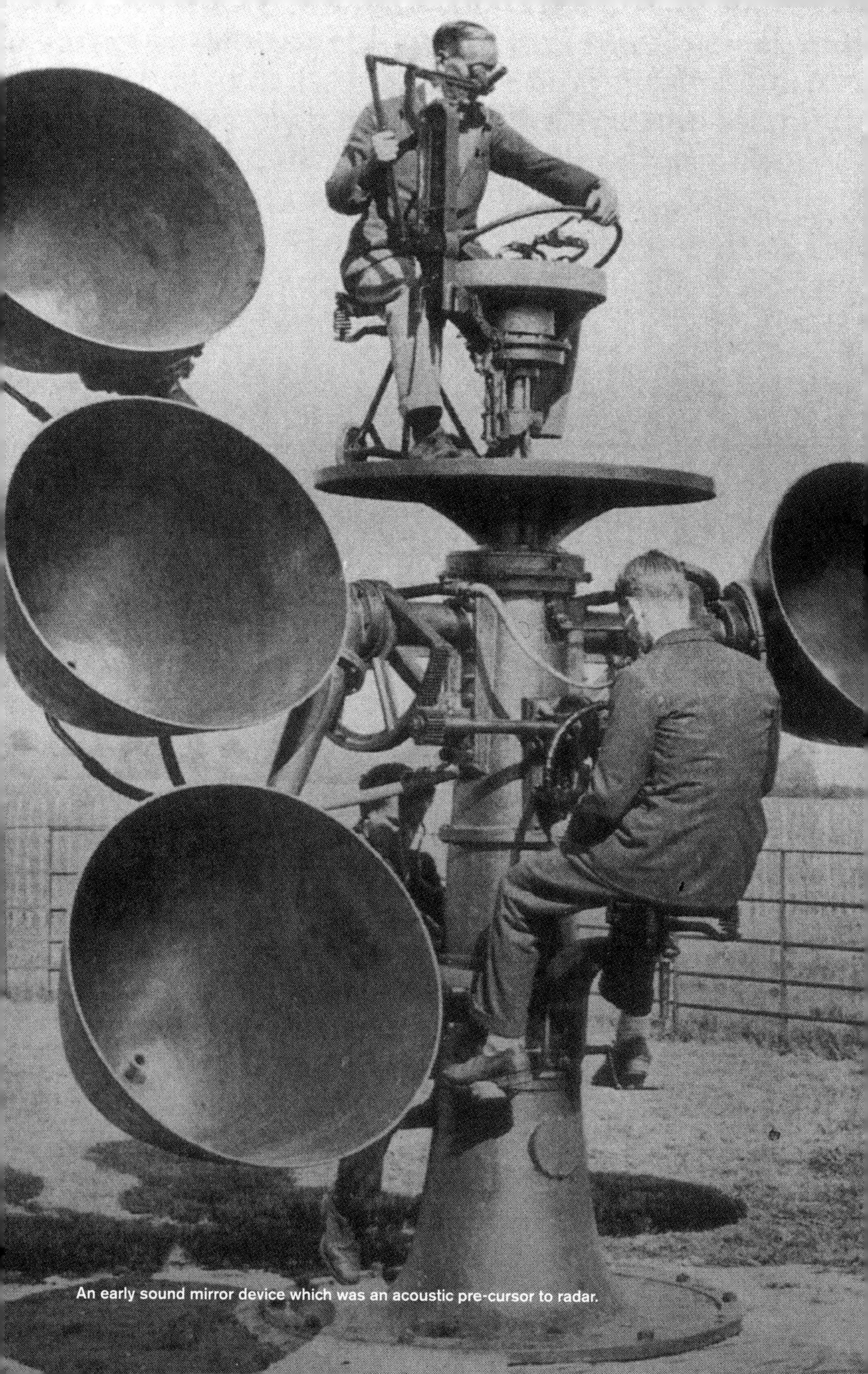

An early sound mirror device which was an acoustic pre-cursor to radar.

Harmonic Tower

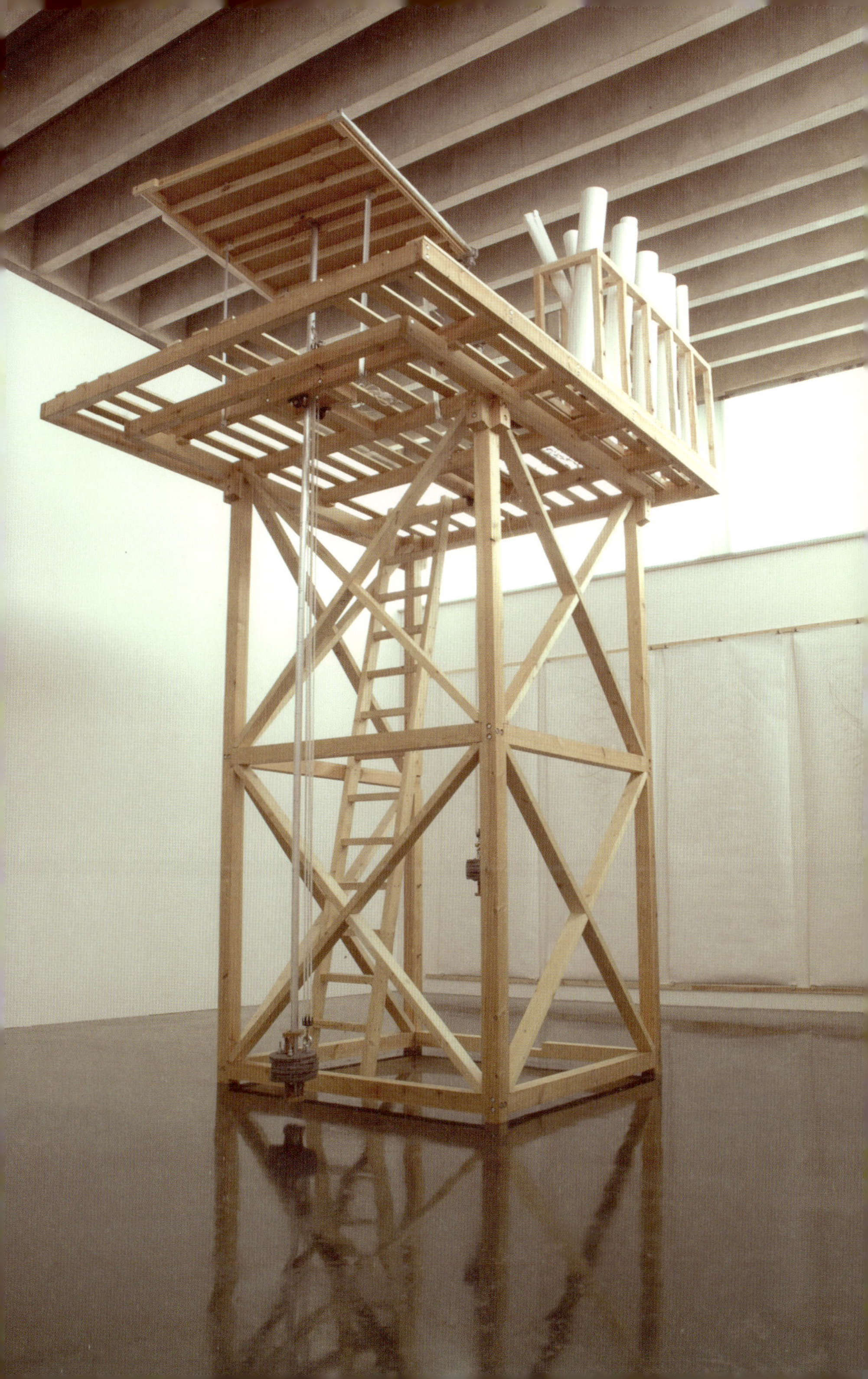

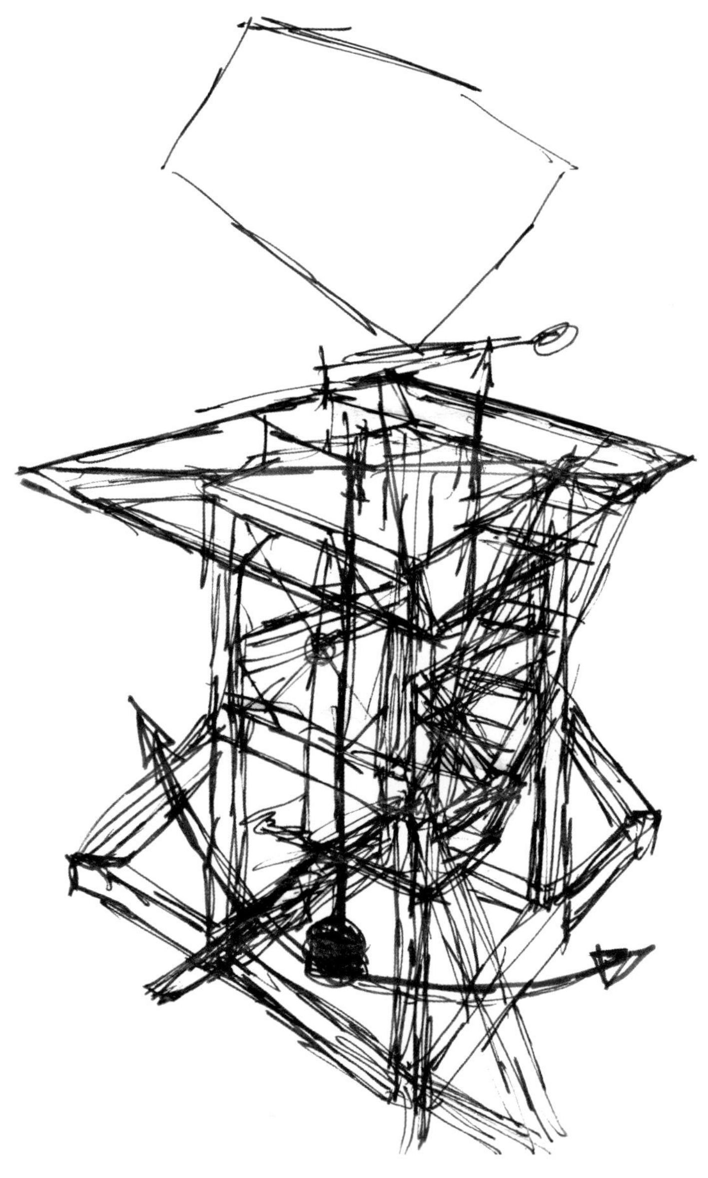

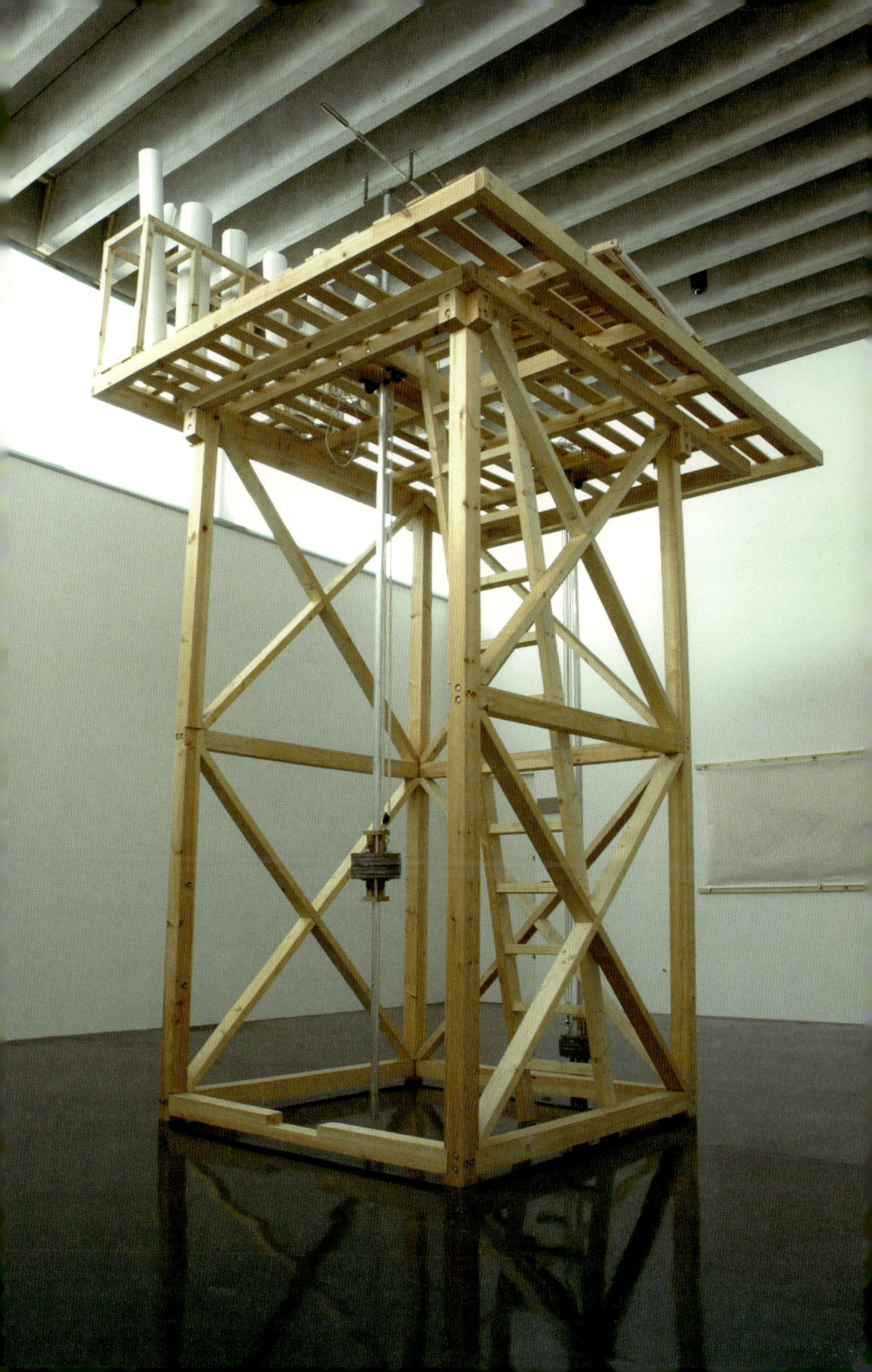

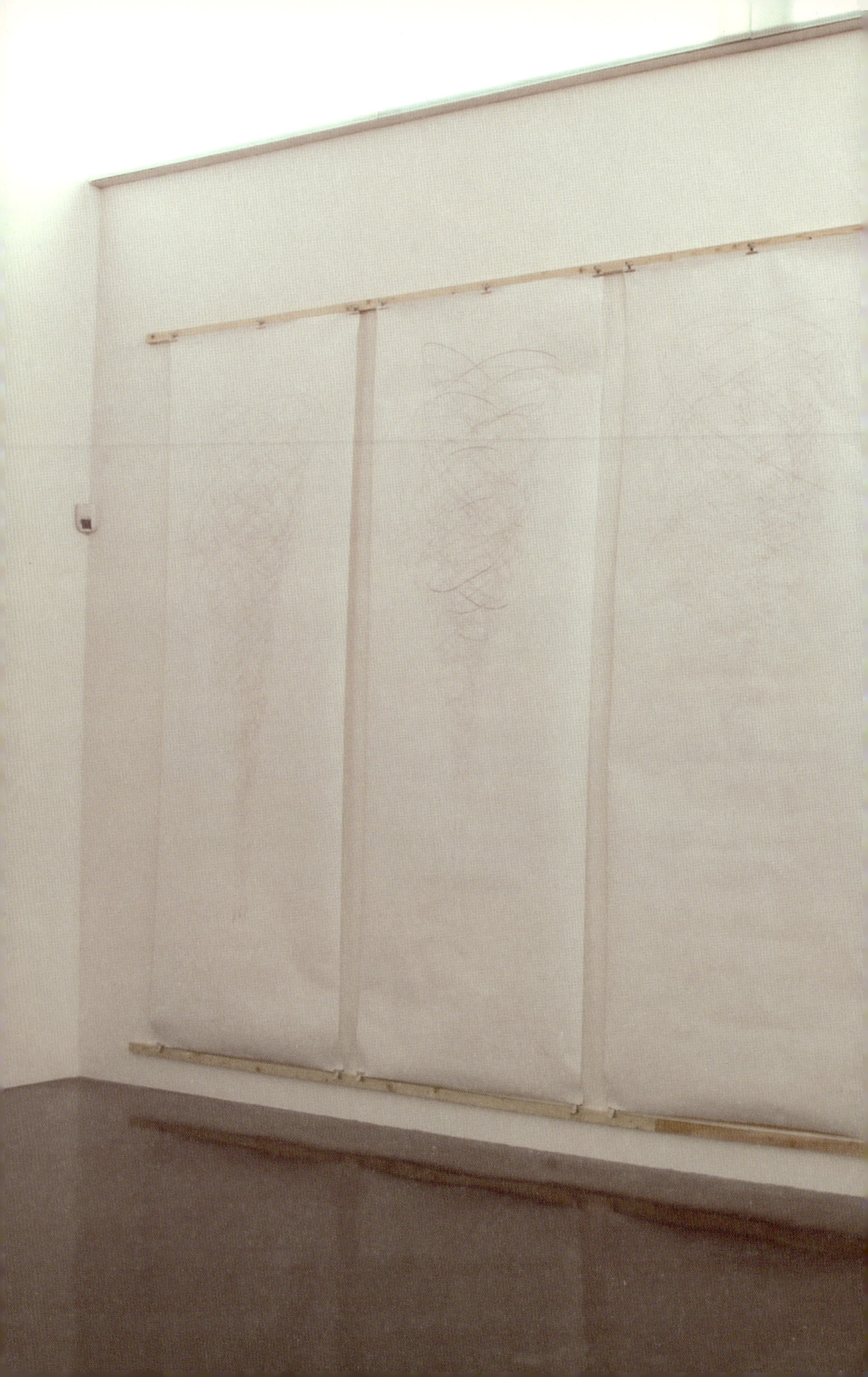

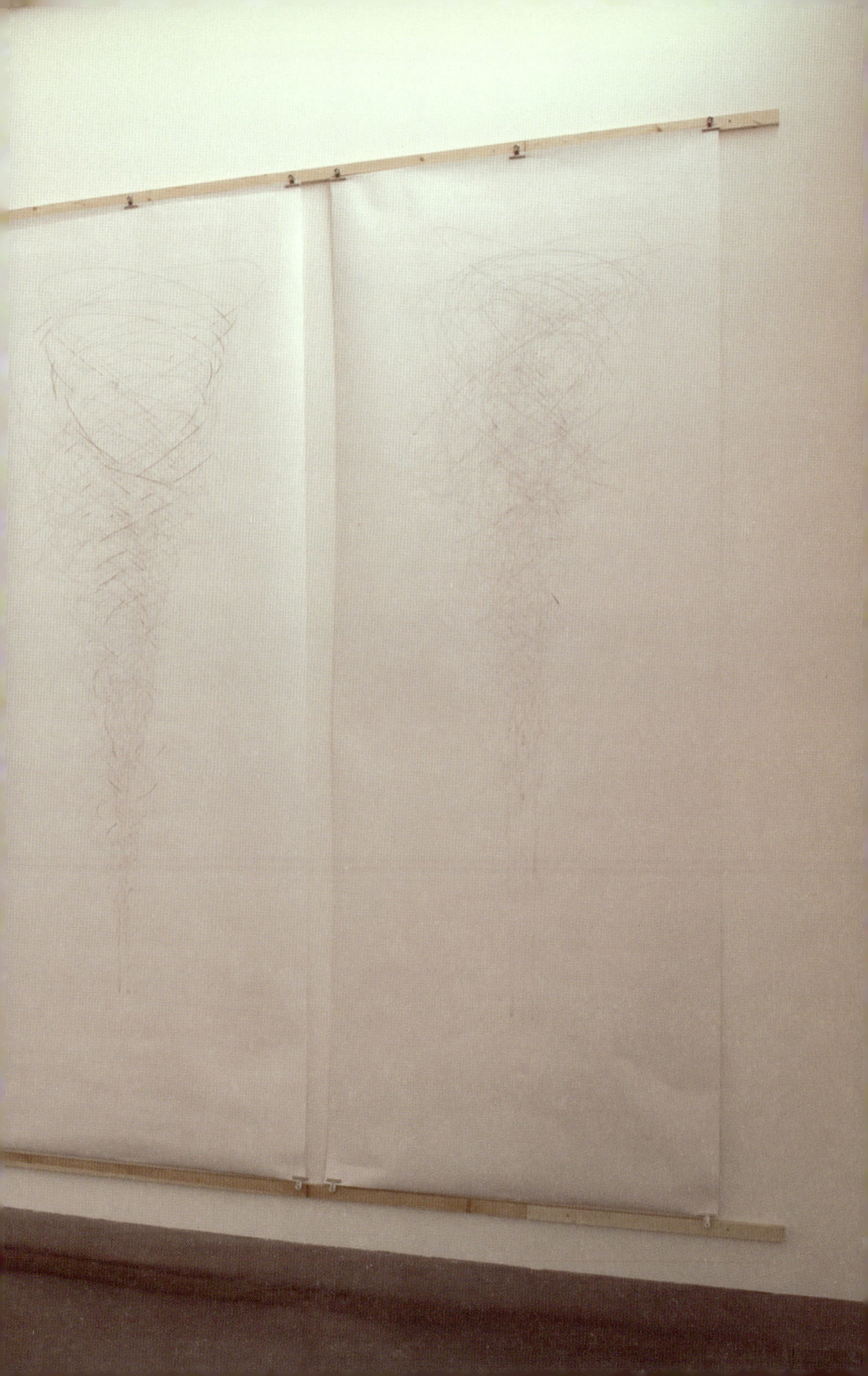

OR 1:10

22cm x ?? PENDULUM = 80CM

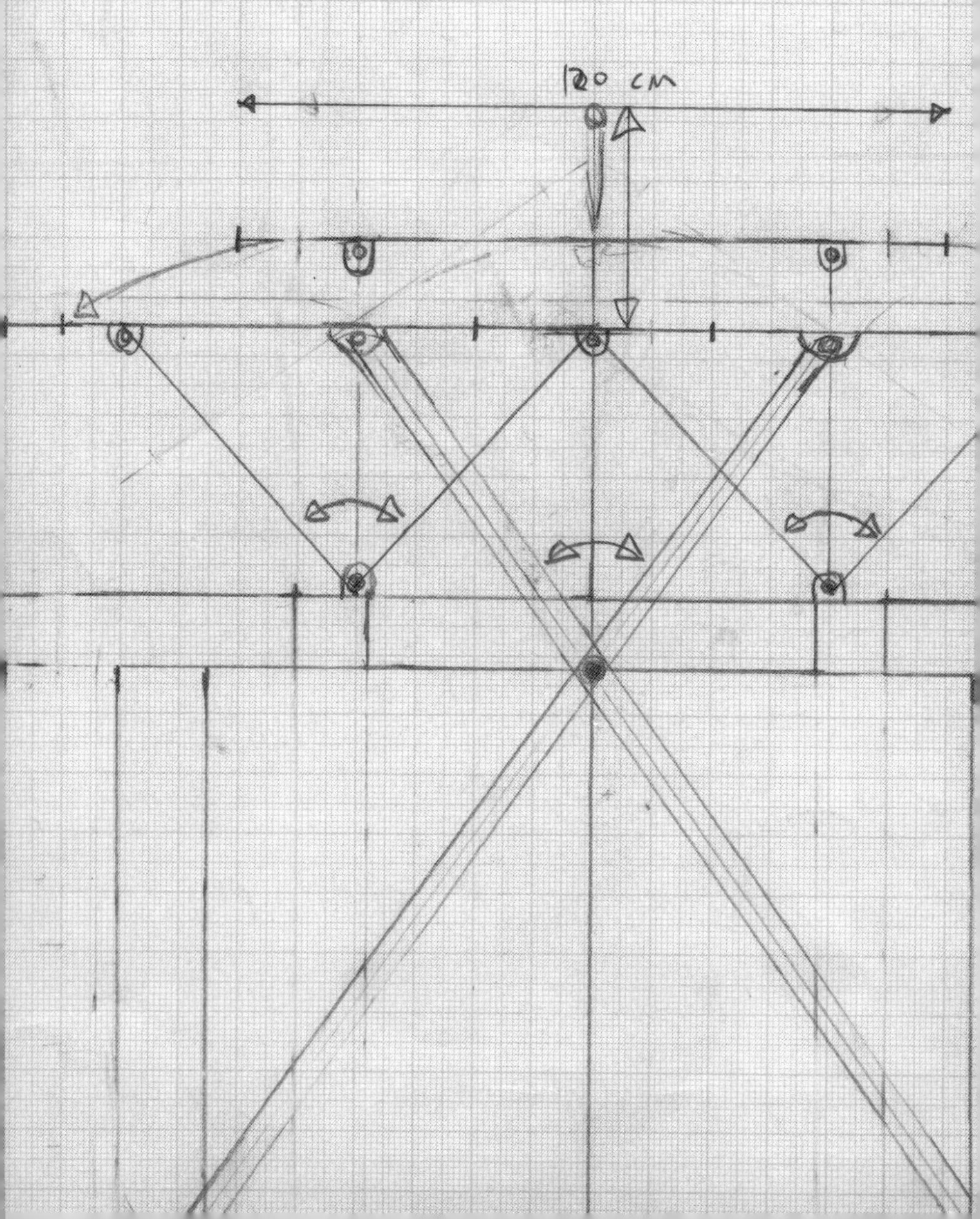

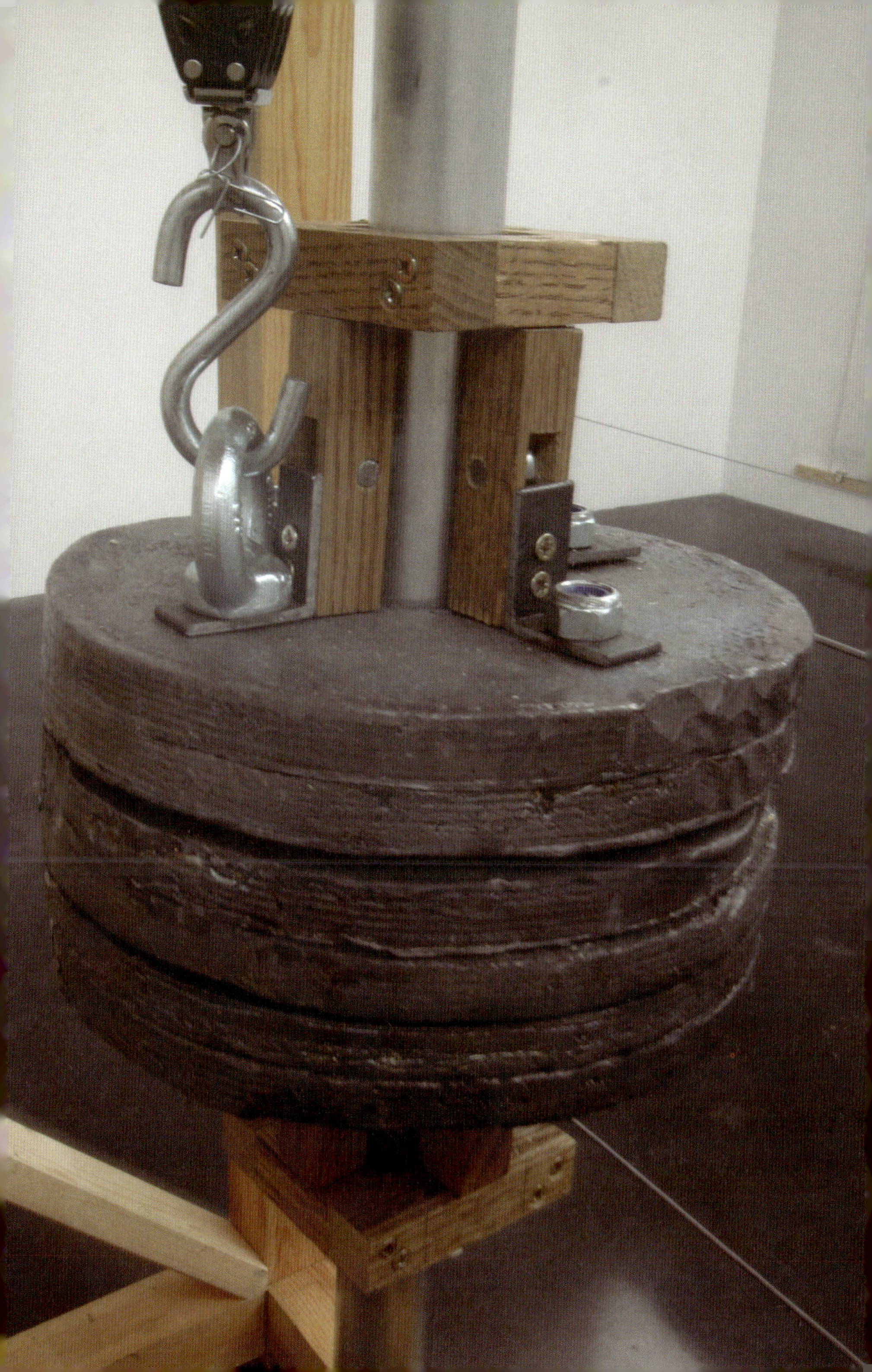

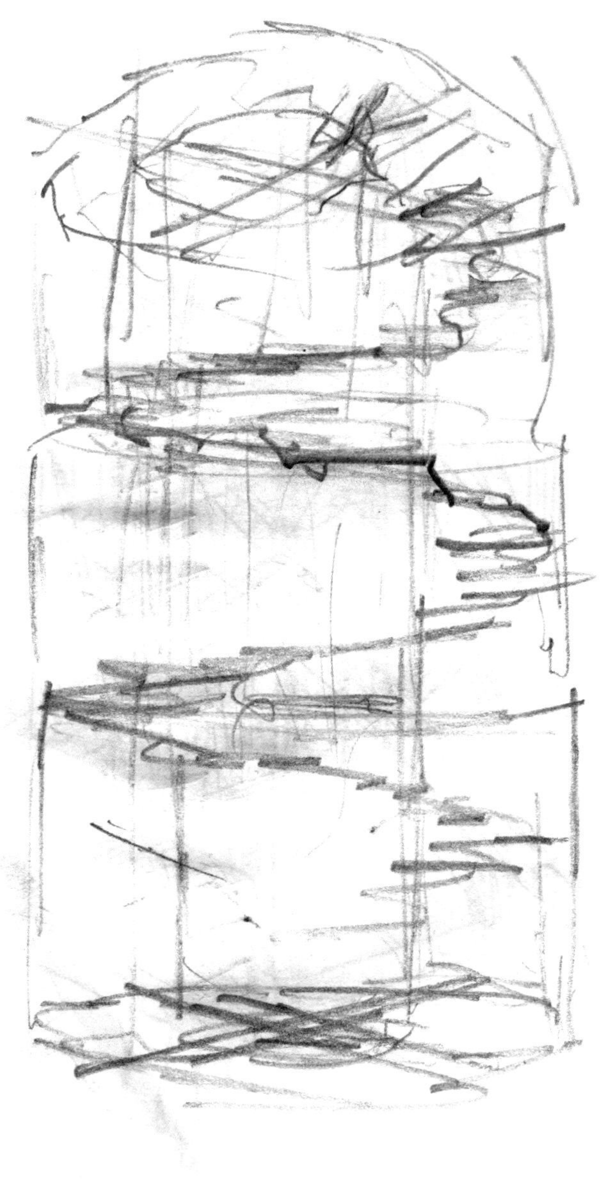

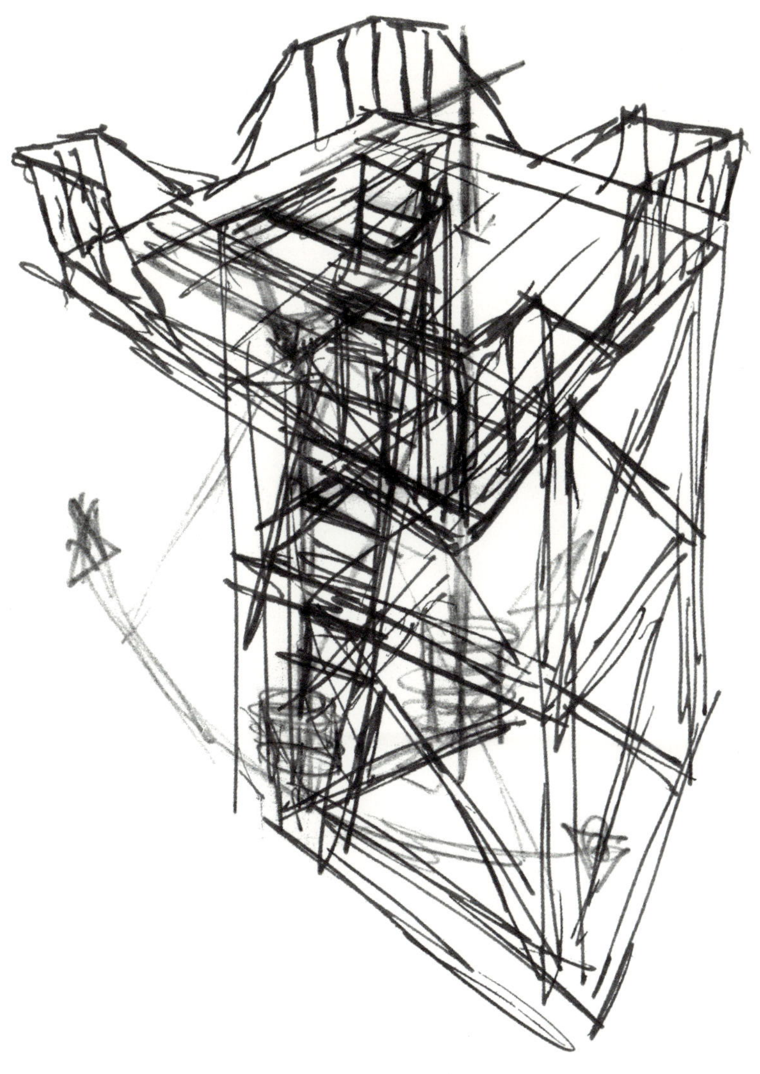

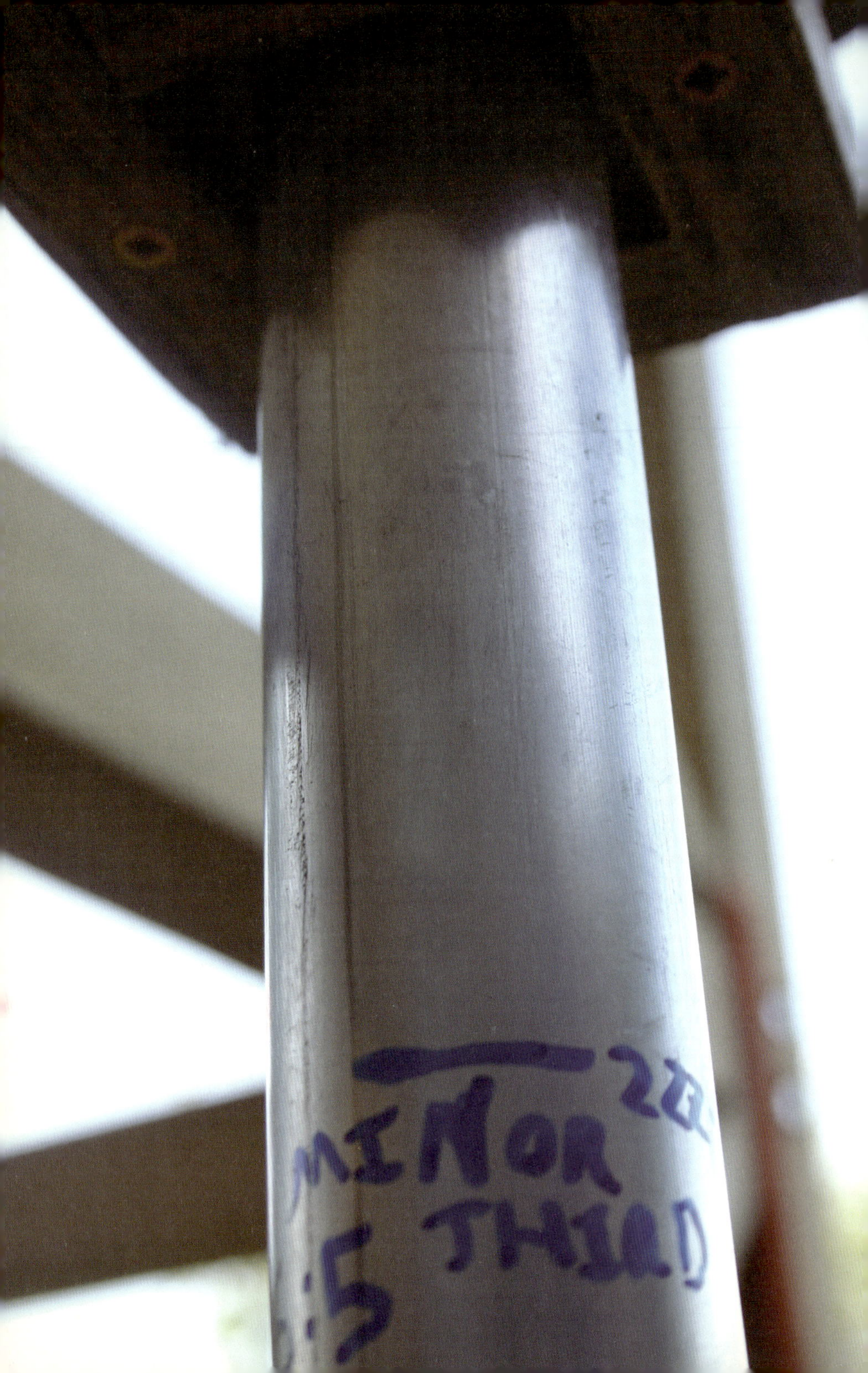
MINOR
THIRD

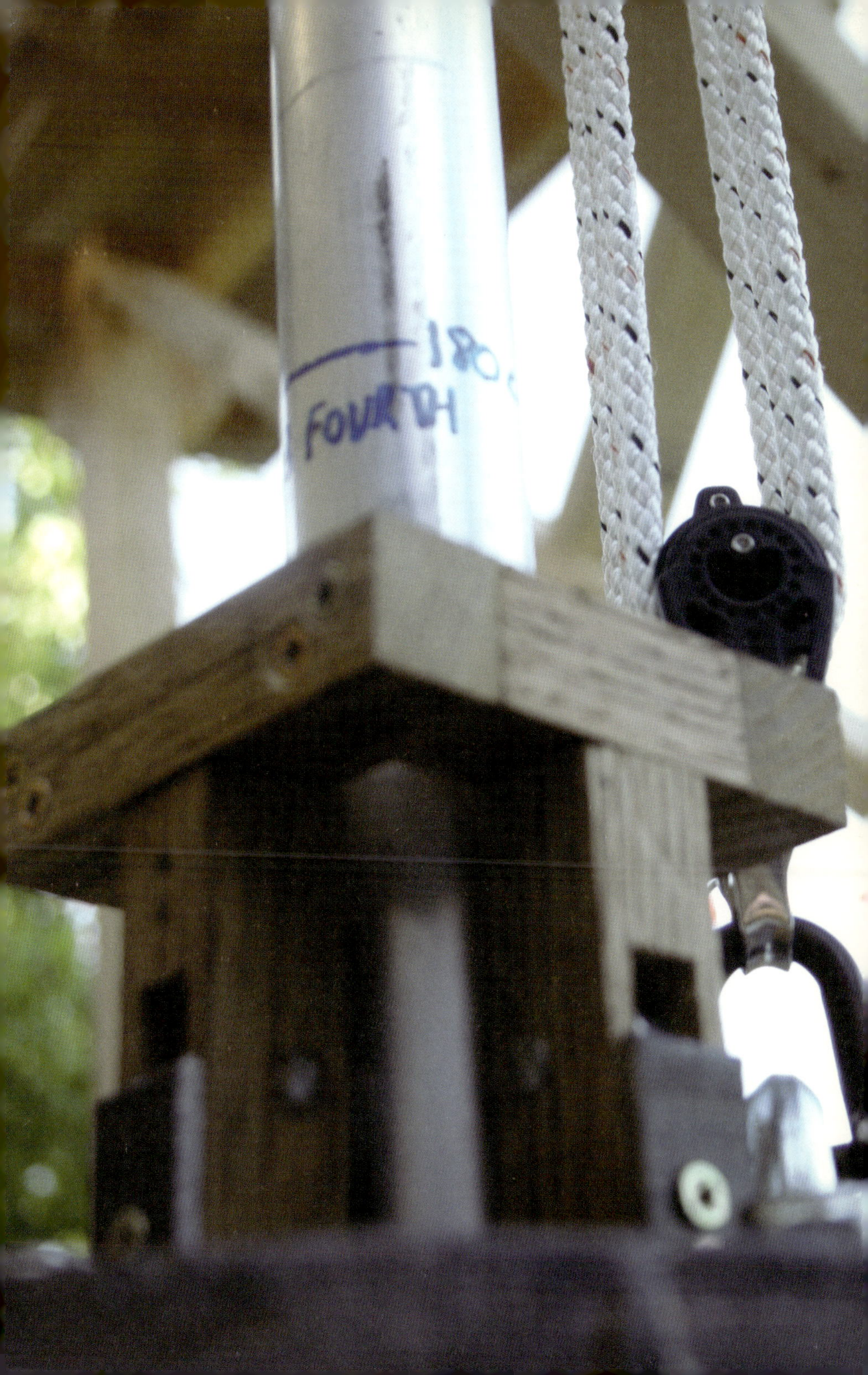
180
FOURTH

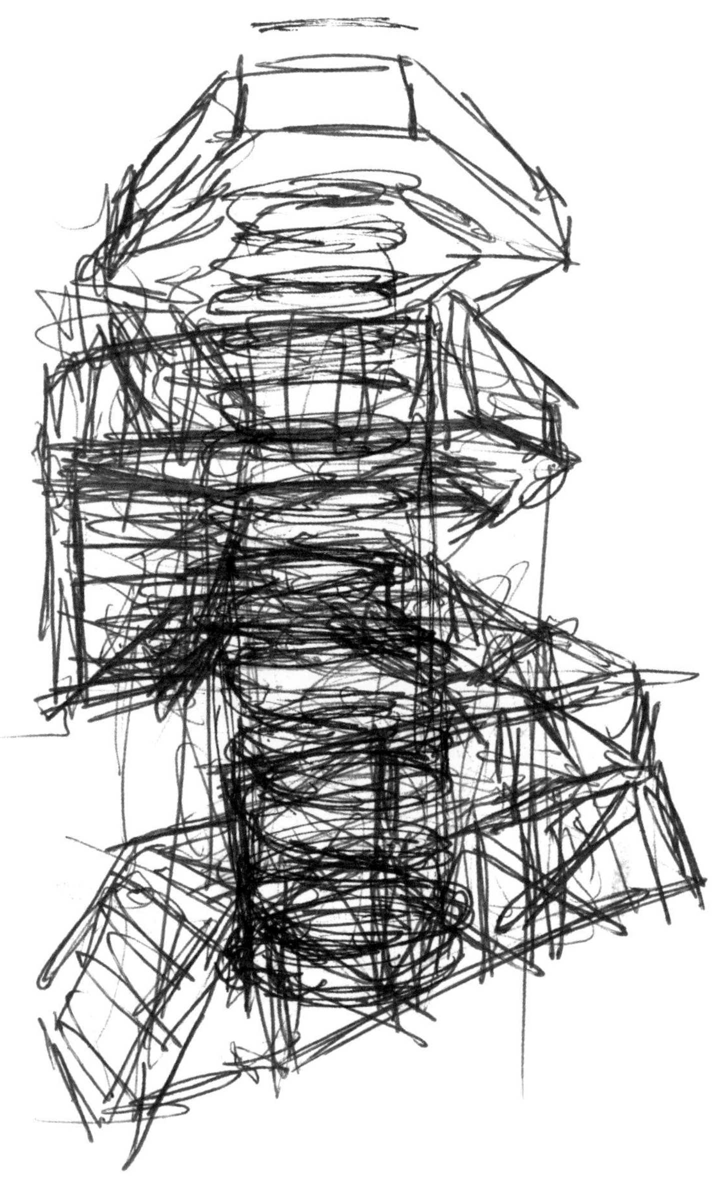

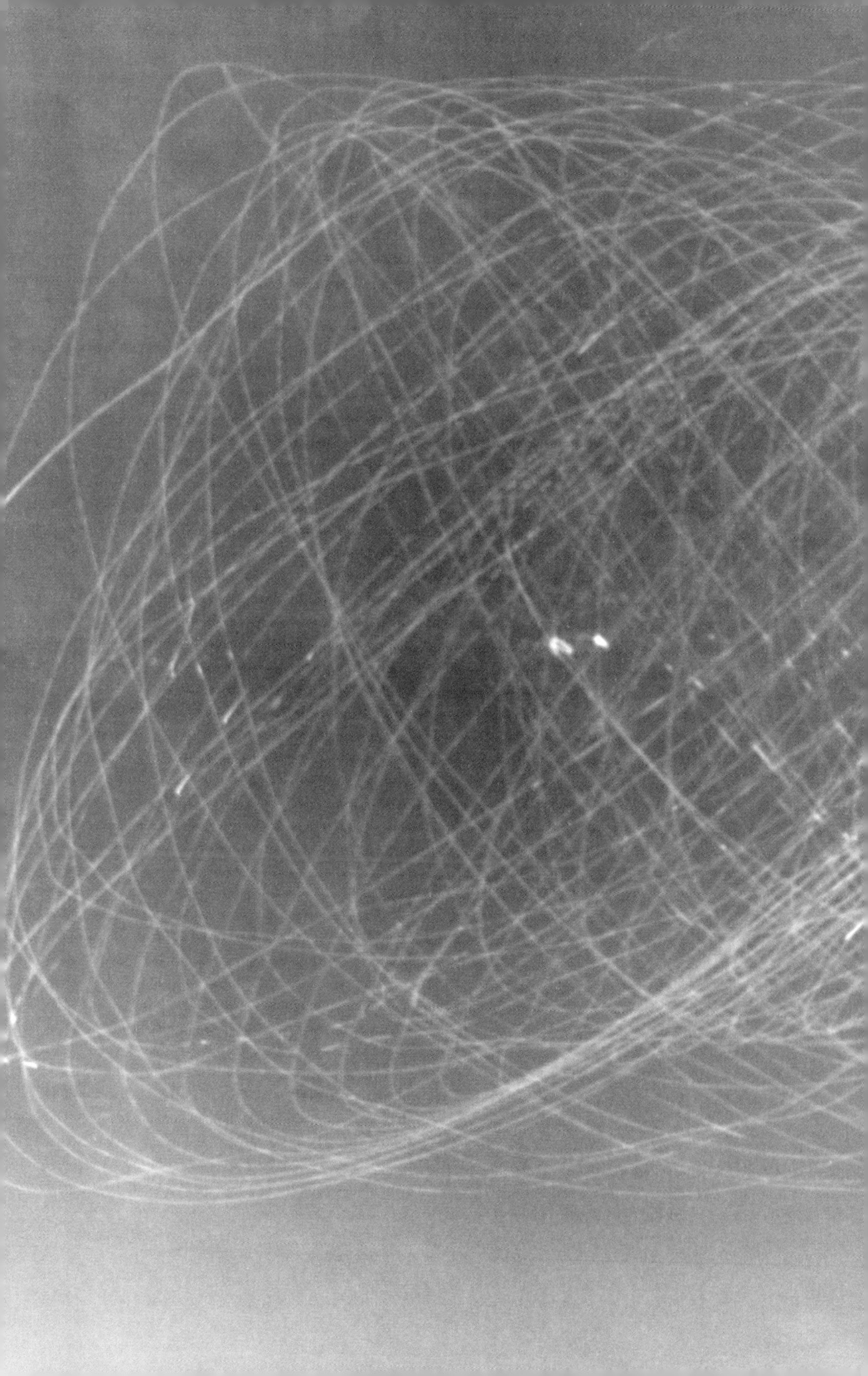

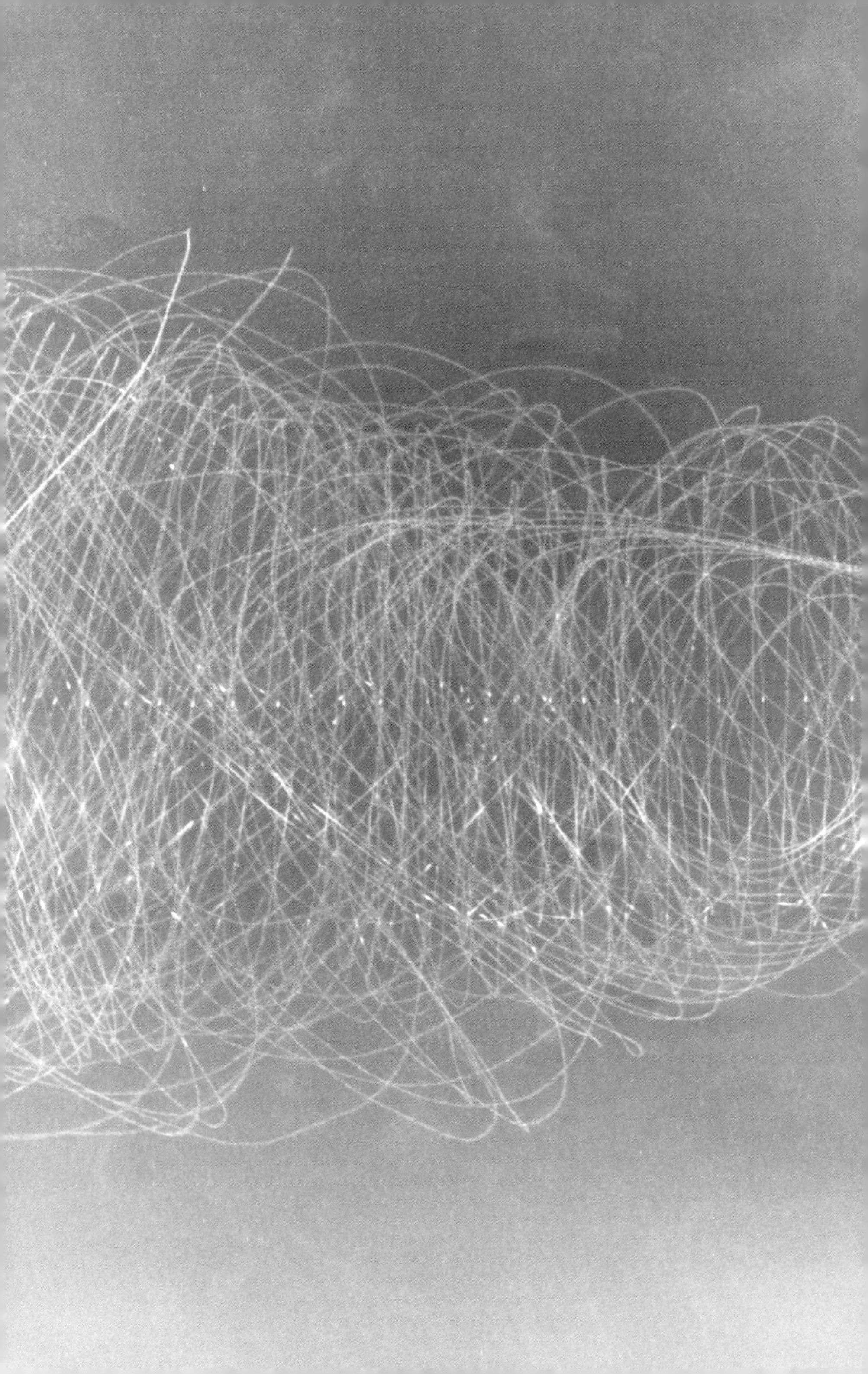

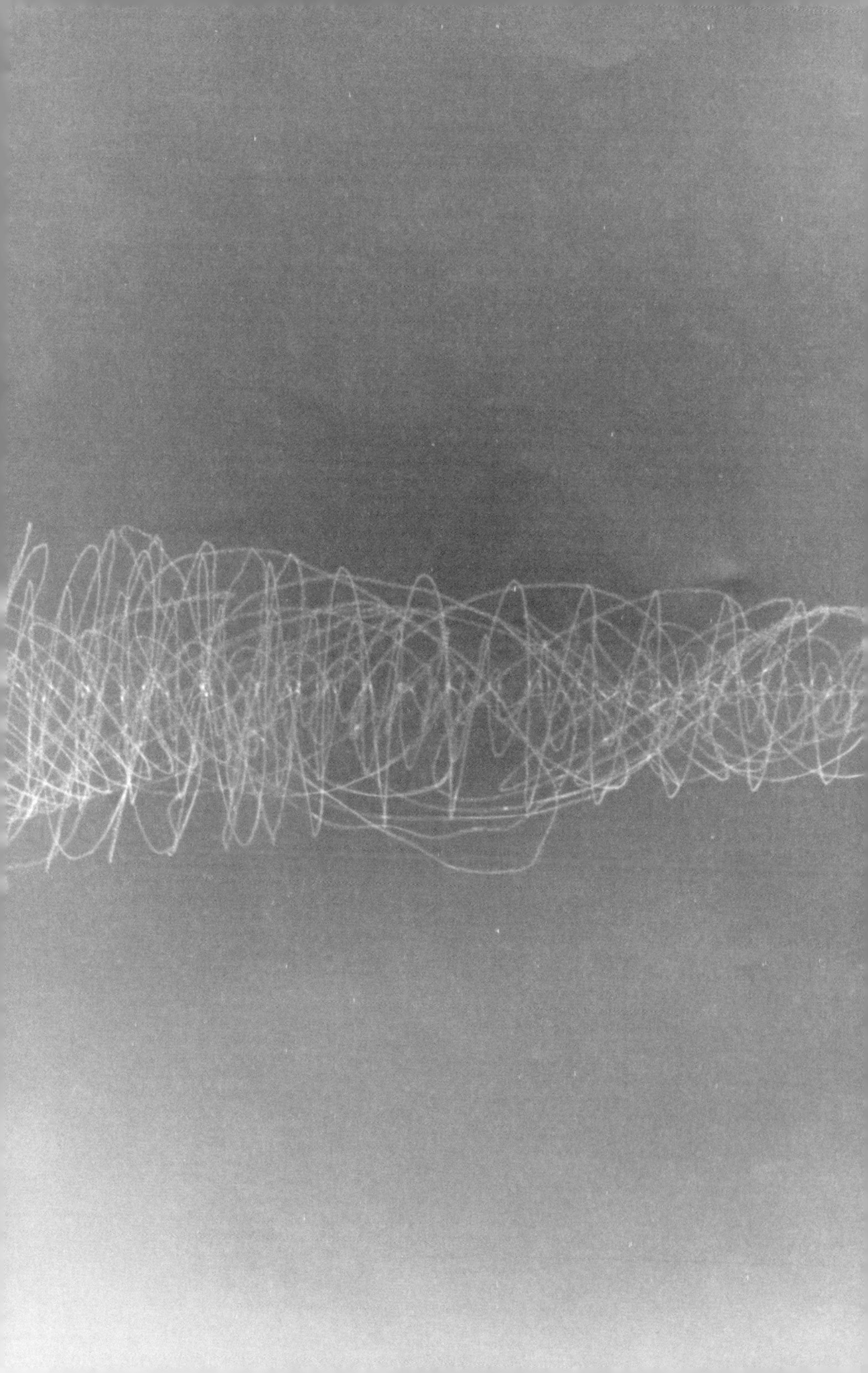

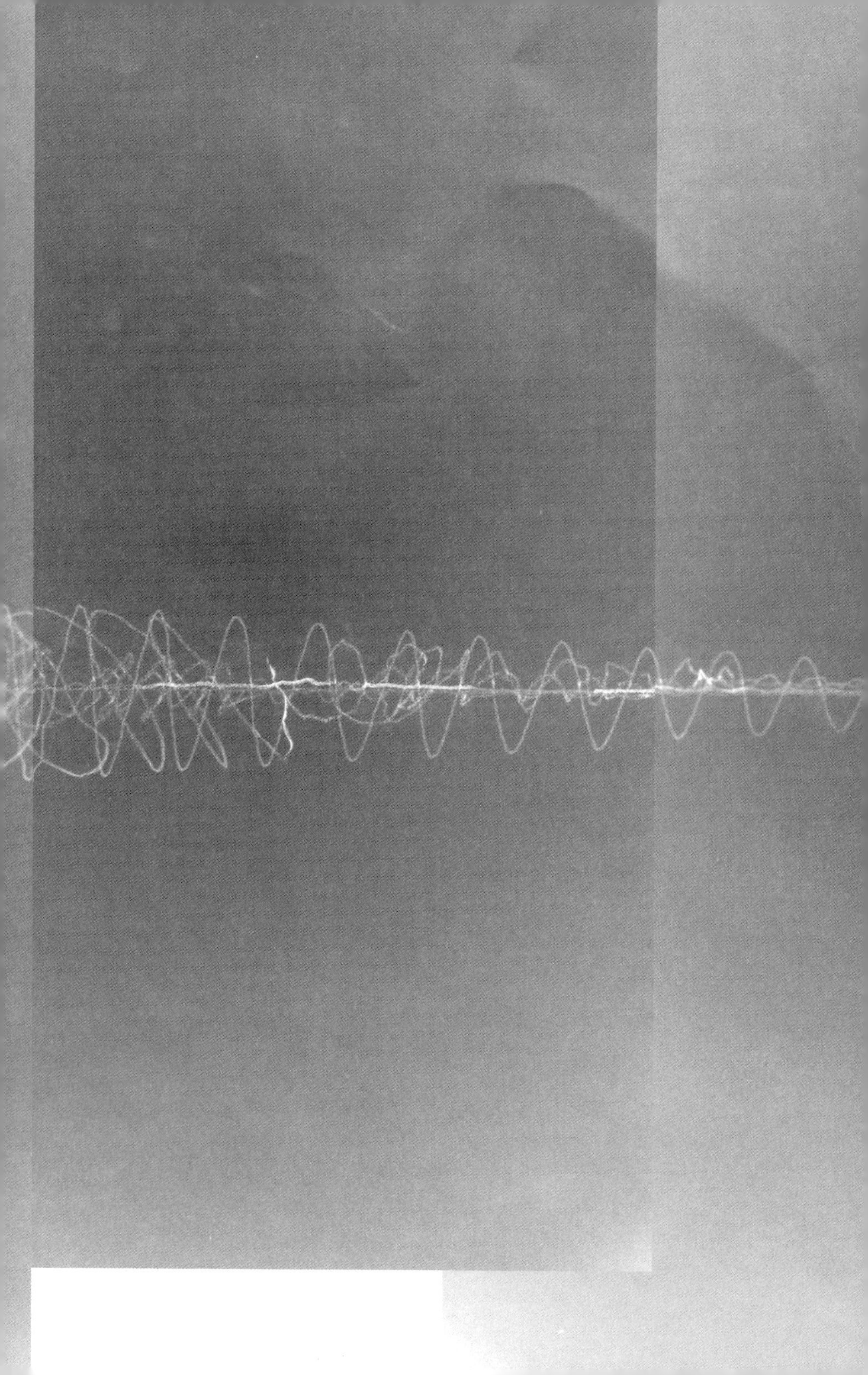

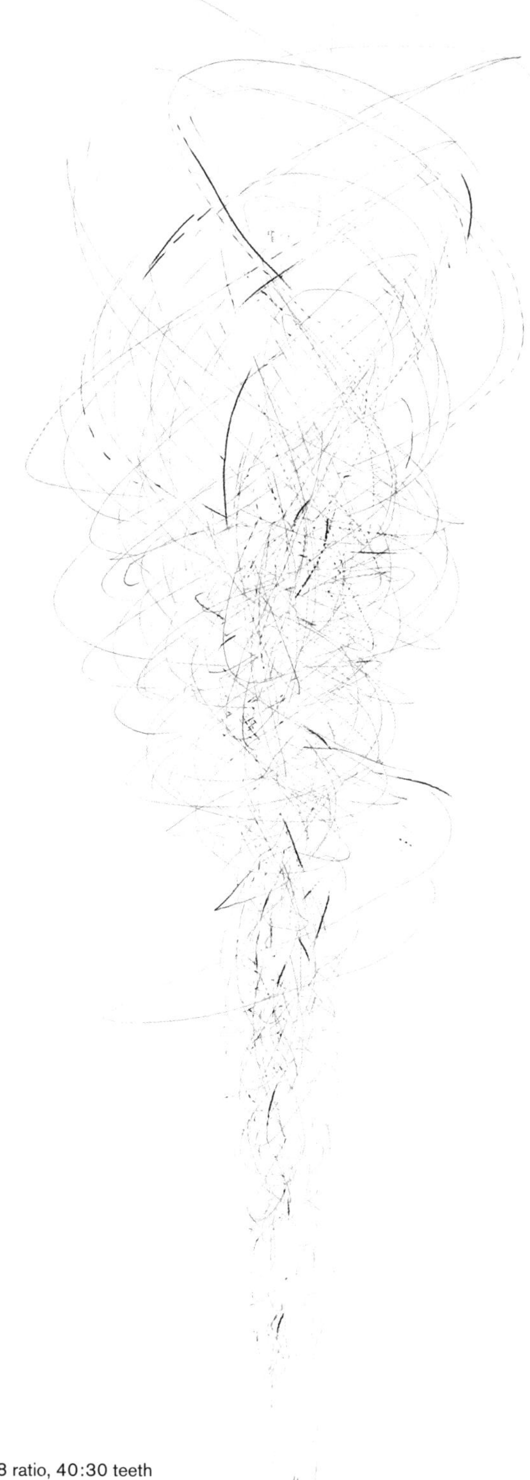

The Second, 9:8 ratio, 40:30 teeth

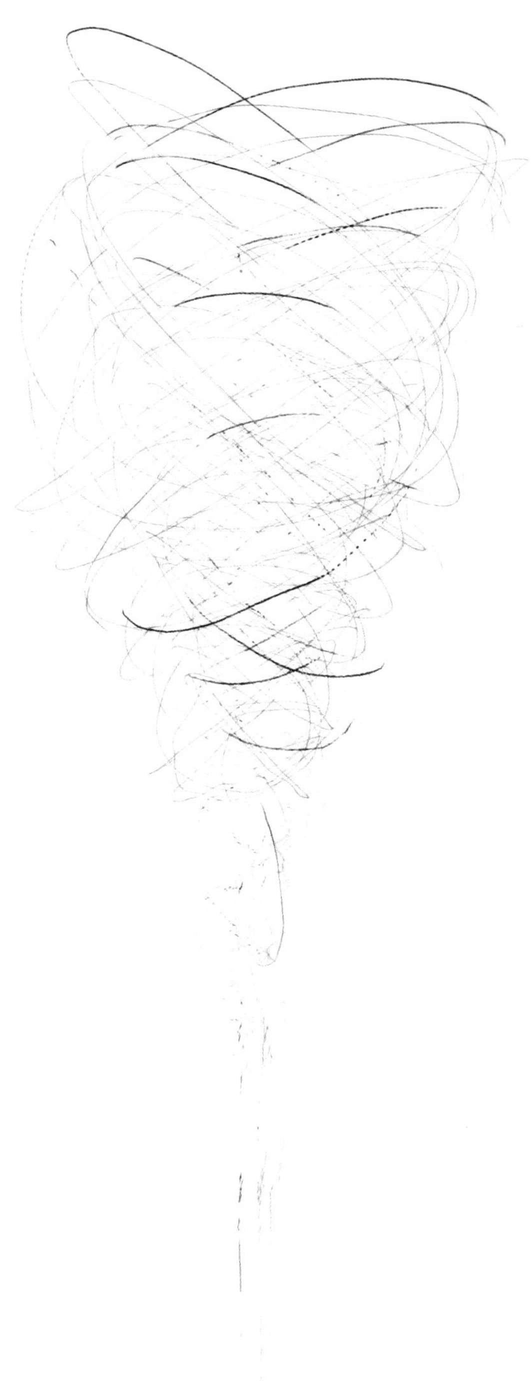

The Third, 5:4 ratio, 50:40 teeth

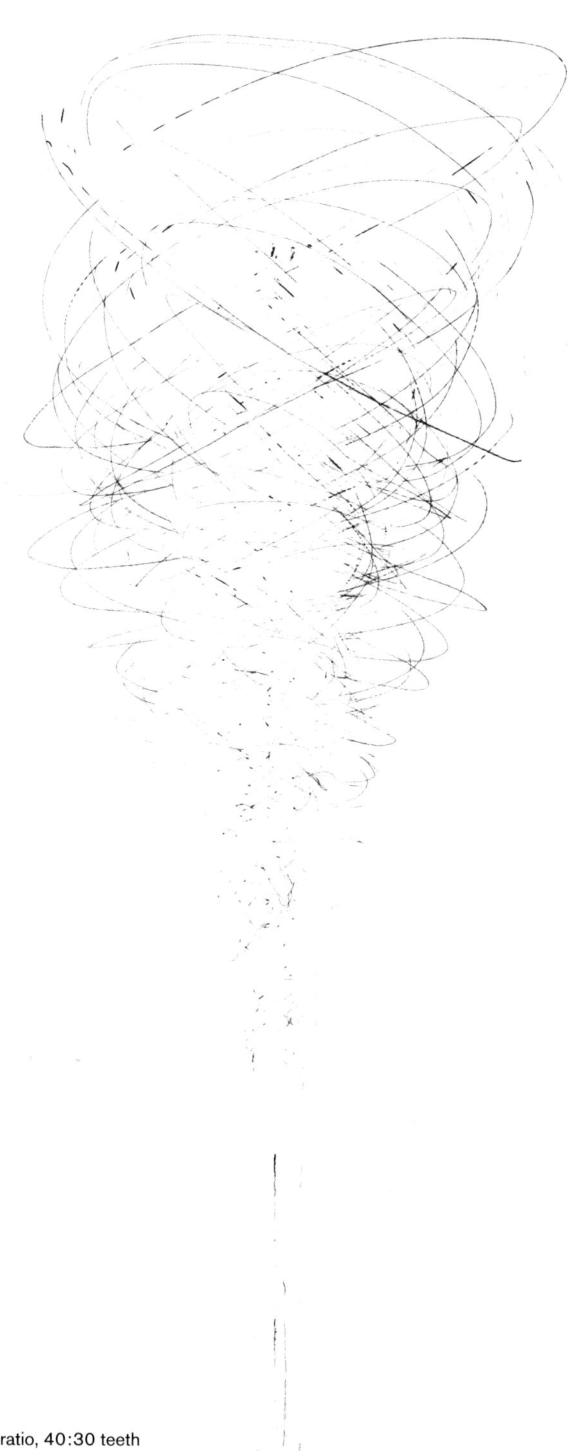

The Fourth, 4:3 ratio, 40:30 teeth

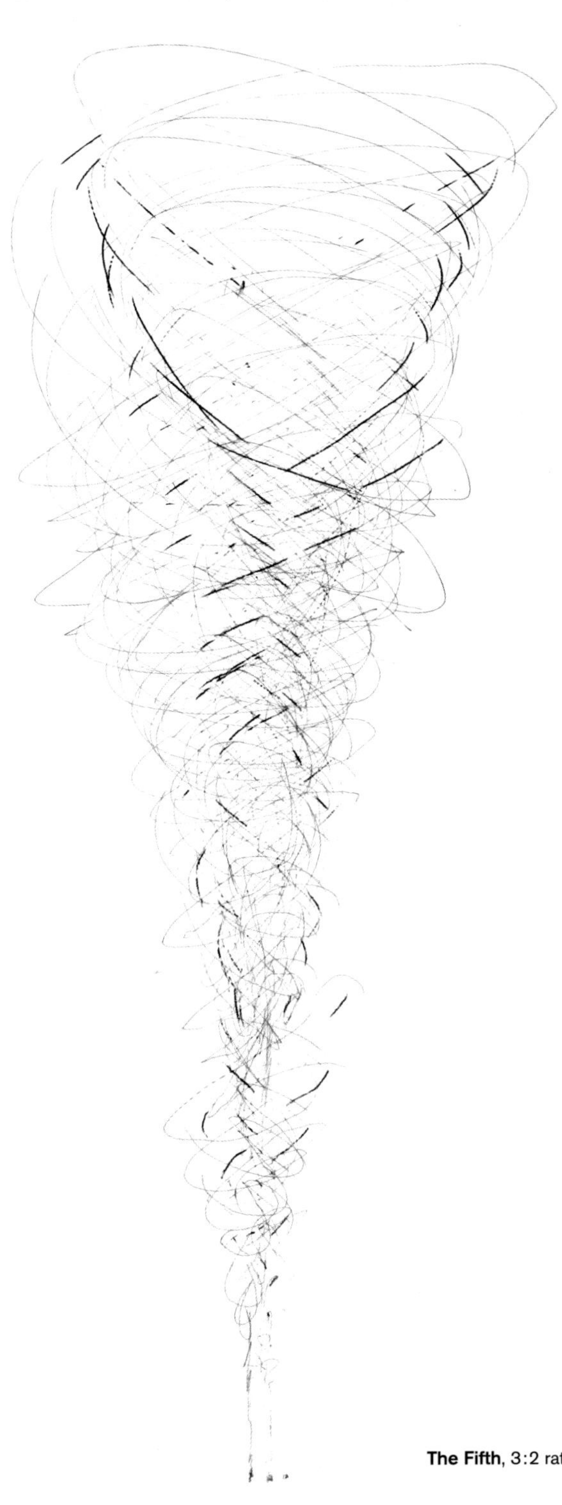

The Fifth, 3:2 ratio, 45:30 teeth

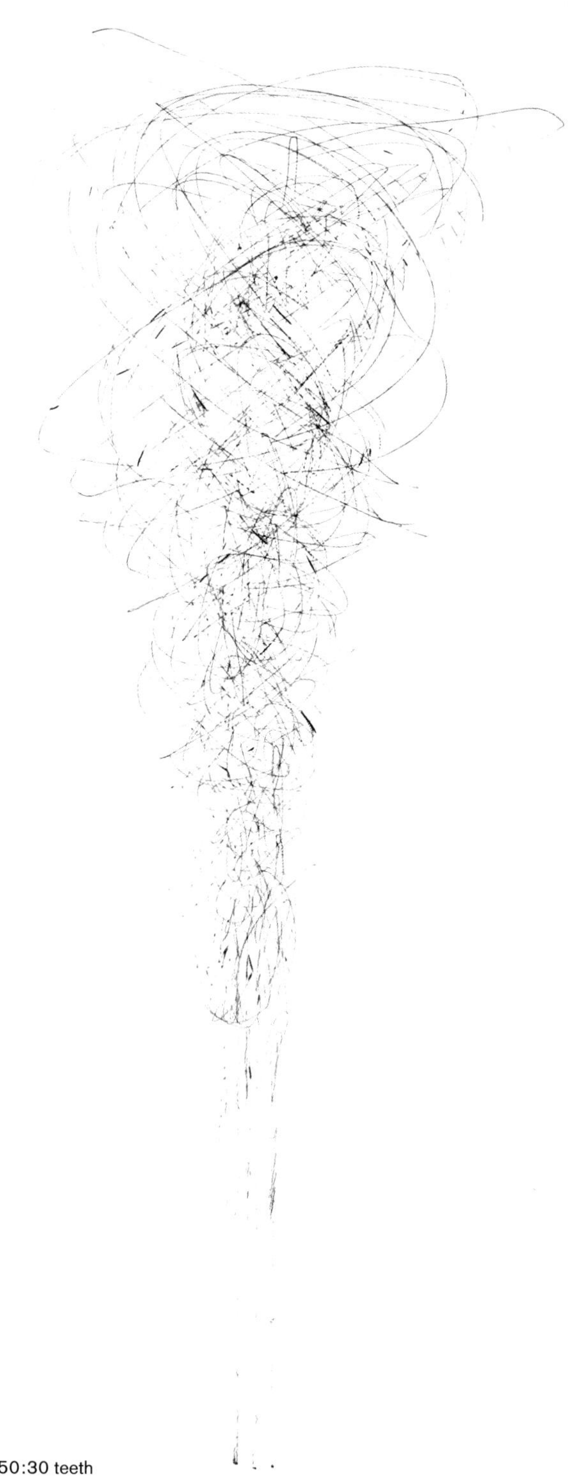

The Sixth, 5:3 ratio, 50:30 teeth

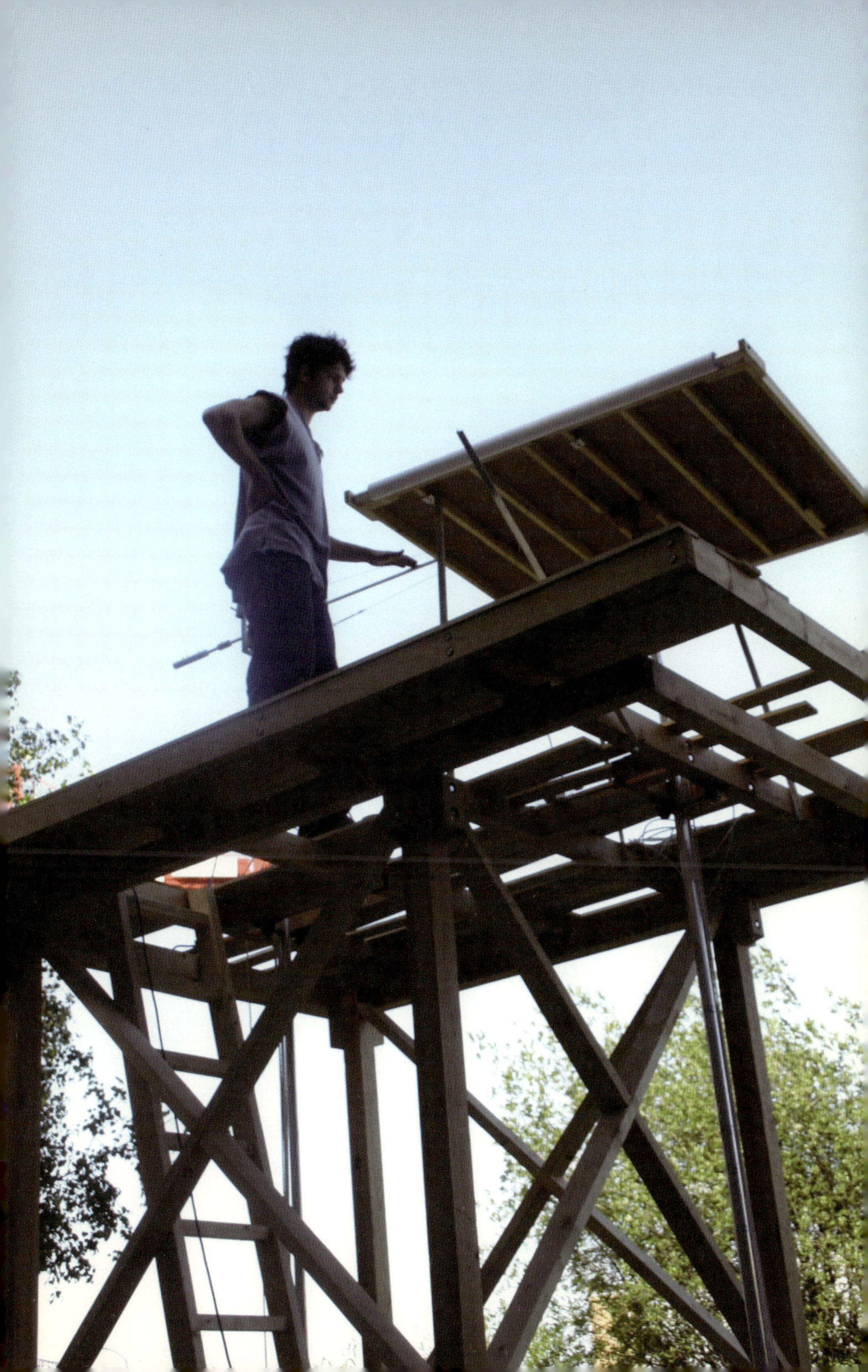

Published to accompany the exhibition

Conrad Shawcross

The Steady States

The New Art Gallery Walsall
16 July – 11 September 2005

Walker Art Gallery, Liverpool
26 November 2005 – 26 February 2006

ISBN: 1-902700-29-5

The New Art Gallery Walsall
Gallery Square
Walsall WS2 8LG
T: + 44 (0) 1922 654 400
F: + 44 (0) 1922 654 401
E: info@artatwalsall.org.uk
www.artatwalsall.org.uk

Walker Art Gallery
William Brown Street
Liverpool L3 8EL
T: + 44 (0) 151 478 4199
F: + 44 (0) 151 478 4190
E: info@thewalker.org.uk
www.thewalker.org.uk

Distributed by Cornerhouse
70 Oxford Street
Manchester M1 5NH
T: + 44 (0) 161 200 1503
F: + 44 (0) 161 200 1504
E: publications@cornerhouse.org
www.cornerhouse.org/publications

Conrad Shawcross is represented by Victoria Miro Gallery, London.

Conrad Shawcross would like to thank his parents and Sophie for all their support. Victoria and Warren Miro and everyone one at the gallery. All the staff at Walsall and the Walker, who have been a pleasure to work with. Lance Entwistle and Monica Chung for all their initial ground work on the project. Nathaniel Rackowe and Brian Gascoigne for their expertise, Fraser Muggeridge for the great design of this book. Everyone in Unit 3 for their support and use of space, Devon and Floyd in New Jersey. Jenny Uglow and Andrea Bellini for their wonderful essays. Len at CNC router Projects and Simon at Darvall. And Rob Dowling for his tireless mortice work.

Edited by Emily Marsden with
Ann Bukantas, Rachel Dagnall and
Deborah Robinson
Designed by Fraser Muggeridge studio
Printed by Orchid

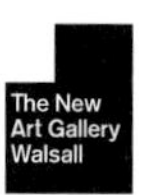

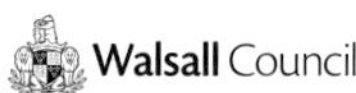

NATIONAL MUSEUMS
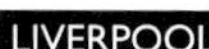

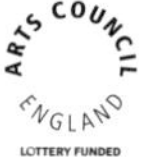

The Henry Moore
Foundation